Mini-Cheers

Carving Miniature Santas

Ron Ransom

Text written with and photography by Jeffrey B. Snyder

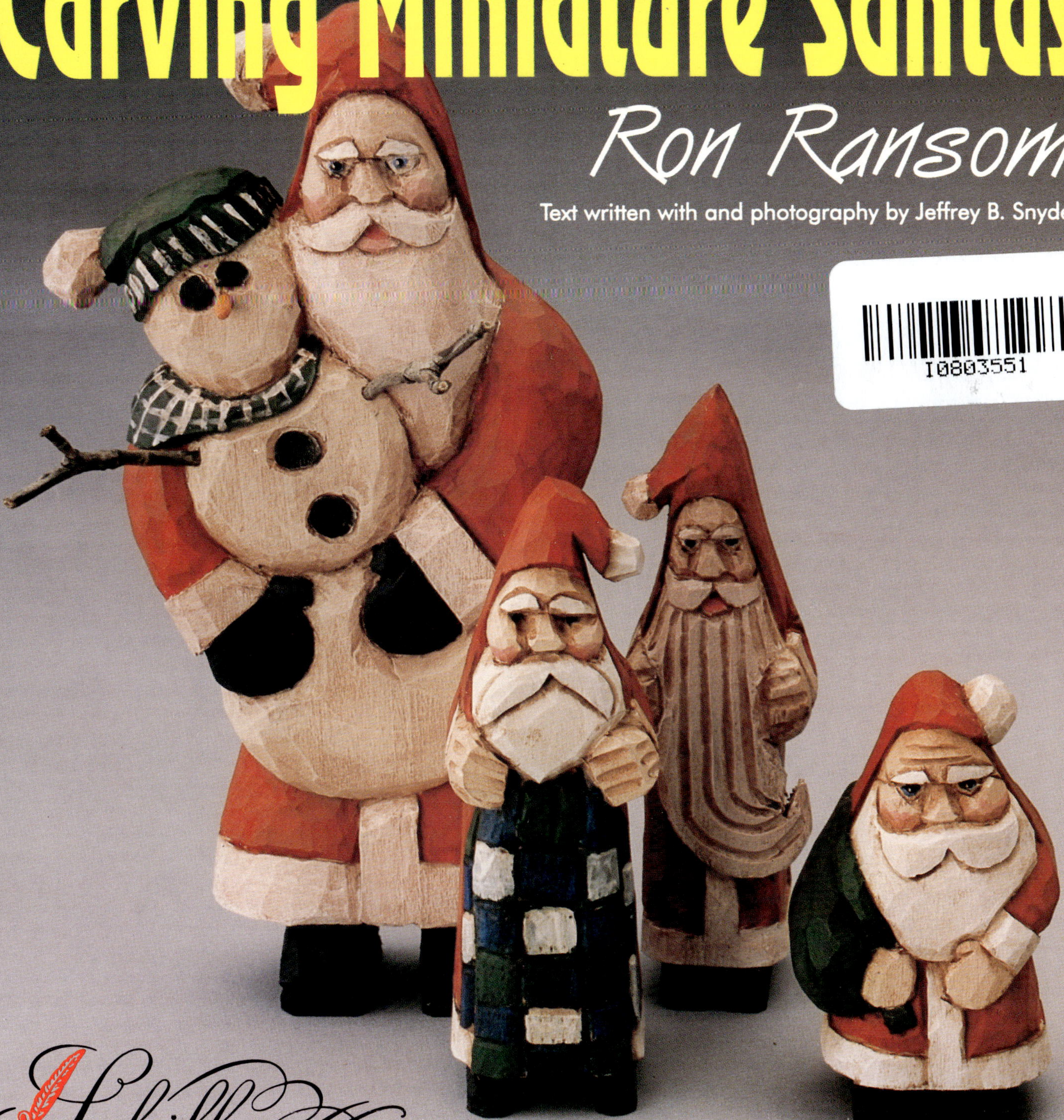

Schiffer Publishing Ltd

77 Lower Valley Road, Atglen, PA 19310

Dedication

Since 1953 when my wife Evelyn and I married, many times I've heard "never marry a man who was reared with five sisters." Evelyn thinks I was spoiled. Of course, this is absurd.

I dedicate this book to my four remaining sisters, Mary, Erma, Alice and Corintha.

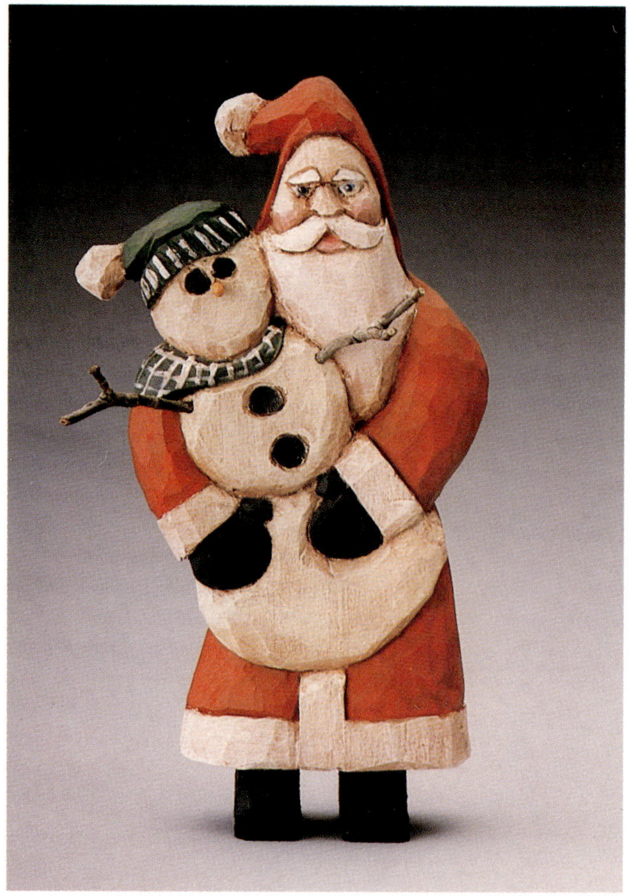

ISBN: 0-88740-824-9
Printed in Hong Kong.

Library of Congress-in-Publication Data

Ransom, Ron.
Mini-cheers: carving miniature Santas / Ron Ransom: text written with and photography by Jeffrey B. Snyder.
p. cm.
ISBN 0-88740-824-9
1. Miniature wood-carving--Patterns. 2. Wood-carved figurines. 3. Santa Claus in art. I. Snyder, Jeffrey B. II. Title.
TT199.7.R363 1995
731.4'62--dc20 95-7246
CIP

Published by Schiffer Publishing, Ltd.
77 Lower Valley Road
Atglen, PA 19310
Please write for a free catalog.
This book may be purchased from the publisher.
Please include $2.95 postage.
Try your bookstore first.

We are interested in hearing from authors with book ideas on related subjects.

Contents

Introduction

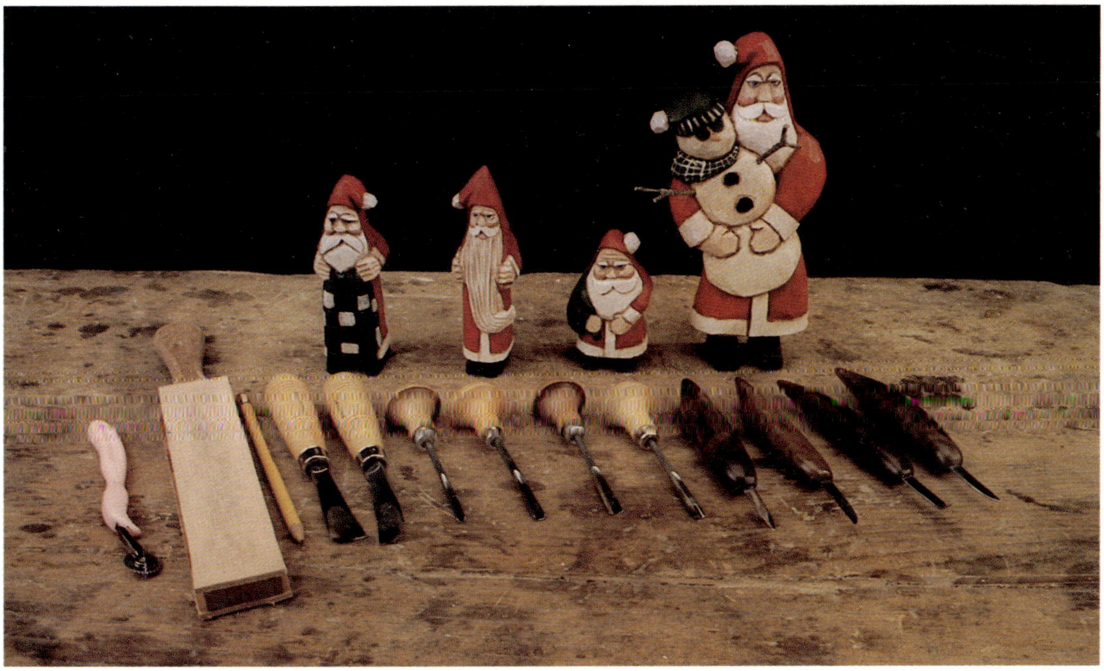

These are the Santas we will be carving and the tools we will use to carve them. Everything I'm doing can still be done with a knife, but I've found that gouges speed up the work.

With my first book, *Santa Carving*, I had no idea what a carver was looking to find. I introduced carvers to my designs and the response was good. From letters, phone calls and personal visits I had a better idea for *Angel Carving* and *Carving Santas with Special Interests*.

Part of the success of these books has been explained by people telling me that my designs and instructions didn't intimidate them. They felt a presentable Santa or other design could be carved.

Many of you have asked for ideas on what to do with scraps of basswood too small for other patterns and too big to throw away. I think you will find these patterns can be used on smaller pieces of wood and will also work on one inch thick wood.

I have also included a Santa with Snowman favorite. It is a guaranteed seller.

I apologize to you who have been patiently waiting for my new book. I was ready to begin in early 1993 but a little carving by my heart surgeon curtailed that effort.

I have also recently retired after 30 years in public recreation and I now plan on some private recreation with my wife.

If you have any questions or comments, please send a self-addressed, stamped envelope to:

Ron Ransom
Box 4101
Marietta, GA 30061

Tools, etc.

As with most carvers, I have tried a great number of tools, sharpening methods and styles. I find that I enjoy my method of carving and envy those who carve the difficult pieces. For want of a better excuse, I'll use "You can't teach an old dog new tricks." I think this dog is probably a little lazy.

I like the knives made by Bob Lominack. They arrive extremely sharp and hold an excellent edge with minimal sharpening. Bob can be reached at P.O. Box 1189, Abingdon, VA 24212.

The various gouges are from a set of Swiss made, palm handled carving sets sent to me from Woodcraft. The numbers I show in the text of this book correspond to this set. Woodcraft and many others sell fine tools and equipment.

I also use a MINIMITE drill from Dremel which I've found to be useful for tight areas. It will also do fine detailing.

If you are not a member of the National Woodcarvers Association, you should be. Their bimonthly issues are loaded with information on what other carvers are doing, patterns and just about everything a beginning or advanced carver needs to know.

Annual membership dues are eight dollars and include a subscription to the magazine "Chip Chats." Foreign memberships are ten dollars annually. The address is:

National Woodcarver's Association
P.O. Box 43218
Cincinnati, OH 45243

The Generic Santa

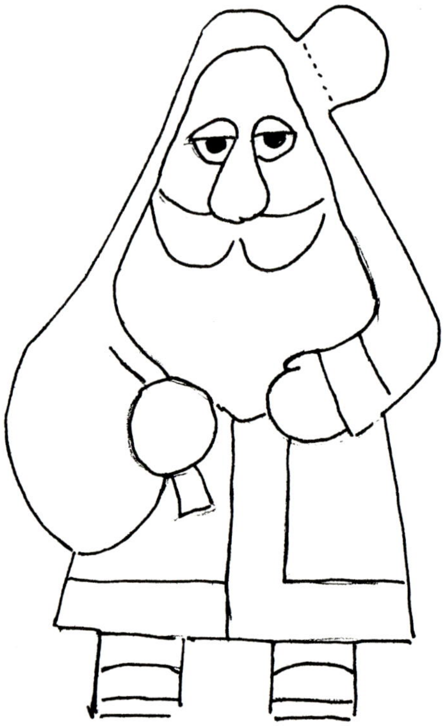

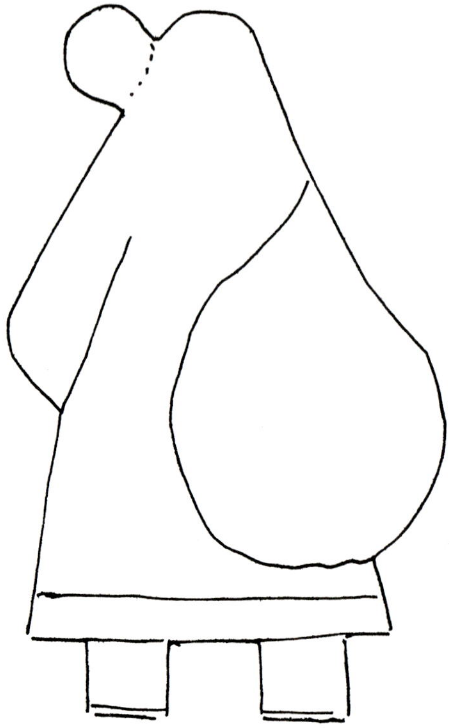

Once your tools are sharp, we'll start carving with the small generic Santa. He may be carved on a 1" piece of wood. In fact, we are carving all our Santas from left over pieces of wood. These sell well if you are interested. Many ask me how to price these to sell. I have no idea where you live or how popular Santa's are in your area. Use your best judgment.

To begin, first transfer the pattern to your wood and cut it out with the band saw. Of course, not everybody has a band saw, but most have the coping saw or reciprocating saw. So, cut out the blank with whatever you have.

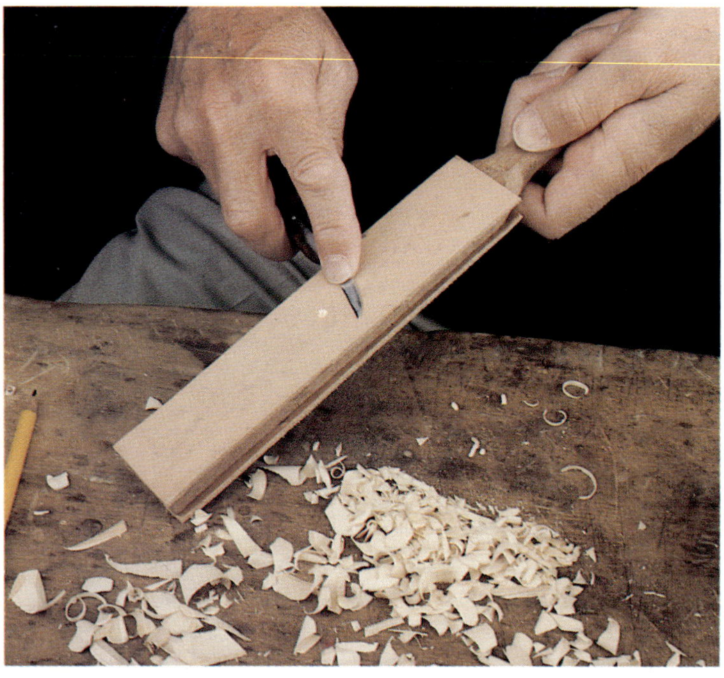

When you start, make sure your knife is good and sharp. I use a narrow piece of wood with smooth leather glued to one side and a rough piece of leather on the other side. On the rough side, spread aluminum oxide powder and neatsfoot oil. Sharpen the knife with the cutting edge trailing the stroke. Don't roll the stroke or you'll dull rather than sharpen. Six or eight passes on this side should be sufficient. Finish sharpening the edge on the smooth side after applying a few drops of neatsfoot oil. Follow this procedure about every twenty minutes and you'll keep a sharp tool.

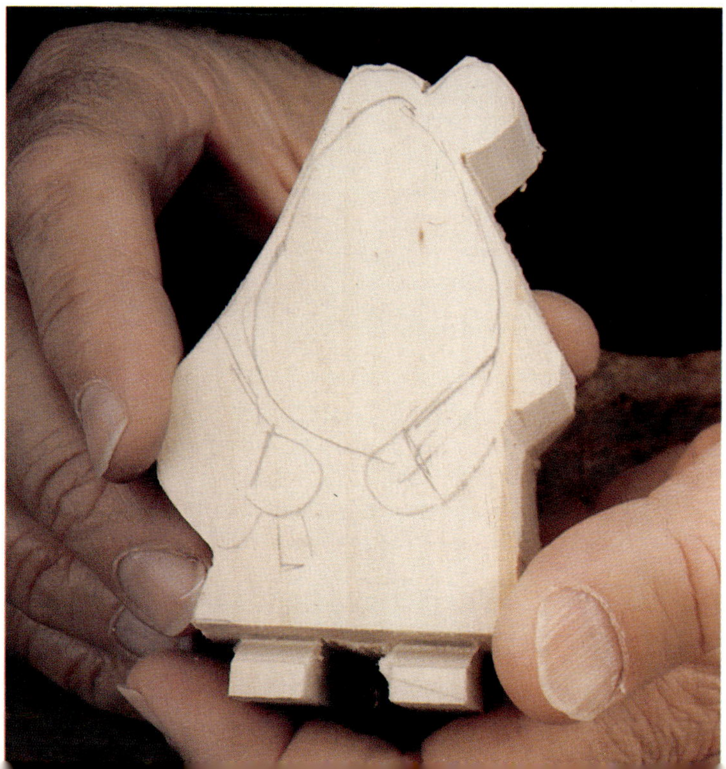

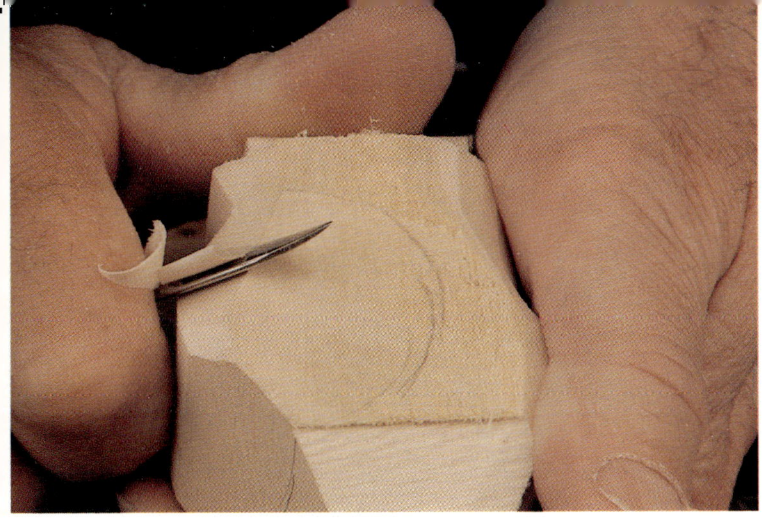

Start rounding. Keep your thumb out of the way as you round off the edges. If you like to leave the edges square, I don't care. If you cut off the pencil lines, it doesn't matter. They can be redrawn.

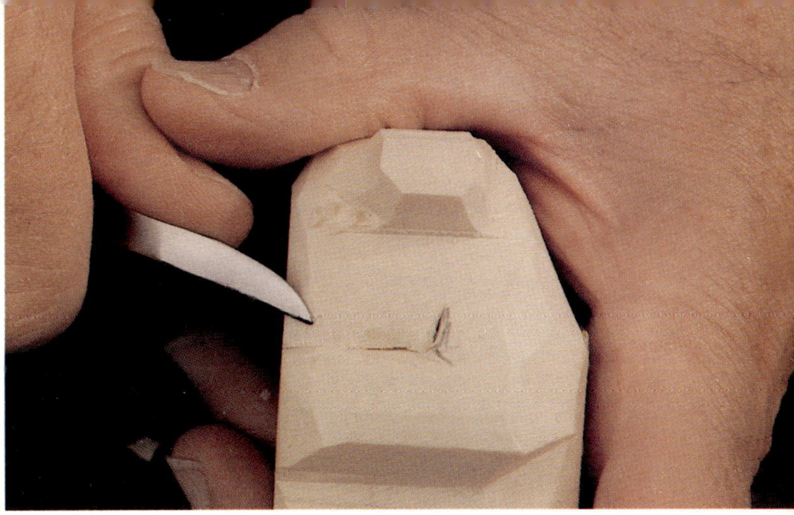

Take the piece out from above to give the arm some definition.

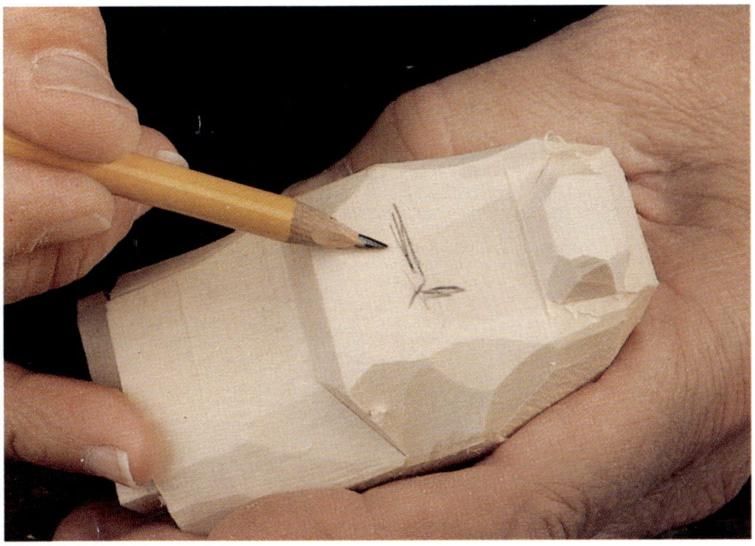

I've drawn in the arm because it's time to start a little incising to get that arm in place.

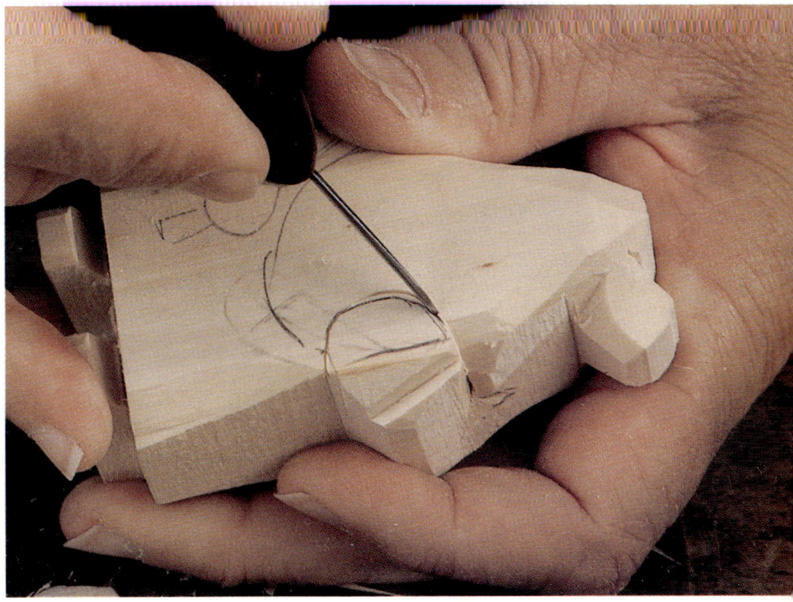

I'm incising or scoring where the hand will go. Stick the blade in as far as you want because this cut will not show.

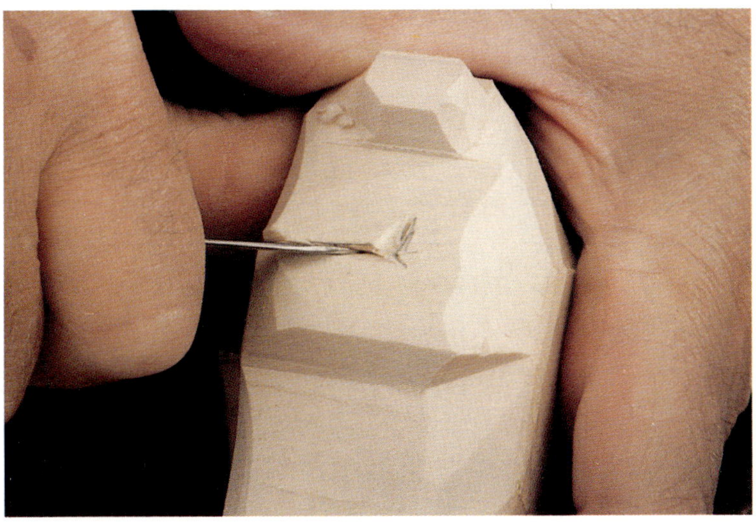

I've decided to move his arm up a little bit to overlap the beard. If you want to move the position of the arm, that's fine. Put it where you want it. Make a V cut where the arm is to be.

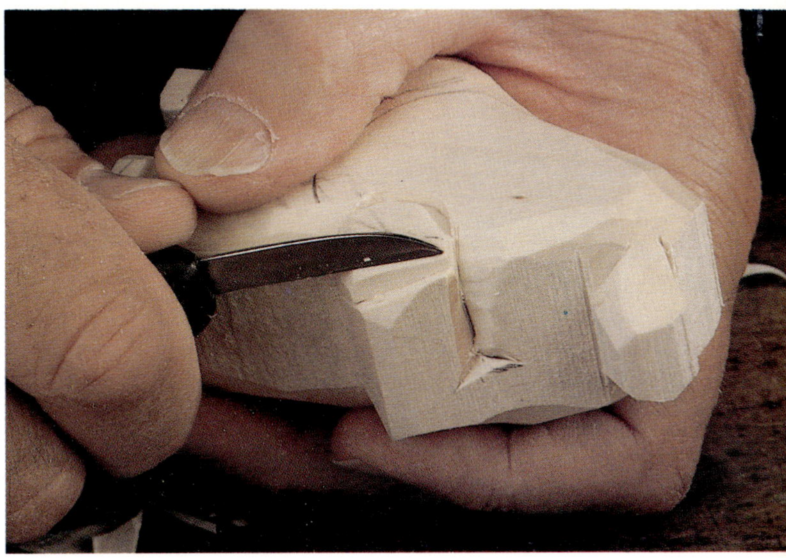

I've done the same thing in toward the sleeve.

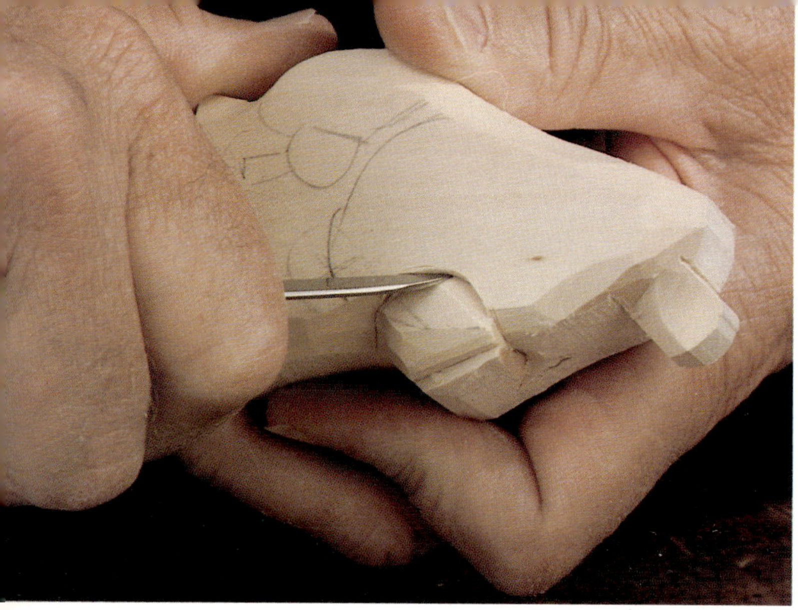

I'm shaping the hand. The fingers are curved; they are not laying out flat.

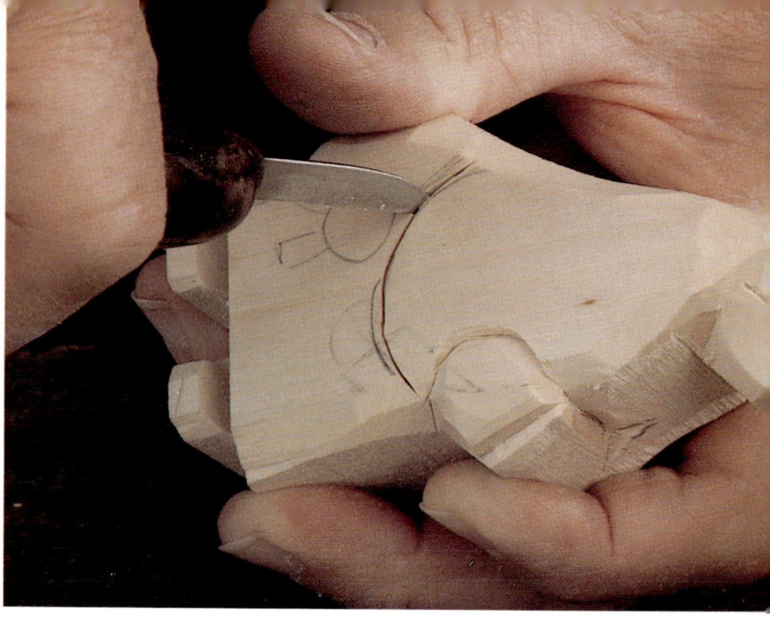

Incise the bottom of the beard.

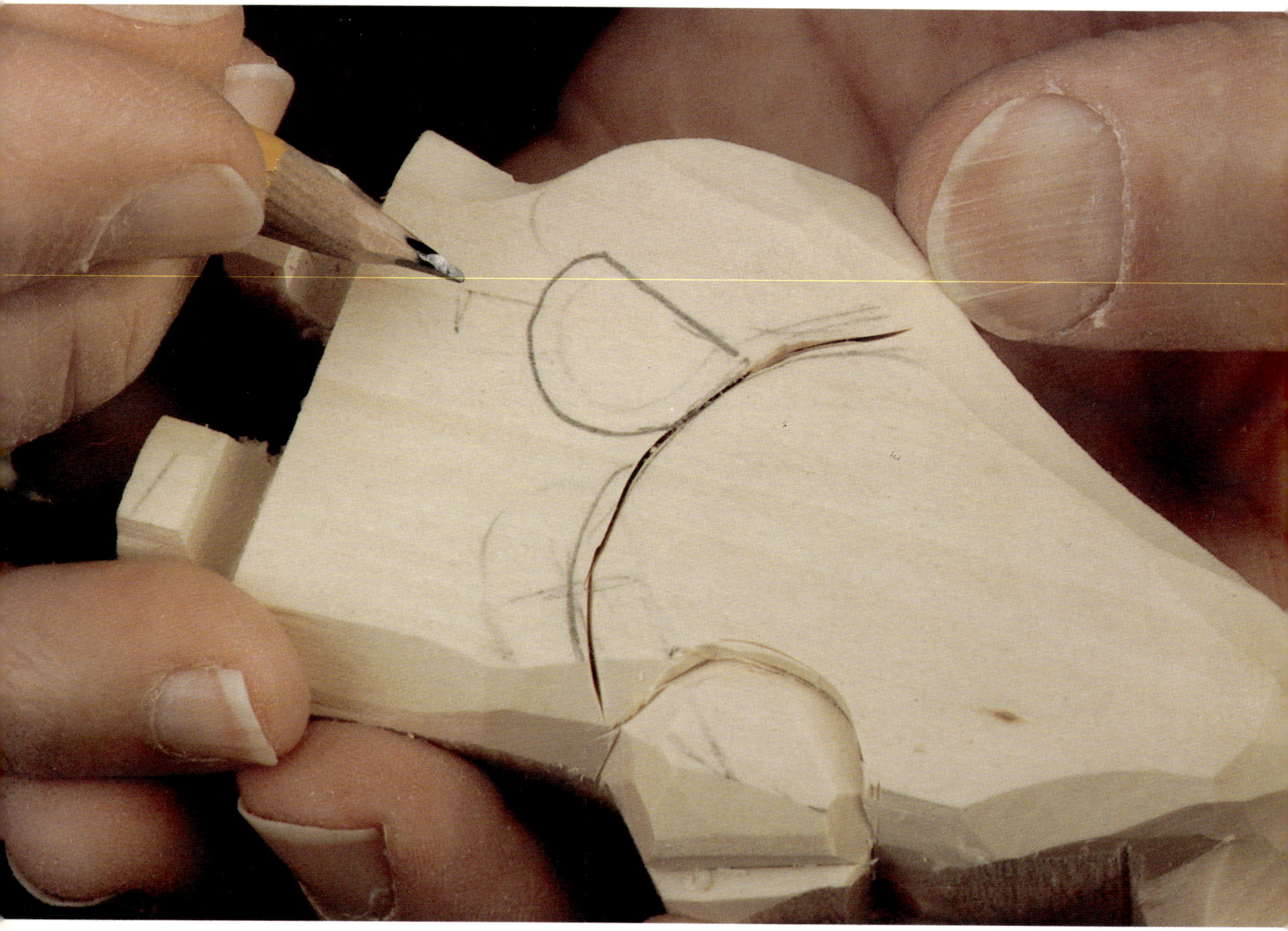

I found, when I moved the first hand, that the second hand would look deformed if I did not adjust it's size. Go ahead and change as you go. You are not working in steel.

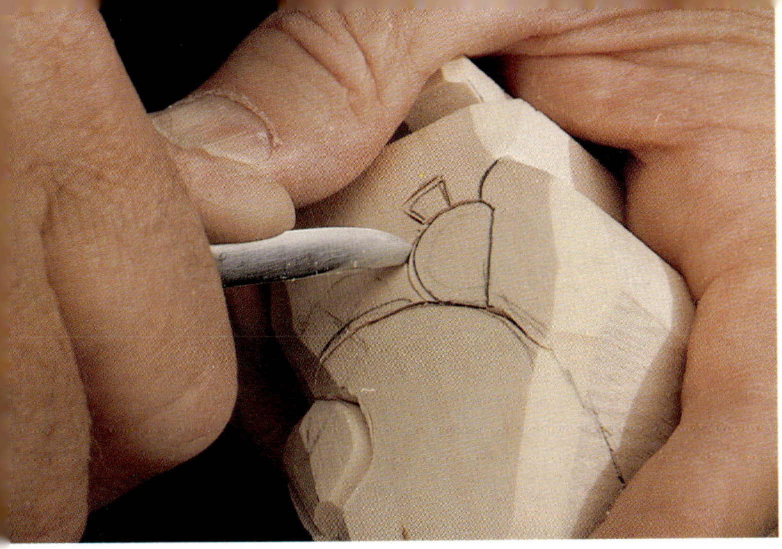

Incise around the hand and the bottom of the bag.

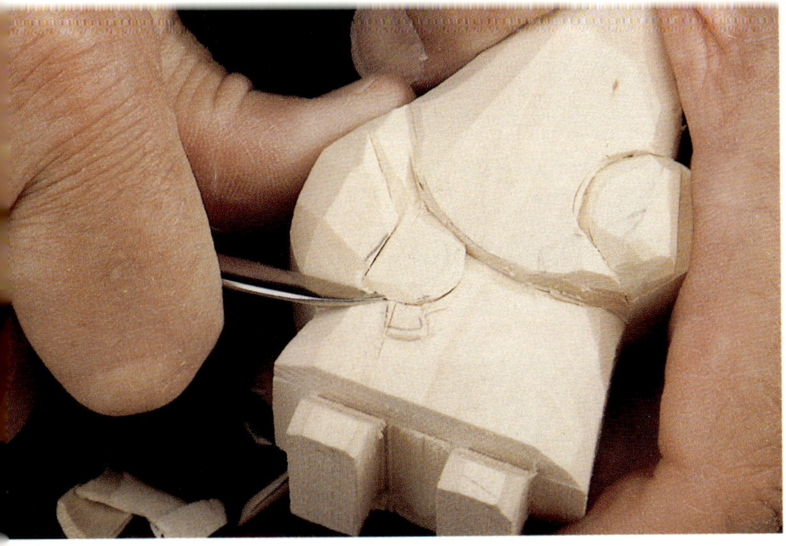

Round up the bottom of the beard and the hand holding the bag. As you round the hand, you will shape the base of the bag as well.

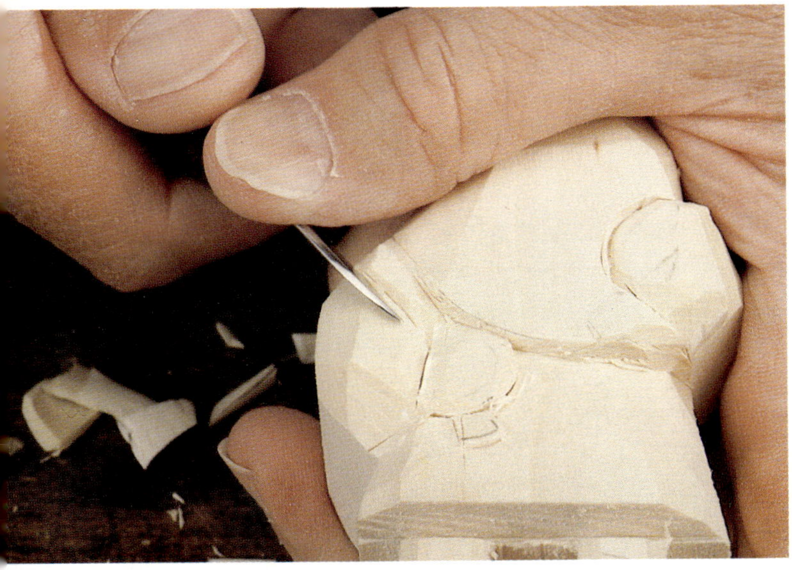

I've cut a little V where the bag of gifts comes into the arm.

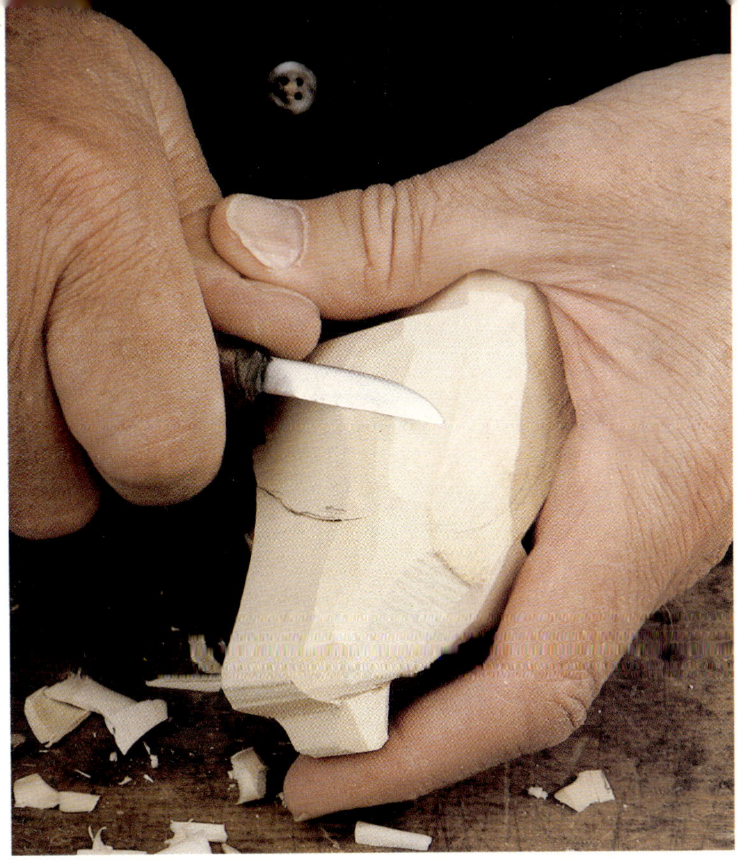

I'm rounding off the back of the bag. Notice how I'm using my left thumb for leverage and control. You're carving a Santa, not peeling a potato.

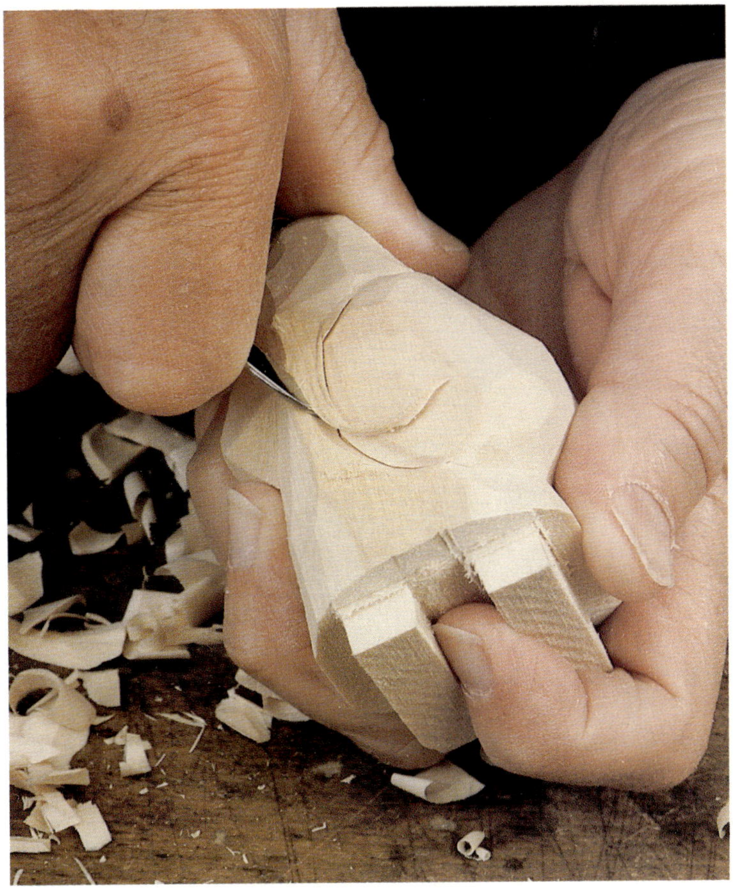

Incise around the bag and rounding the edge now.

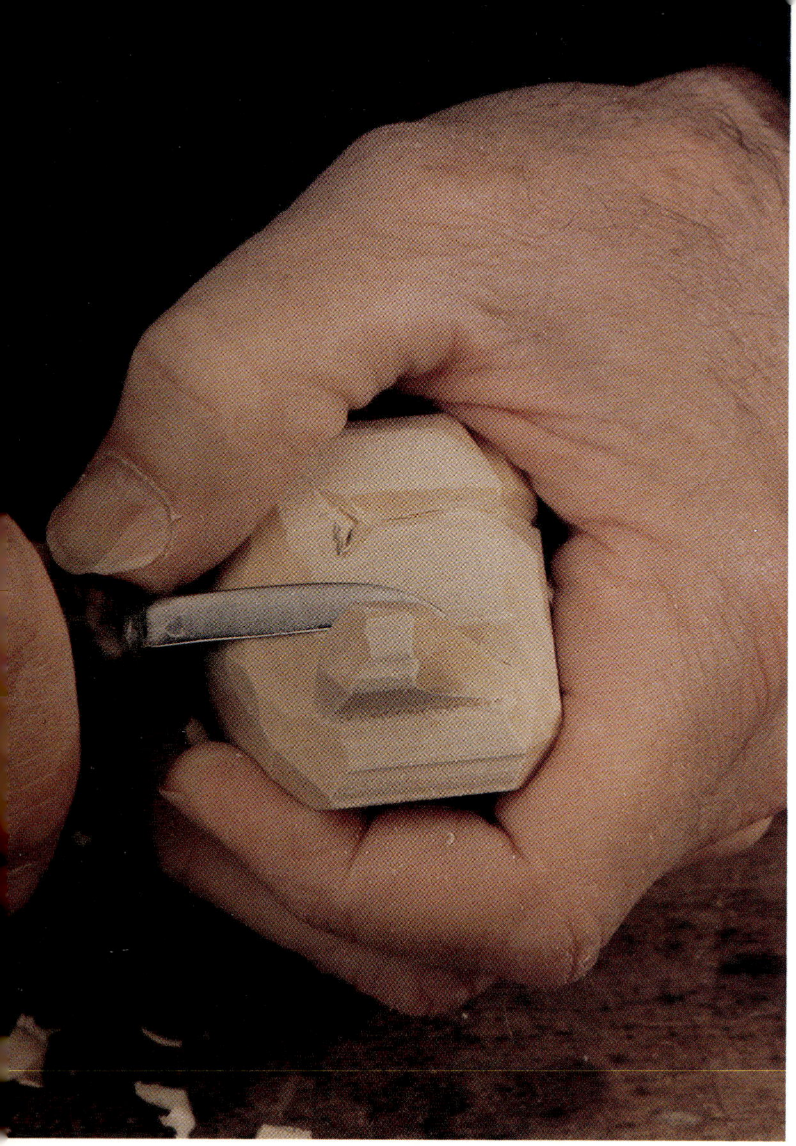

Round the little ball at the end of Santa's hat. Be careful not to cut it off. You wouldn't want a ball-less Santa.

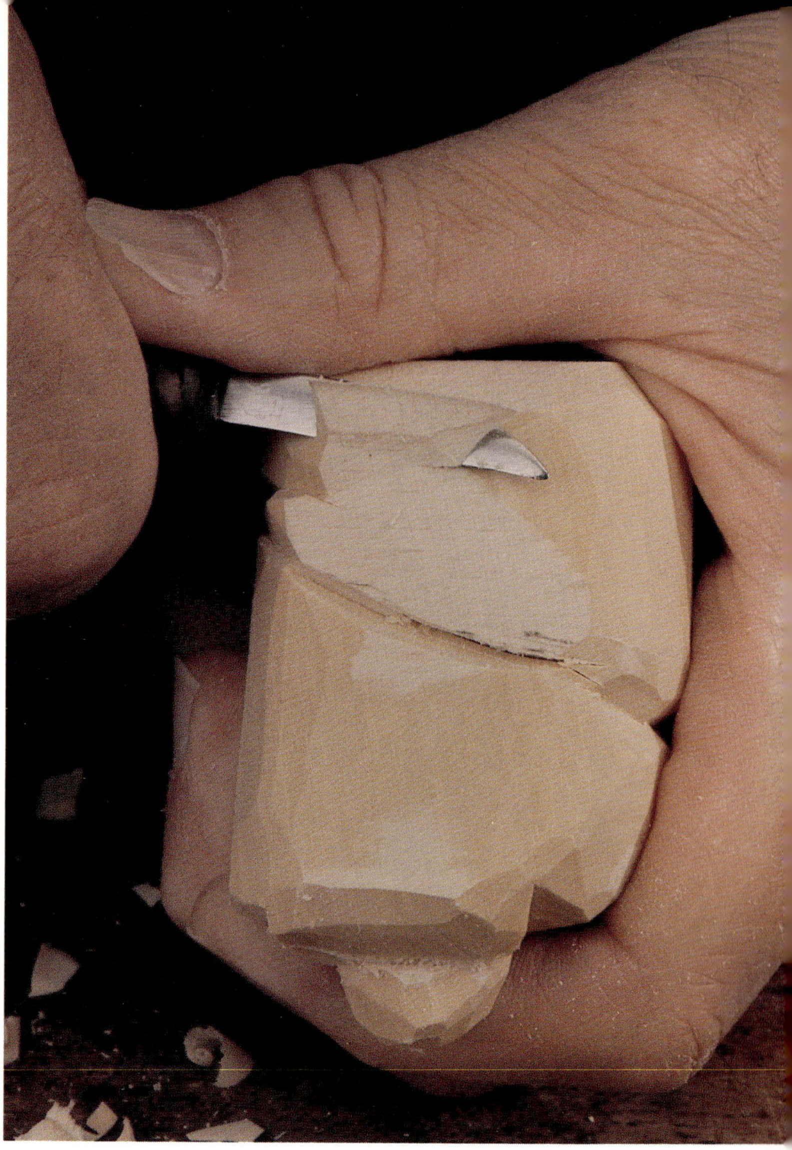

It is a good idea to smooth off all the saw marks and rough spots as you go. I seldom use sandpaper. If you want to use sandpaper, have at it.

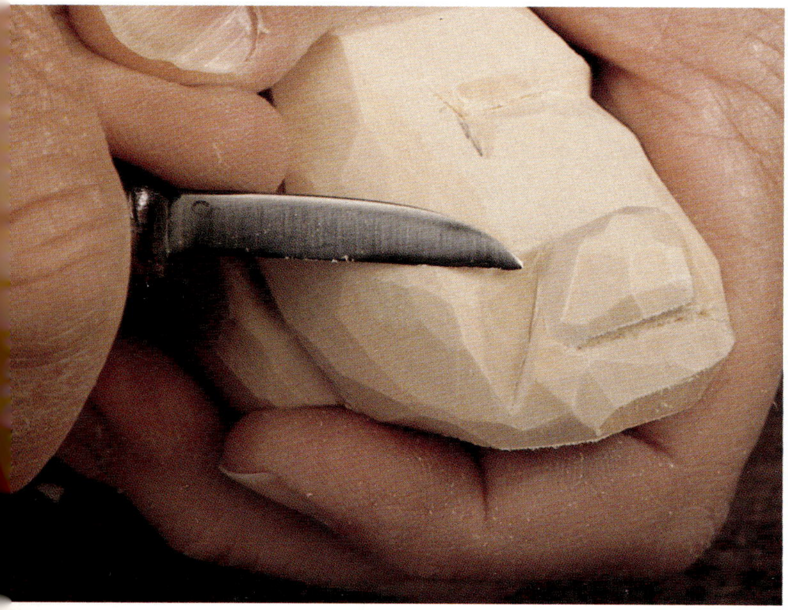

Make a little V cut to tie the ball into the hat.

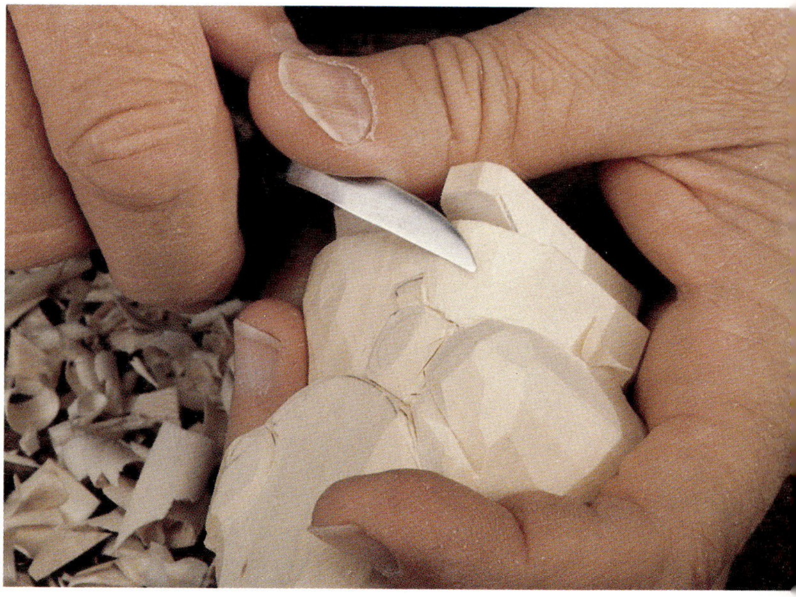

I'm continuing to round to my satisfaction.

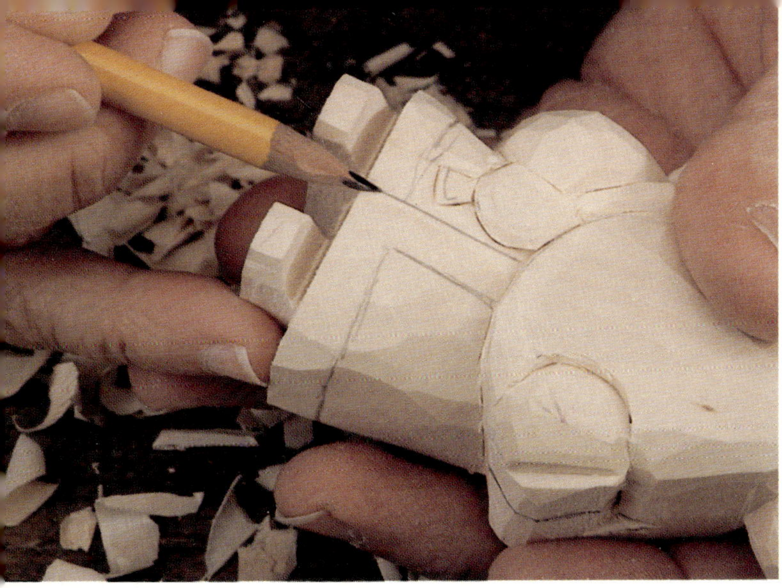

Draw in the fur now.

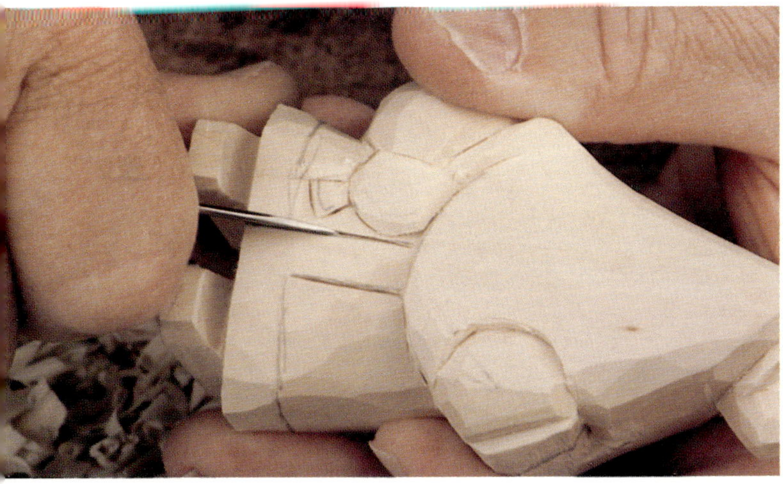

To place the fur, first incise along the line ...

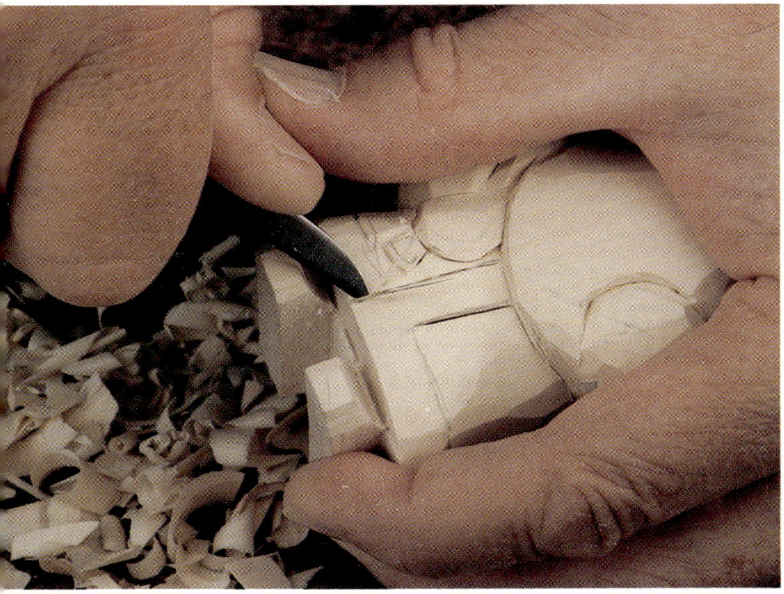

... and then carve at an angle to cut it out. This is very simple and raises the fur up away from the rest of Santa's robe. Continue all the way around Santa's robe.

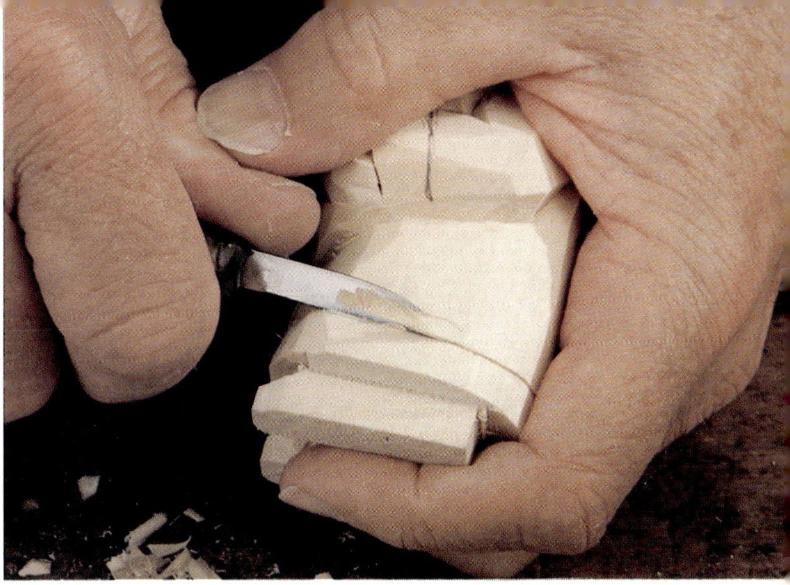

Continuing around. Just bring the knife down to the incised line and flip the wood out.

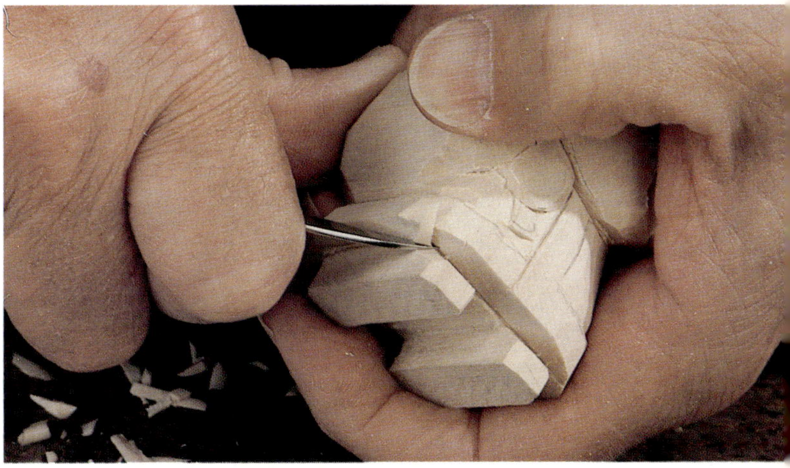

Round the feet and draw in some heels.

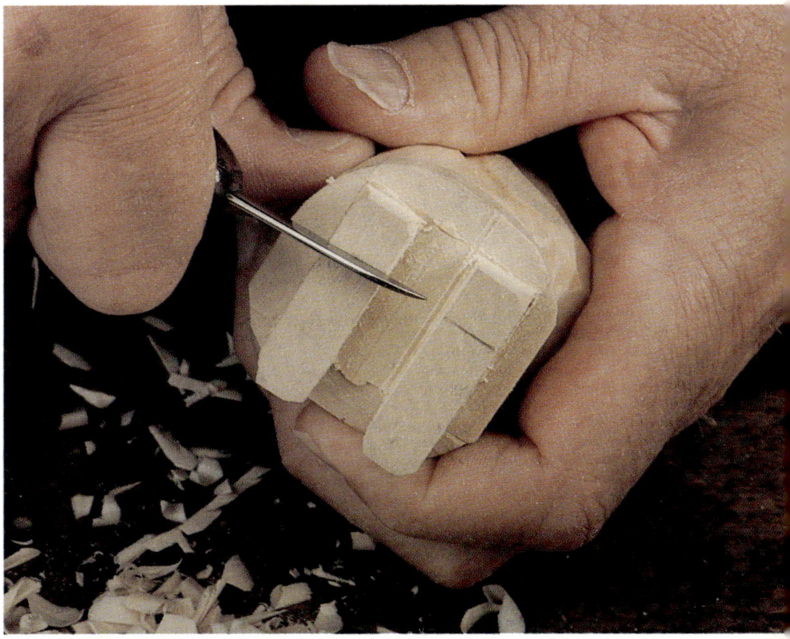

Incise a line for the heels and then ...

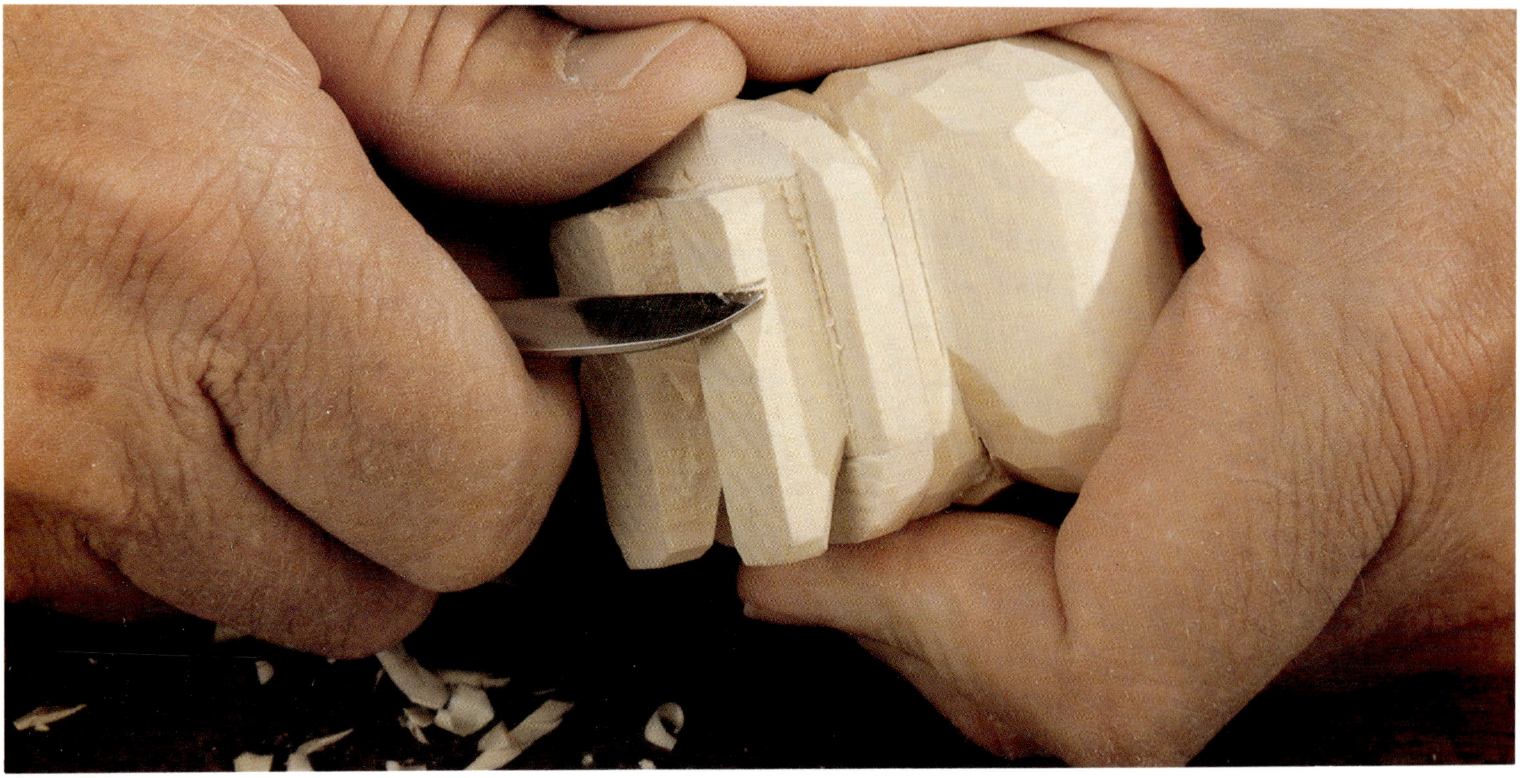

... cut out a little chunk.

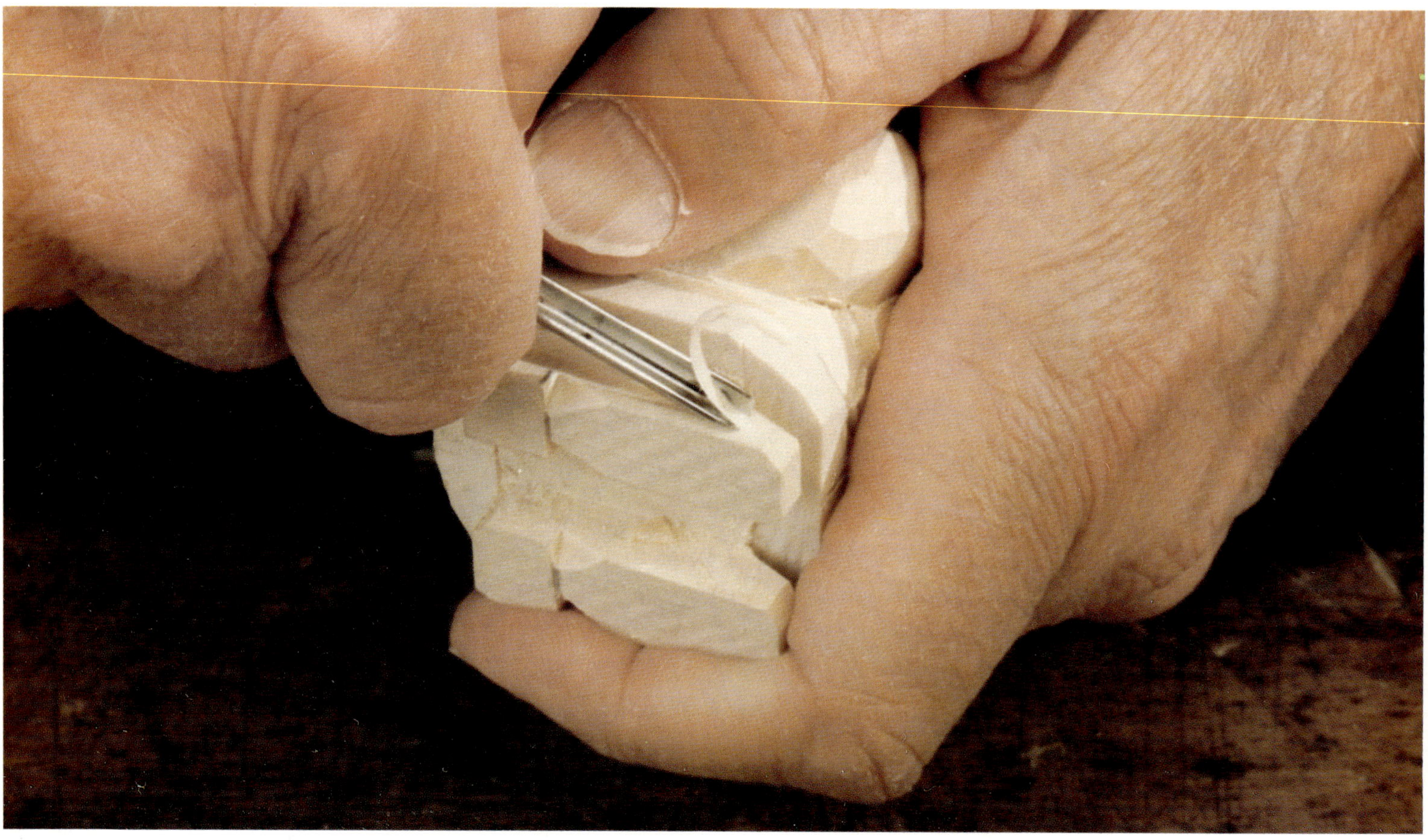

Sometimes I take this #11 gouge and put in the sole. If you don't have a gouge it's not really necessary to include a sole, so don't do it.

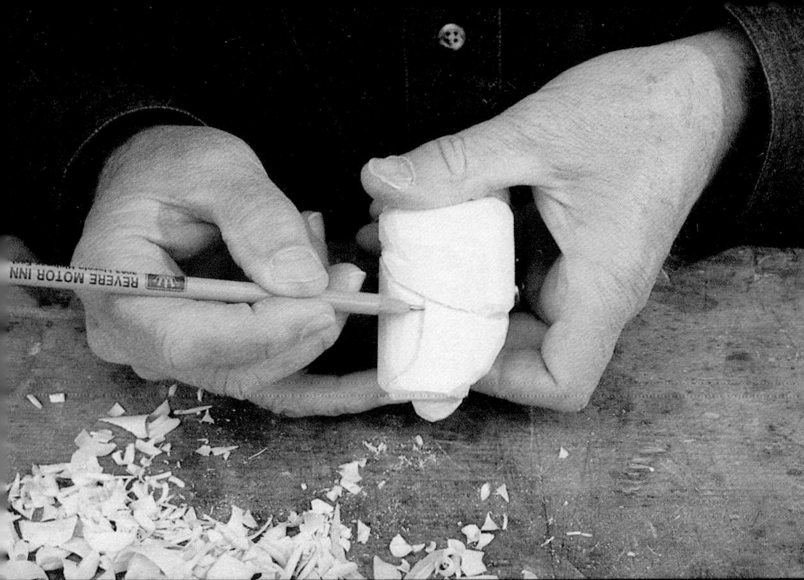

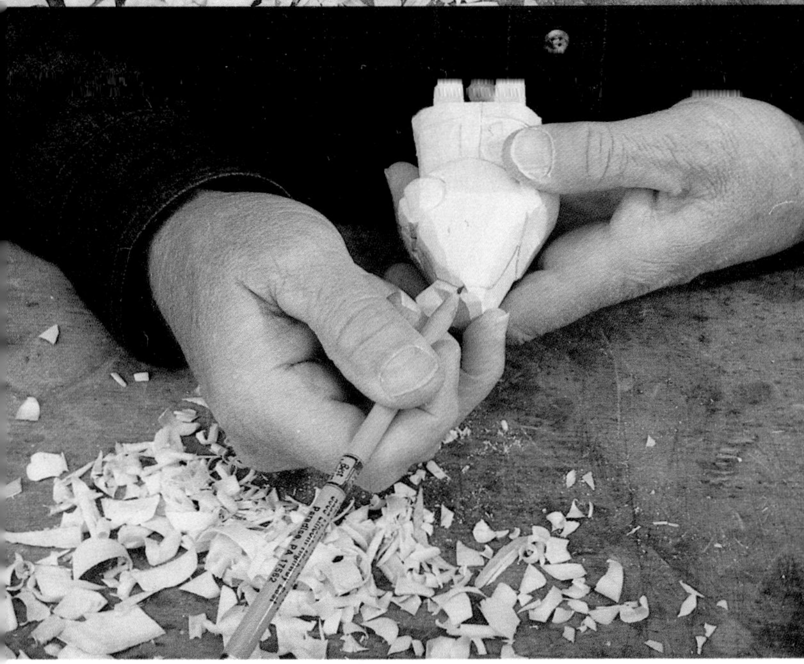

As far as I'm concerned the face is the most important part. Wrinkles in the clothes and other details will not help you market your Santas if the face is not done well. Draw in a line where you want the face to go.

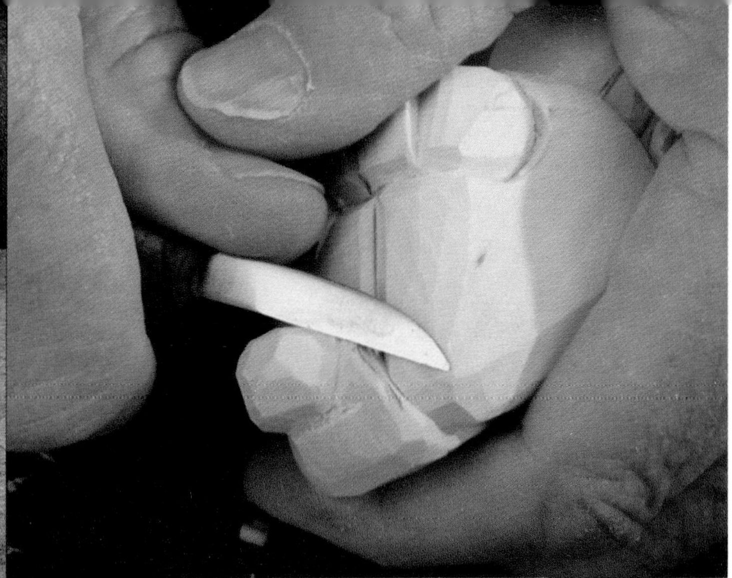

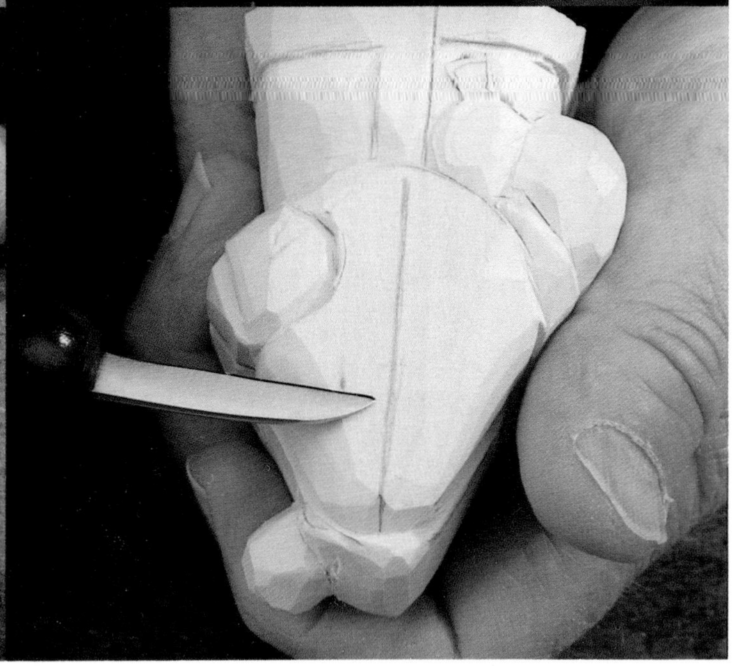

Round off the area of the face. You want roughly an egg shape here. Draw a center line down the rounded face. This will give you something to bring the lines of the face up to later.

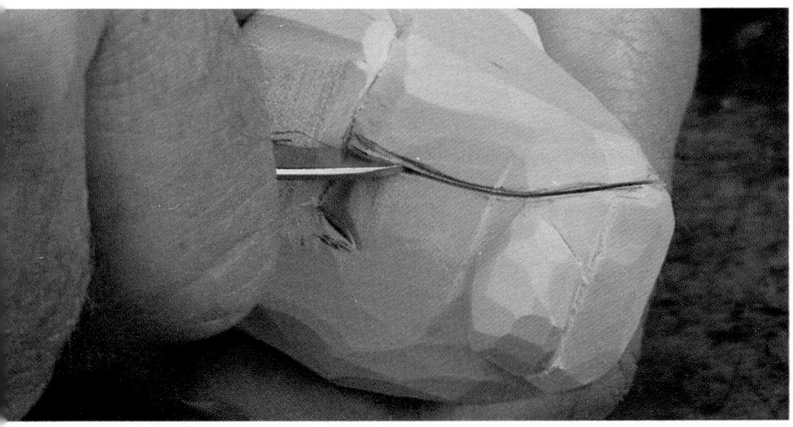

Incise all the way around the head. Notice how deeply my knife blade is cutting, about 1/8" into the basswood.

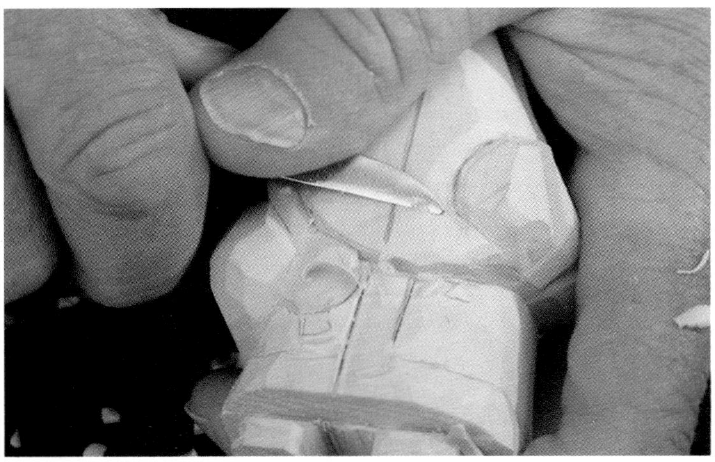

Blend the left hand into the beard now.

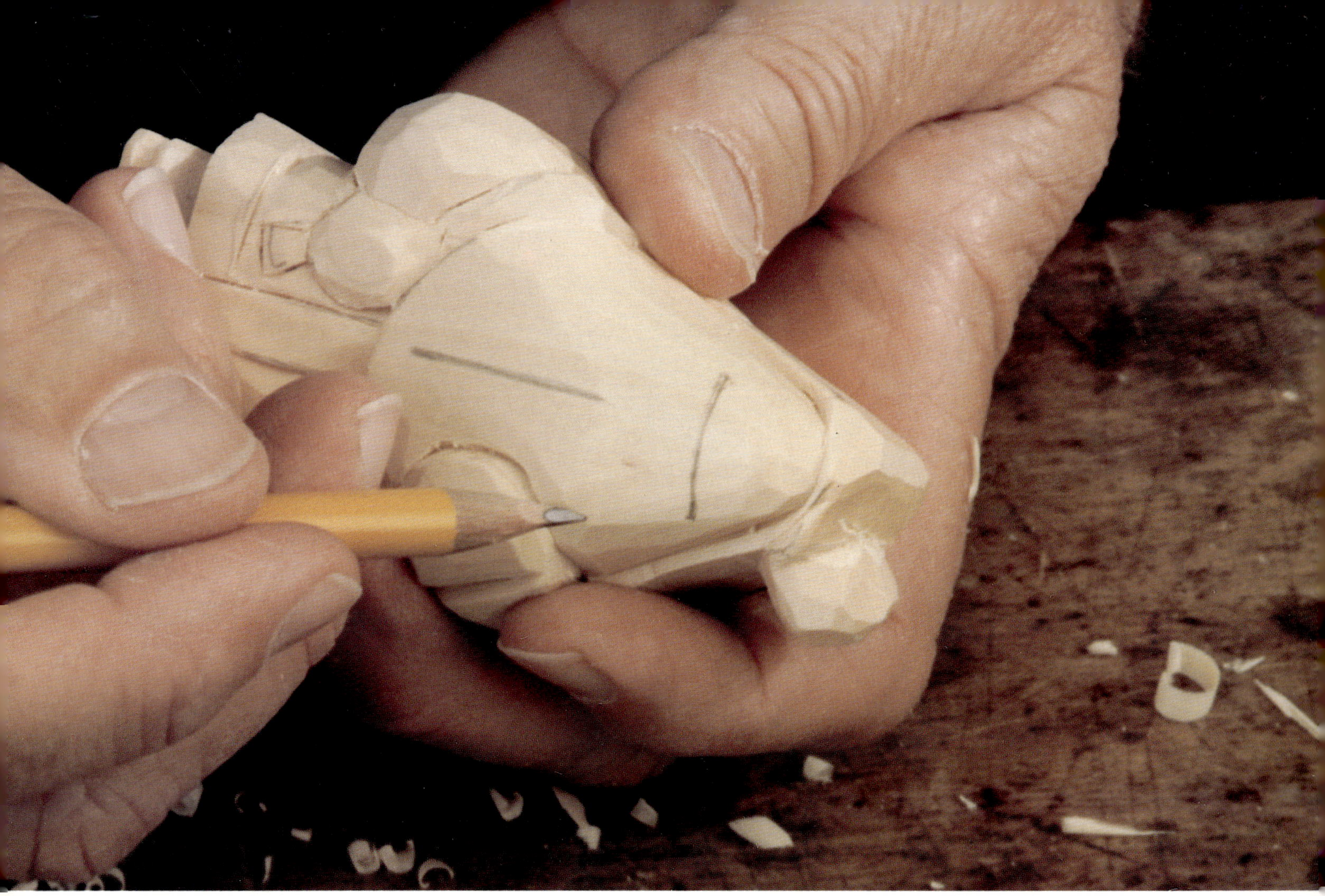

Draw in the face, beginning with a line across for the eyes first.

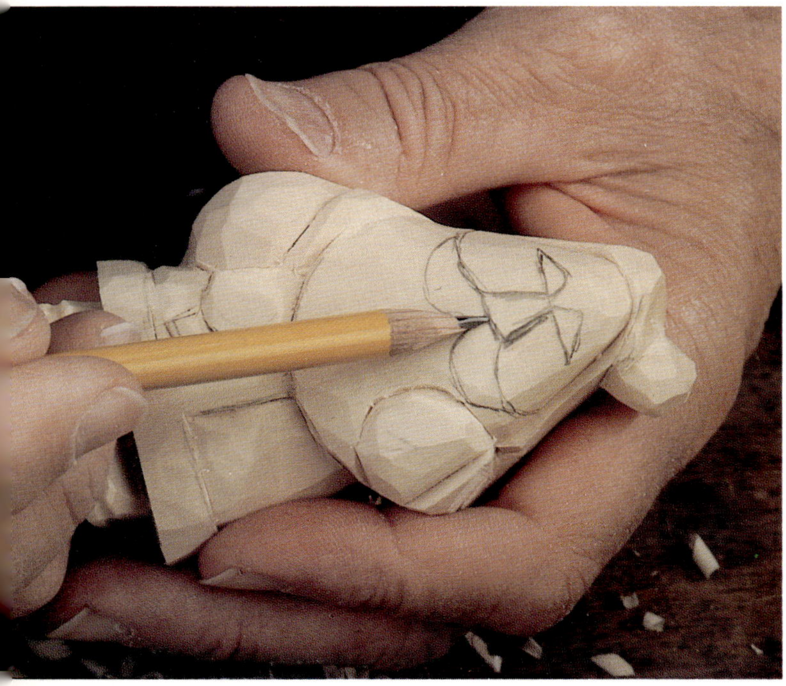

Draw in the rest of the lines for the face. Be sure to leave your nose wide. This is very important.

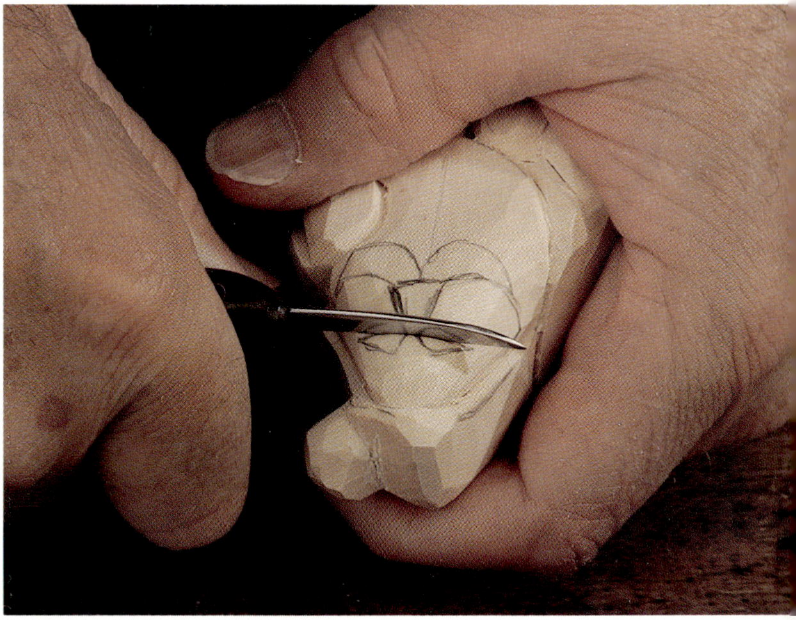

Stick your knife in as deep as you can get it for the eye channel. Both Harold Enlow and Claude Bolton, members of the Caricature Carvers of America, have encouraged me to keep doing this like I do. I abide by the old rule, "if it isn't broke, don't fix it."

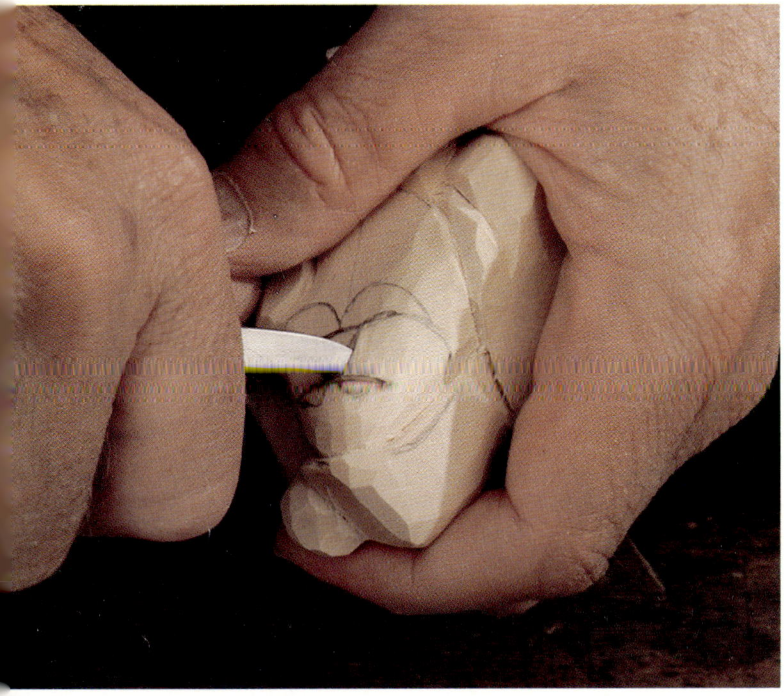

Incise the nose, angling your lines out a bit.

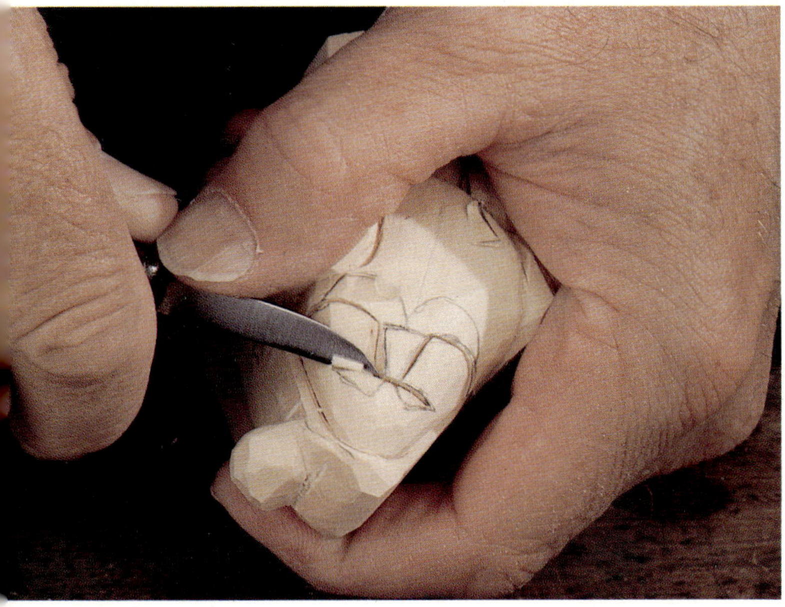

Clean out along each side of the nose. Clip off the outer tips of the nose for nostrils.

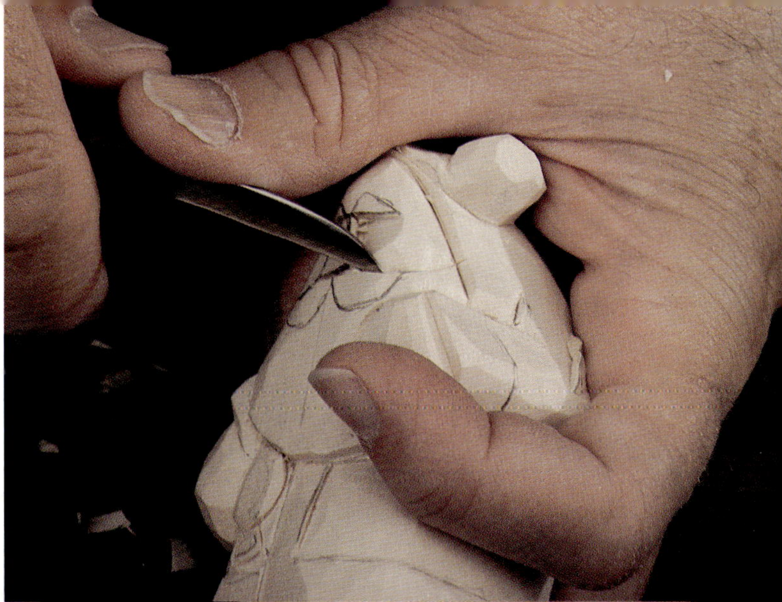

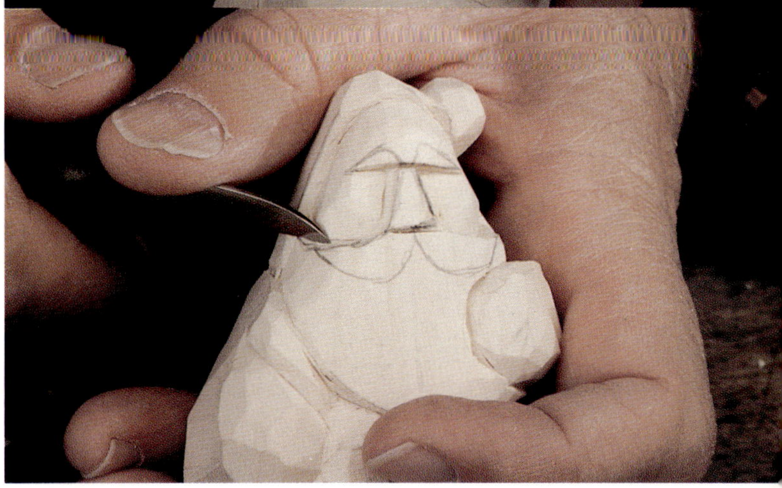

You want a nice round cheek, so keep rounding into the mustache and beard. Don't worry about whether your cheeks match. People who carve realistic faces say some carvers run into problems when they try to make both sides perfect. Look in the mirror. If your face looks perfectly alike on both sides, call Ripley's.

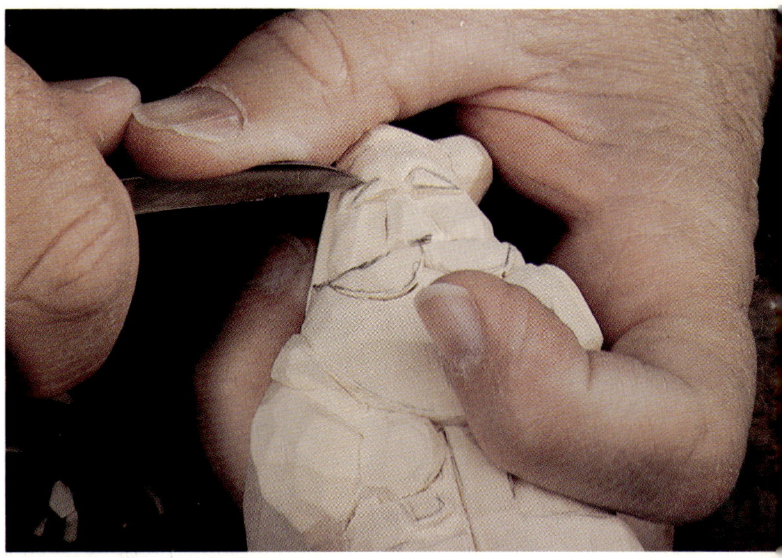

Cutting out around the eyebrows is real important. Incise and shape like the other parts, but be careful or the eyebrows will flip out.

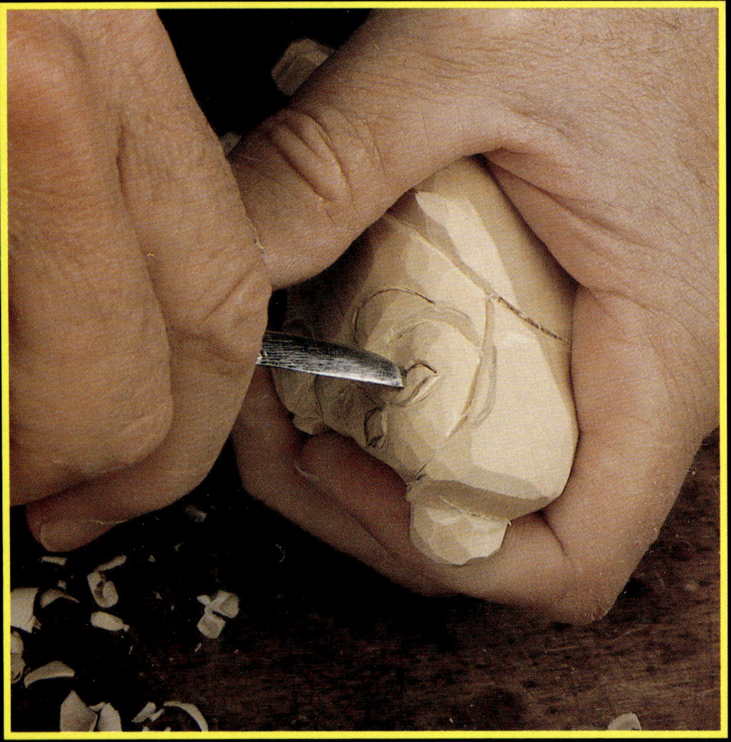

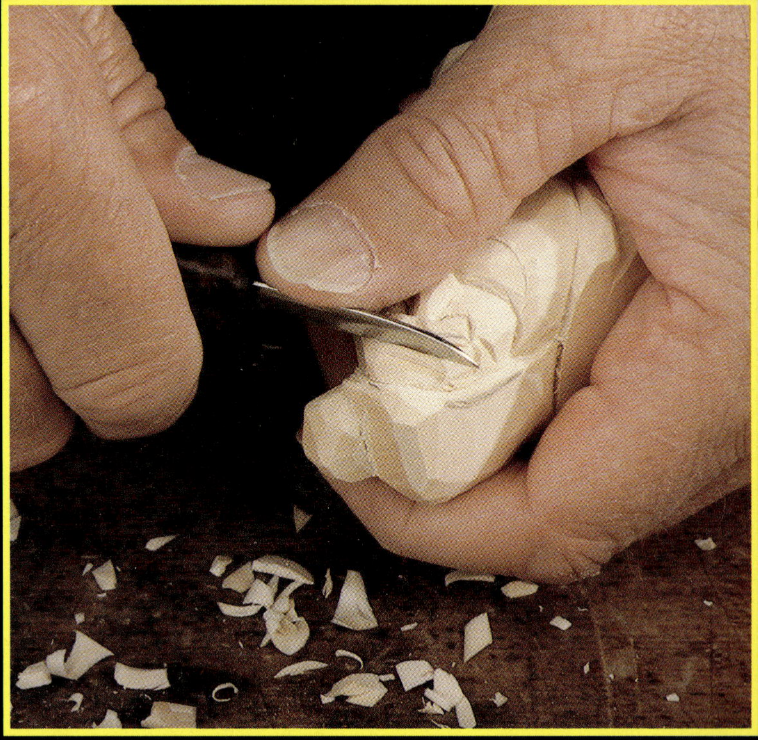

Draw in the eyeballs. These are very small, so you'll need a very sharp knife to carve them. Stick in the blade deep into the corners of the eyes and incise the eyeballs.

Make a couple of little V cuts in the forehead for frown lines.

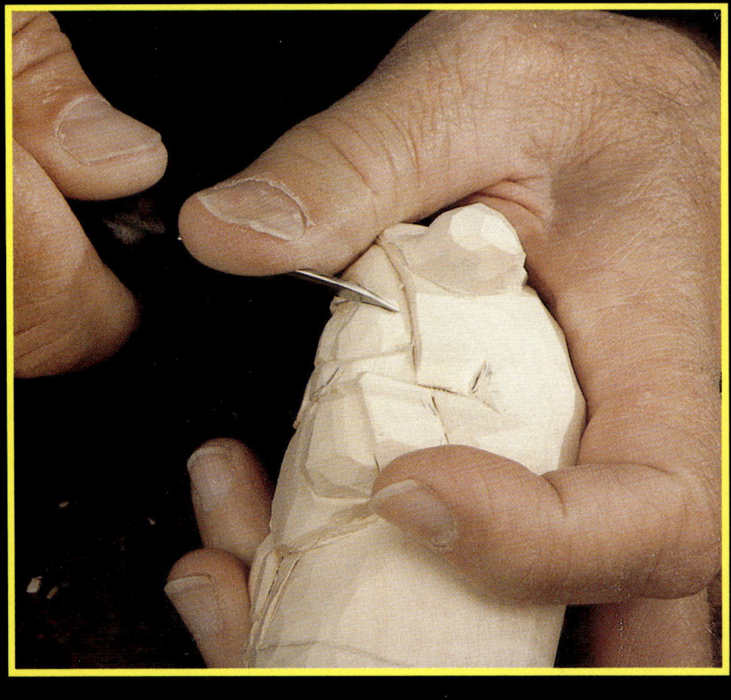

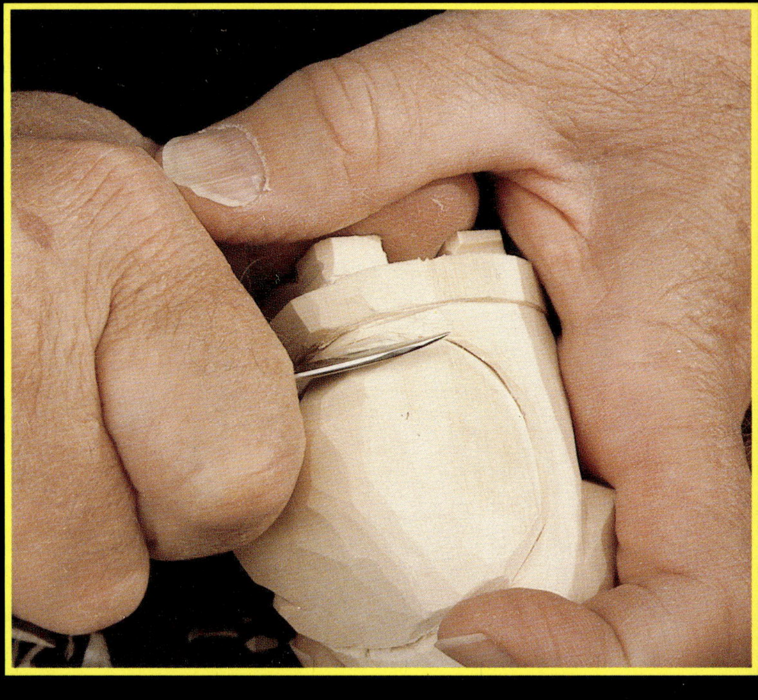

Put in some laugh wrinkles. Stick the cutting edge of your blade straight in and then come in at an angle and take out a little chunk.

Go back now and do some final rounding.

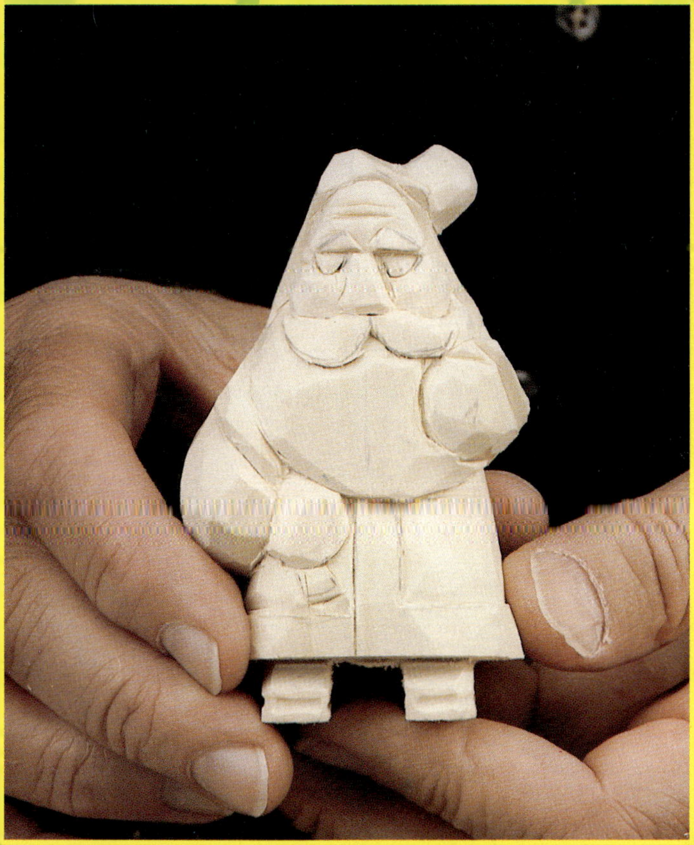
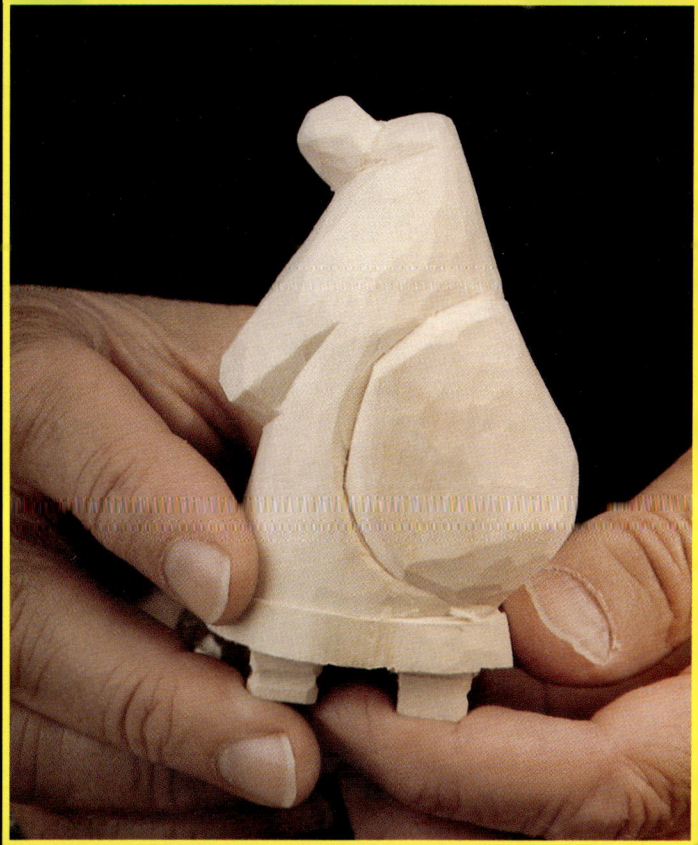
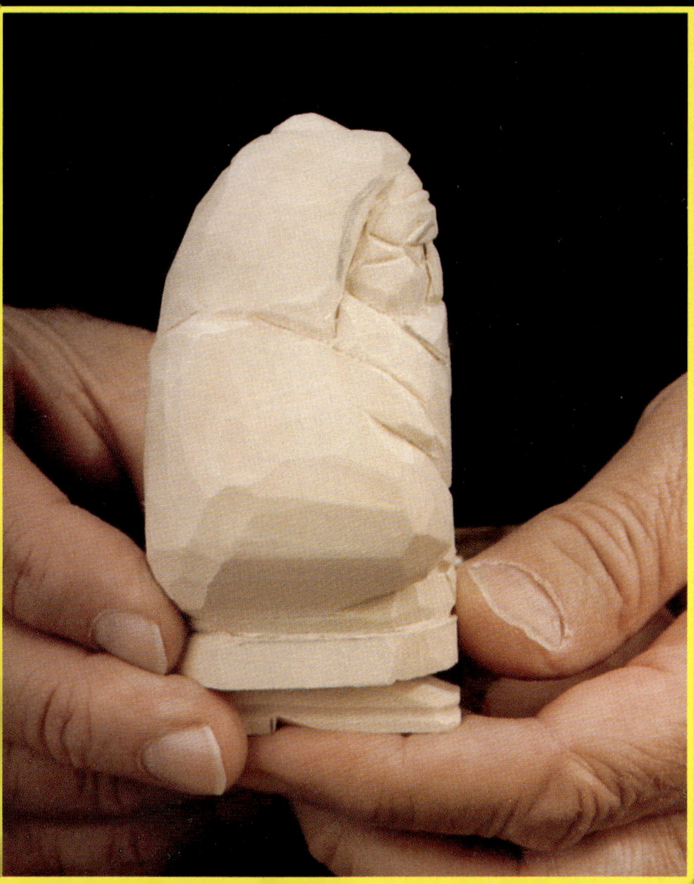
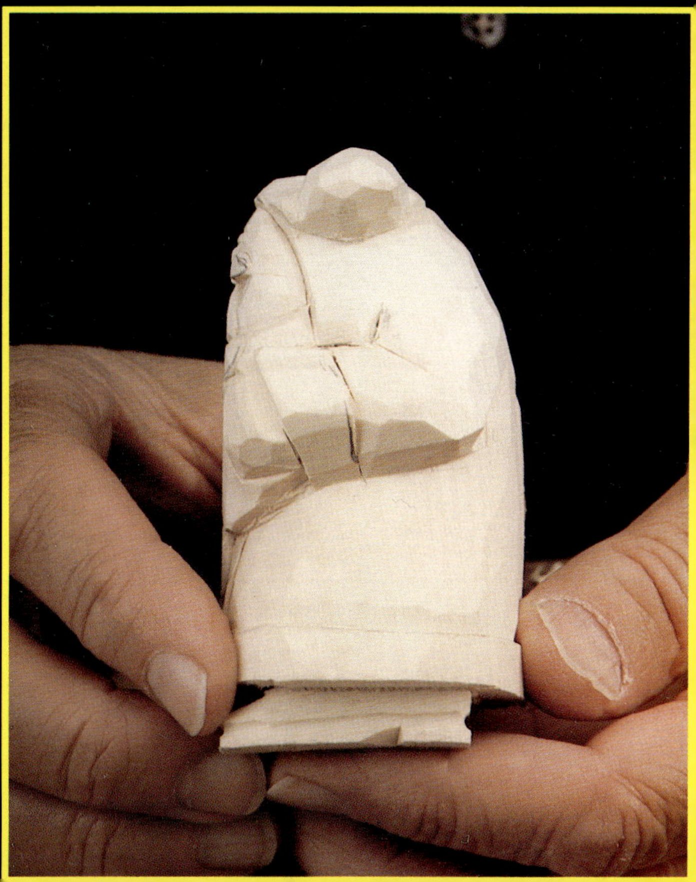

The Tall Santa

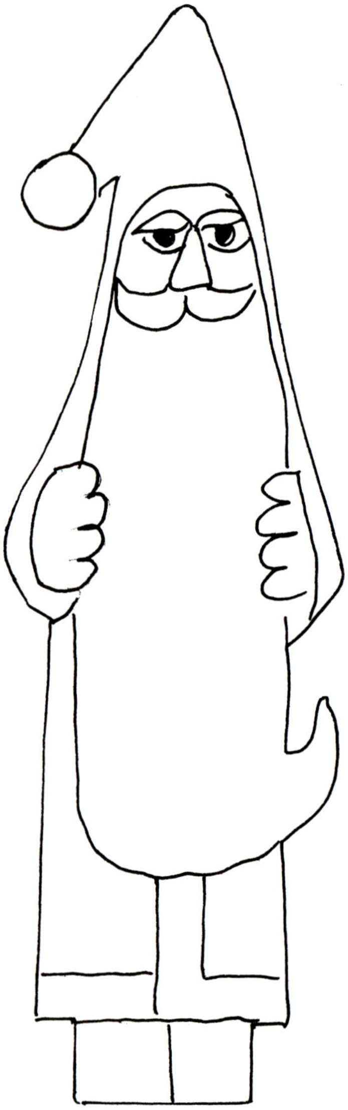

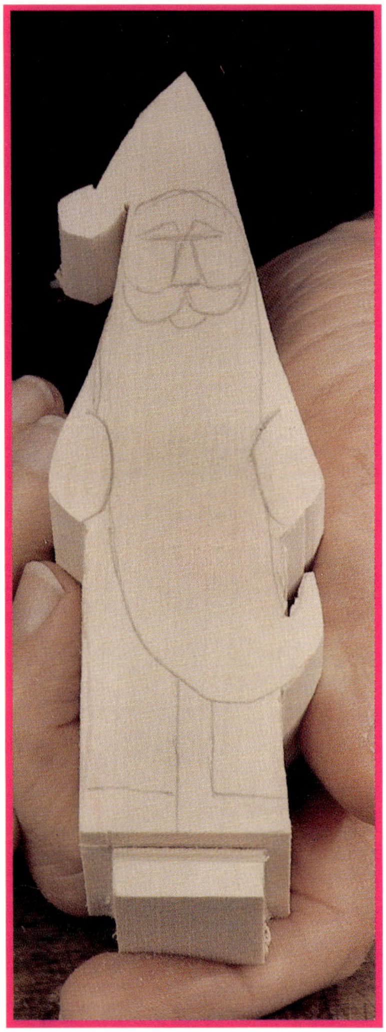

Here's a taller guy more in the Father Christmas vein. He has a curled beard to give you something else to think about.

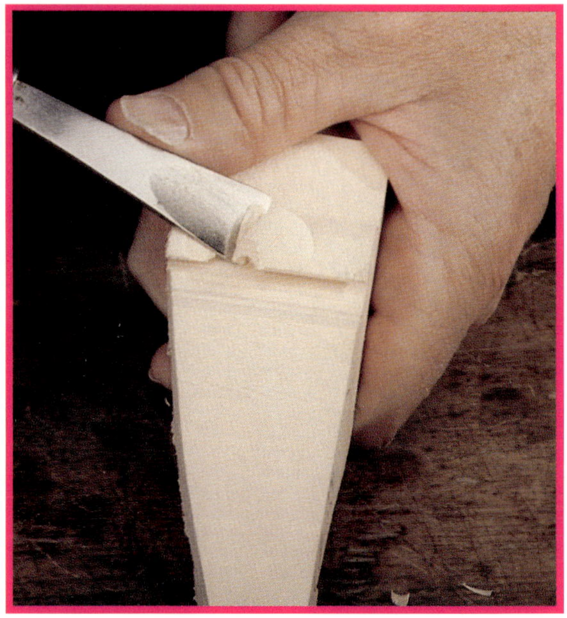

I'm moving to a pretty good sized gouge to get the excess wood behind the beard out of the way. Be very careful not the stick the gouge into your hand.

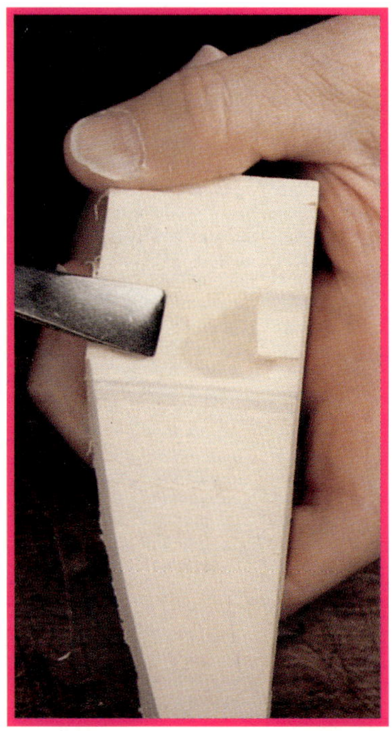

I've removed all but about 1/4" of the beard.

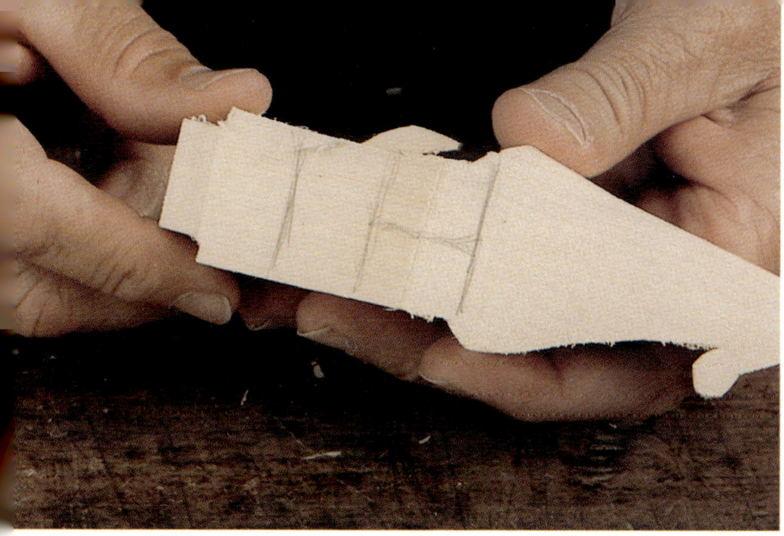

I've decided to make this one the "night after Christmas". Santa's worn out and his backside is hanging out.

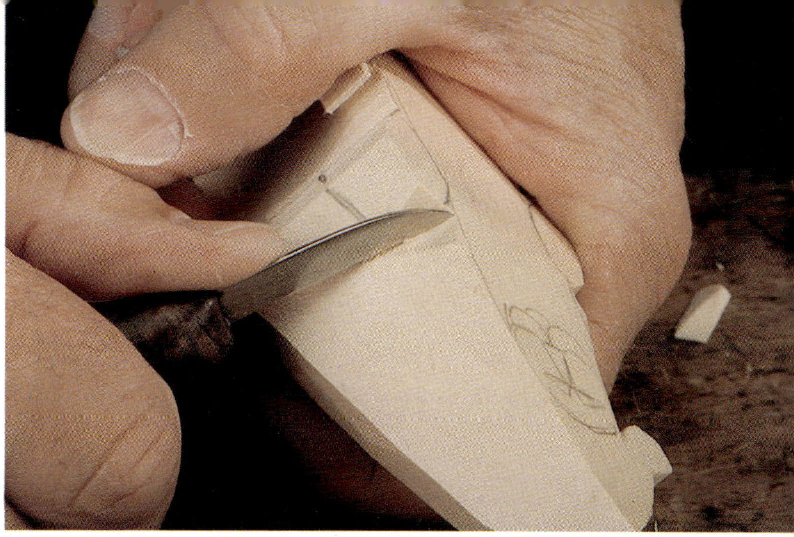

Notch each side where his hands are and ...

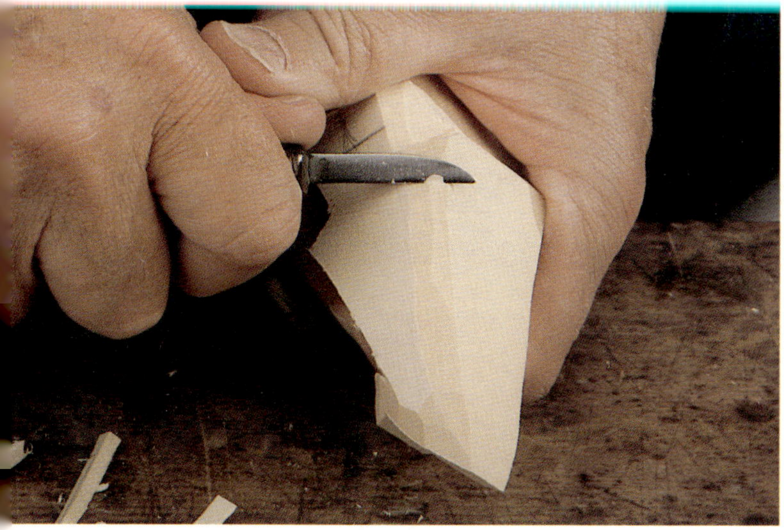

Begin to round Santa down, getting rid of the sharp edges.

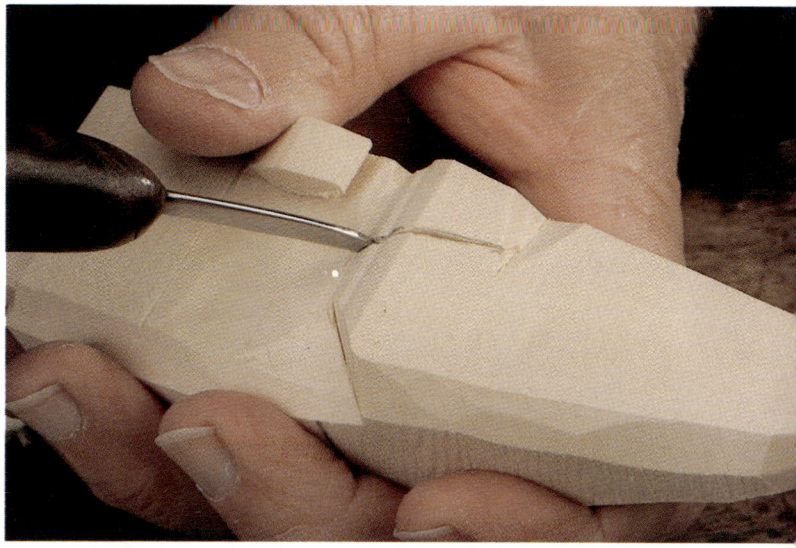

... make a line and incise where each of his hands go into his sleeves.

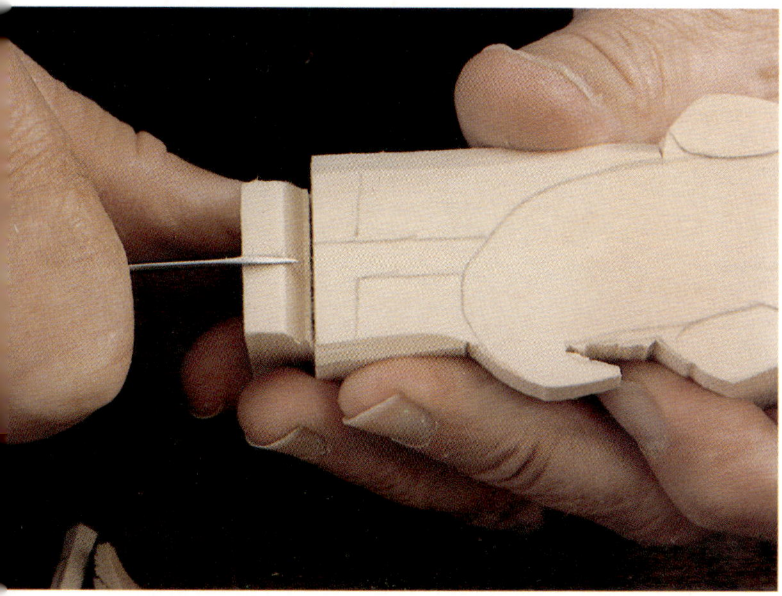

You'll notice that his feet are not separated. Just make a little notch between them.

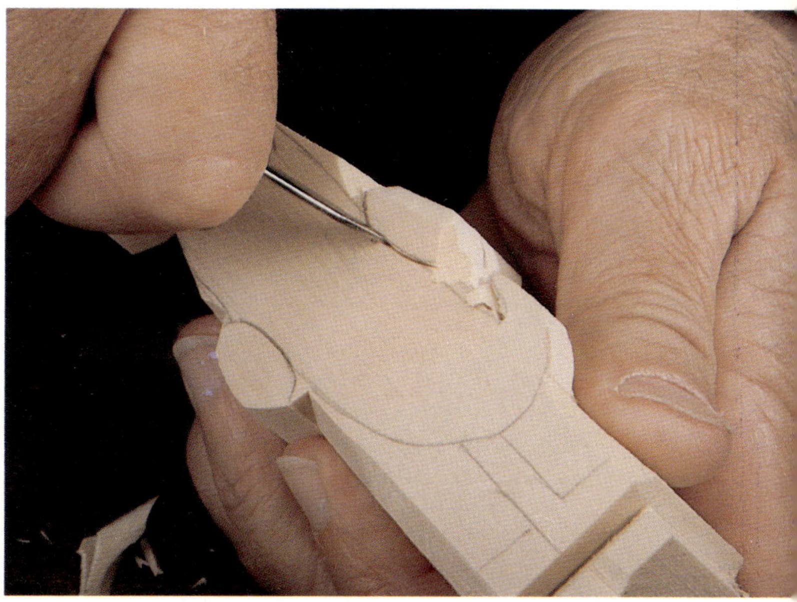

Incise both hands in the front along the beard.

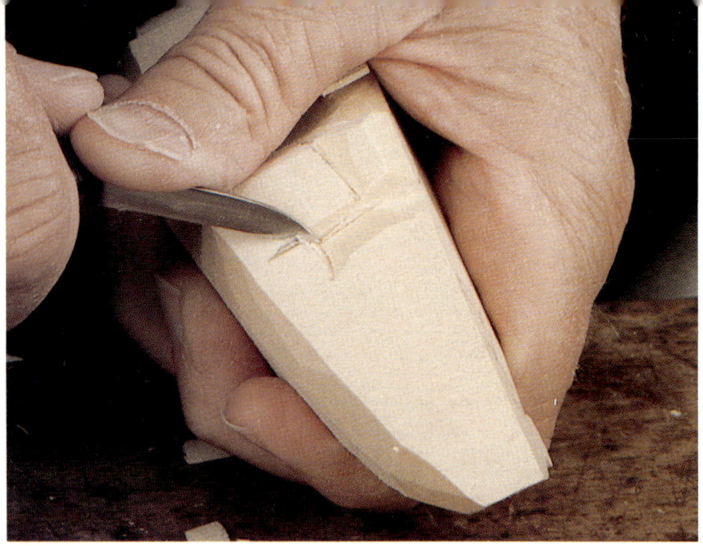

To get the sleeve in, first draw them. They are the same on both sides. Then incise the lines as before and cut out the notch created when you incised the arm.

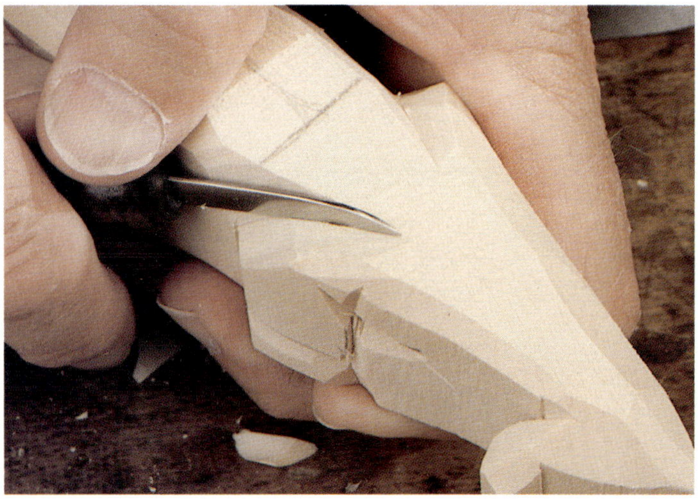

Make a small series of V cuts to define the backs of the arms.

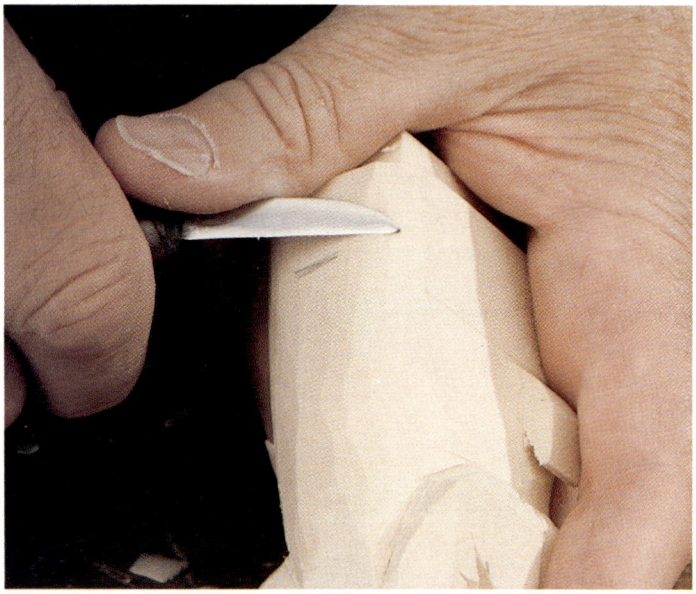

You will notice that I have cut off the lines to Santa's backside while rounding but I will draw them back in.

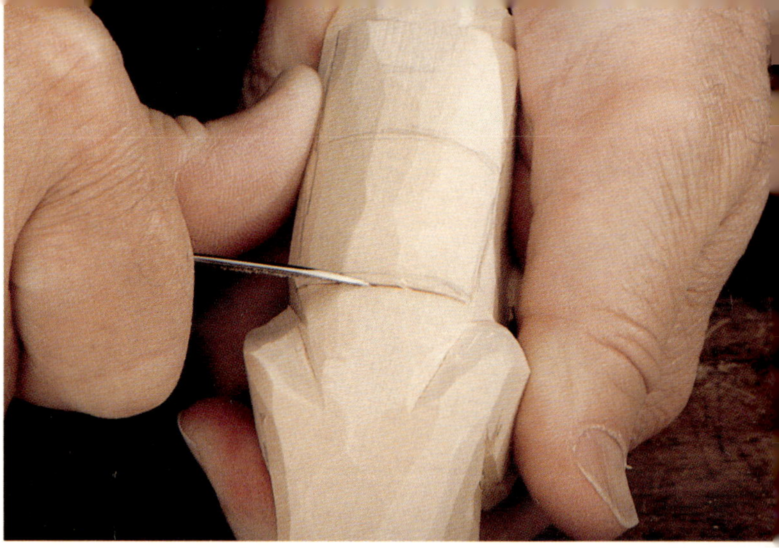

Draw in the flap and incise those lines.

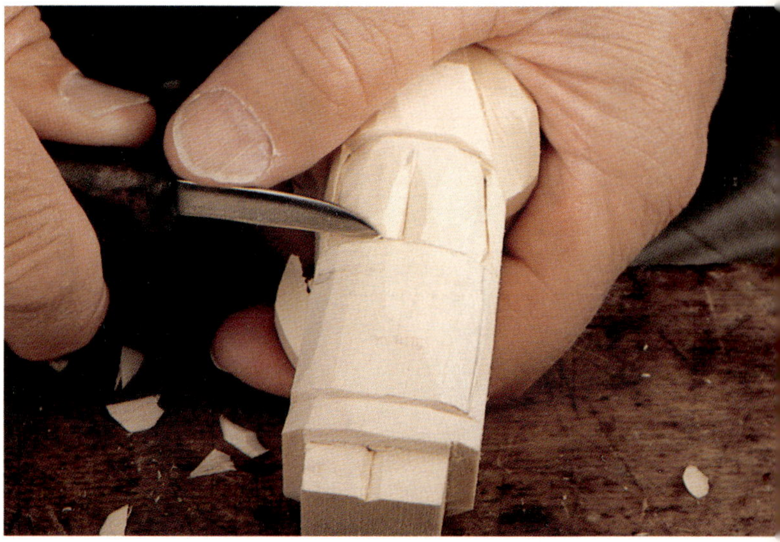

To get the cheeks in, carve them the same way you would the cheeks on the face ... except don't put the nose in.

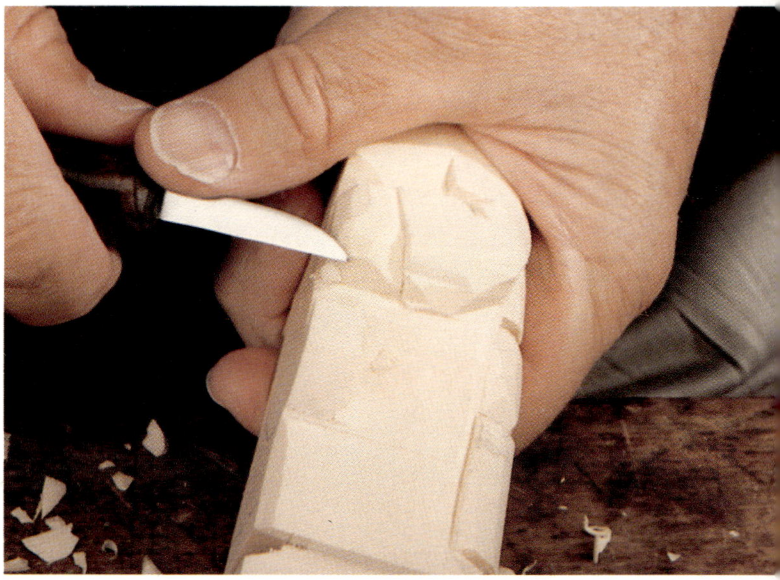

Santa has his fists clenched. Round his fists.

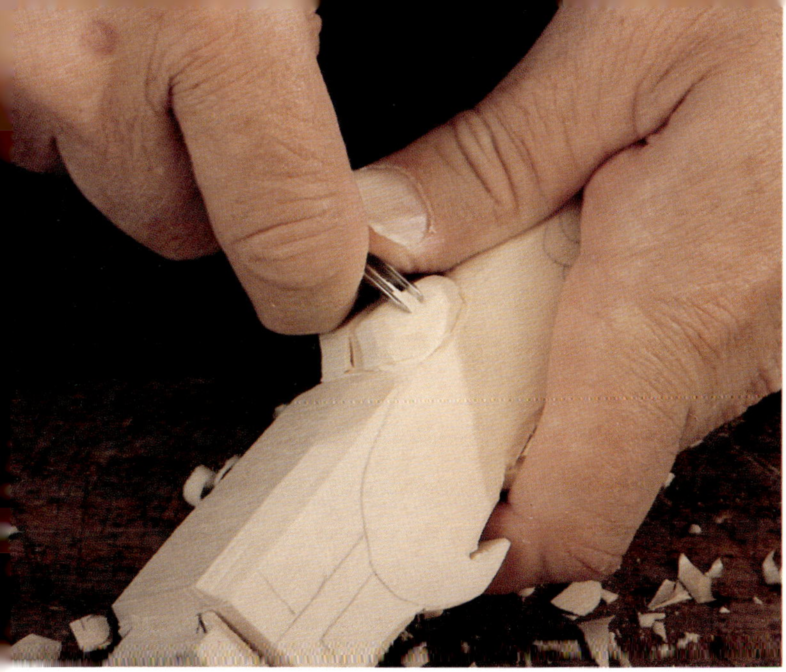

Use the gouge to define the fingers. Begin with the middle finger and work out.

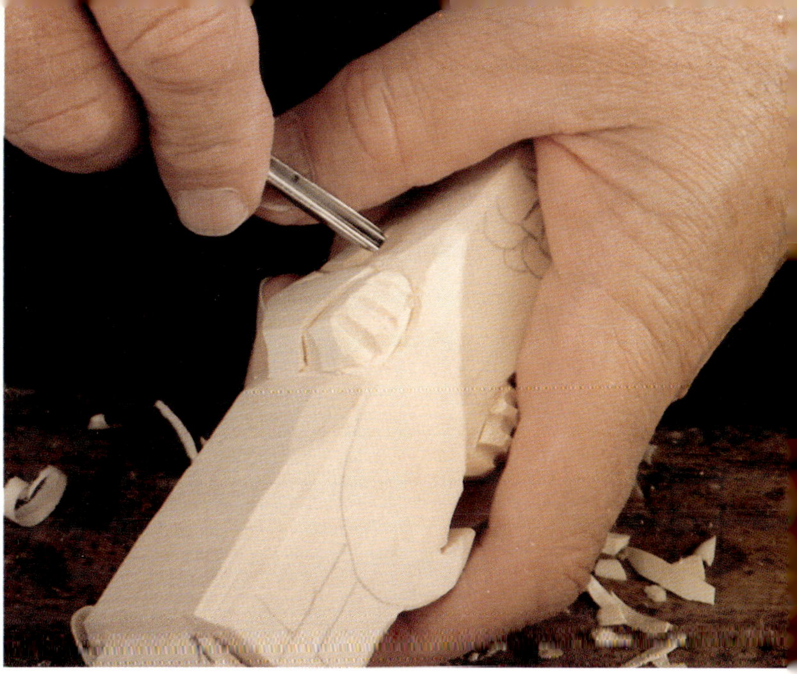

You need four fingers equidistant from each other. The thumb is not visible. It is hooked under the beard.

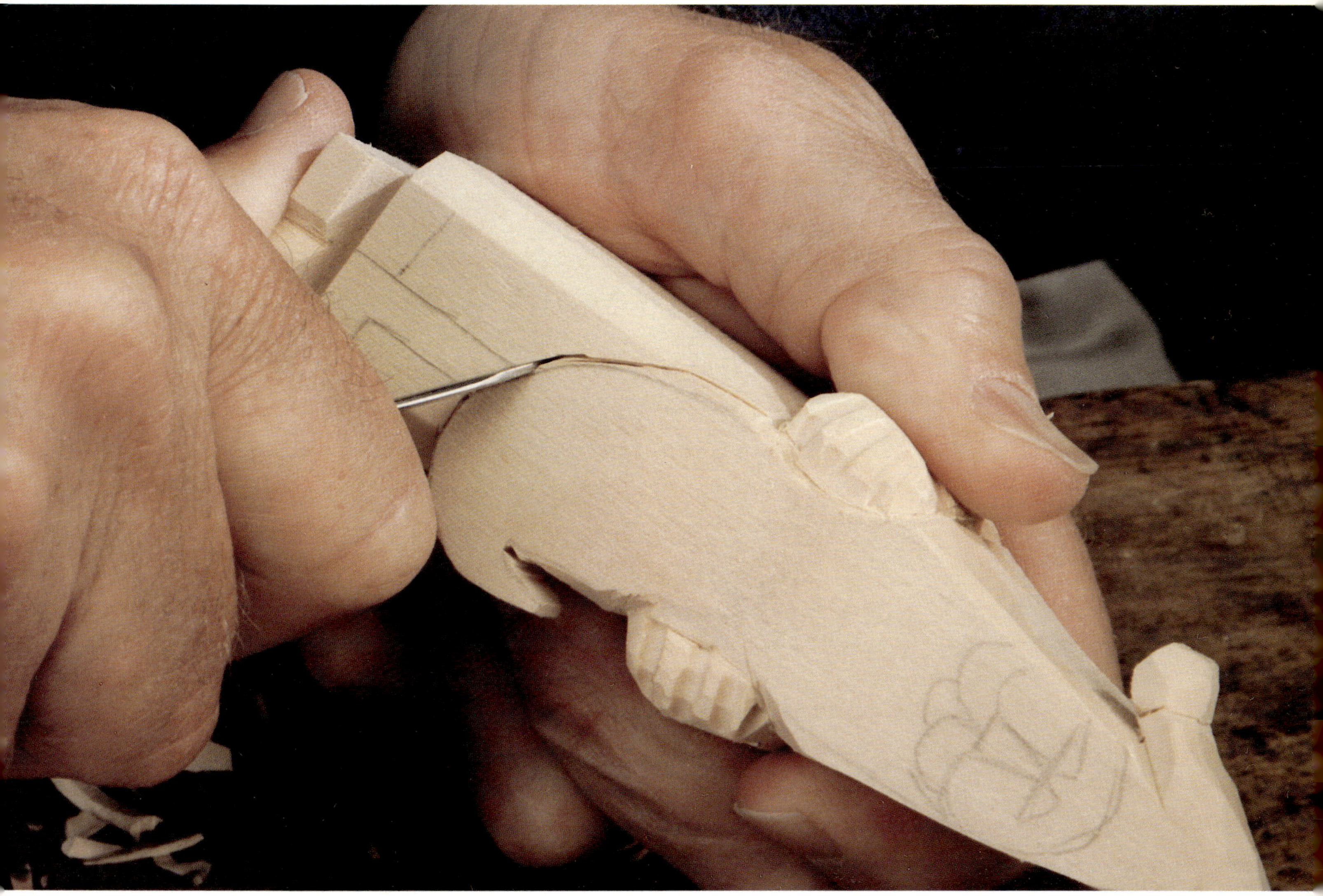

Working on the front, incise the beard.

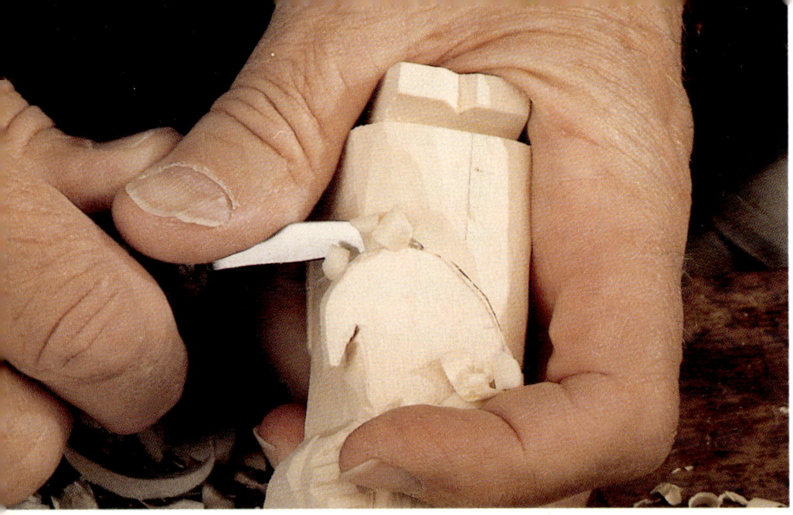

Round the front of the robe up to the beard.

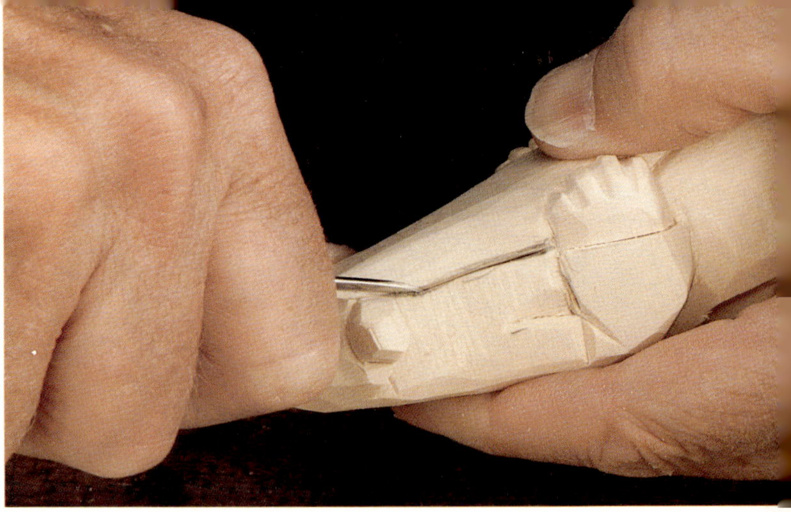

Draw back in the sides of the face. Bring the line down even with the front edge of the sleeve. Incise the line of the face all the way around from sleeve to sleeve.

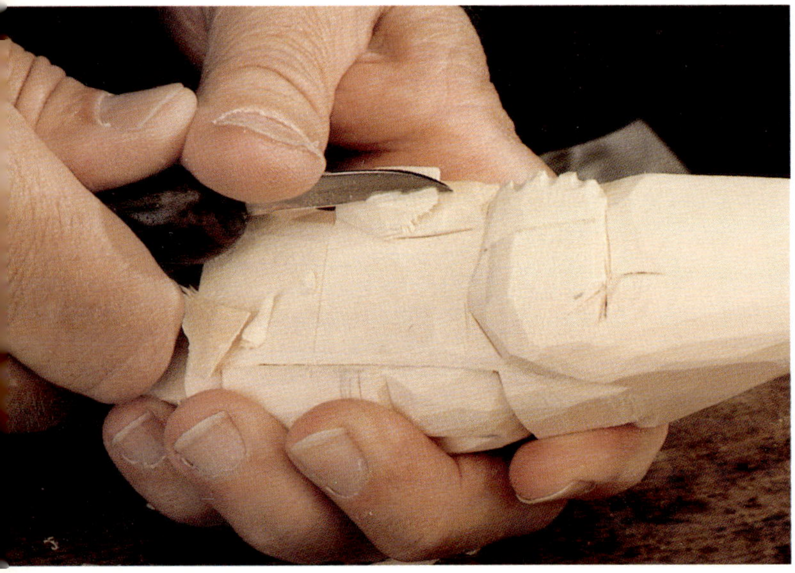

Round off the curled side of the beard.

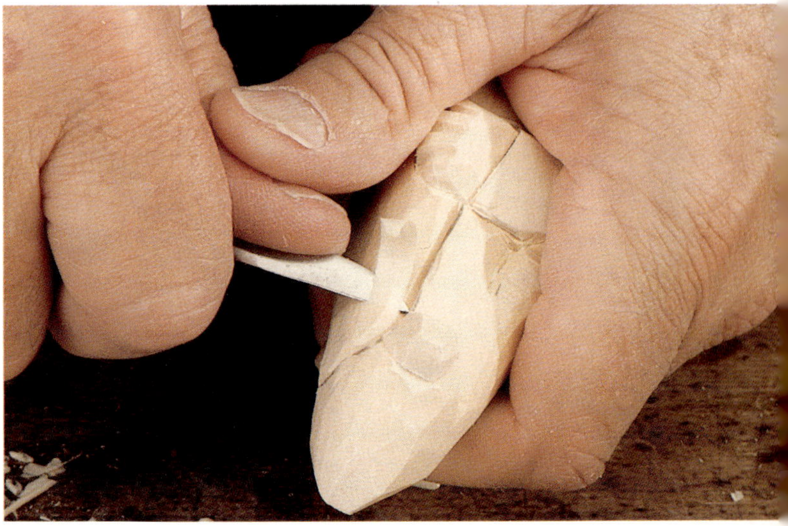

Now round to the incised line of the face ...

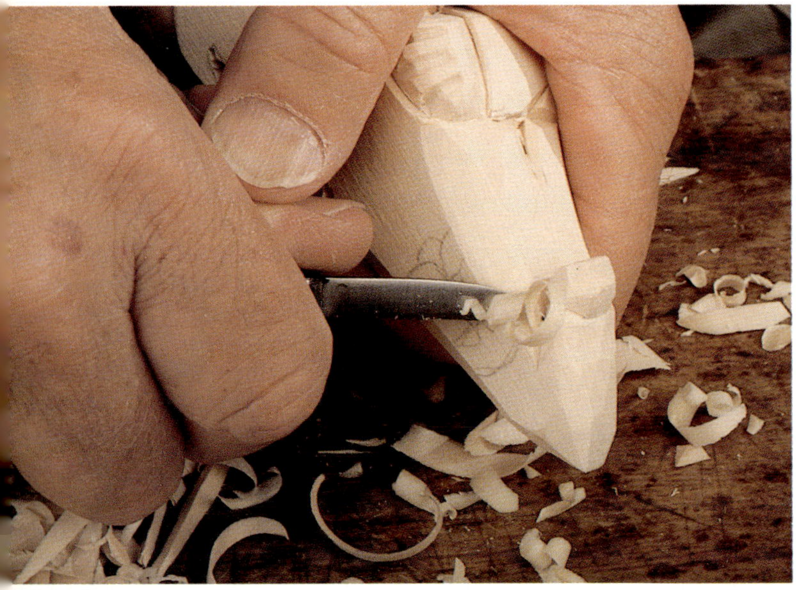

Start rounding up into the face area. You can draw in the face again later.

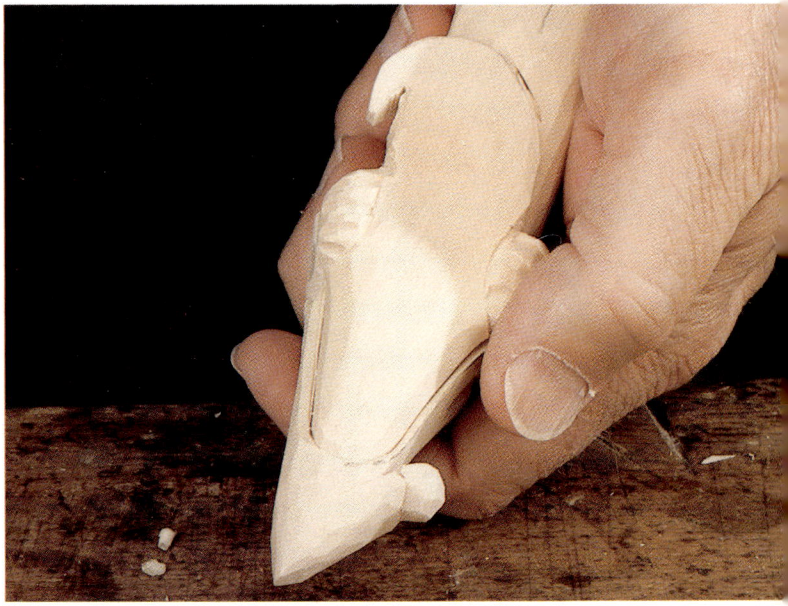

... like this.

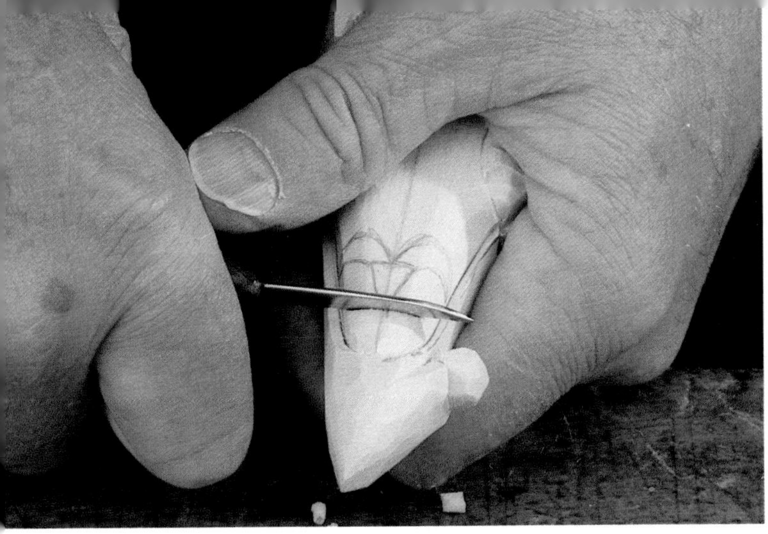

Draw in a center line for a point of reference first and then draw in the face. Even though I draw in the same face, each one ends up looking different. Now cut in the deep channel of the eyes just as we did before.

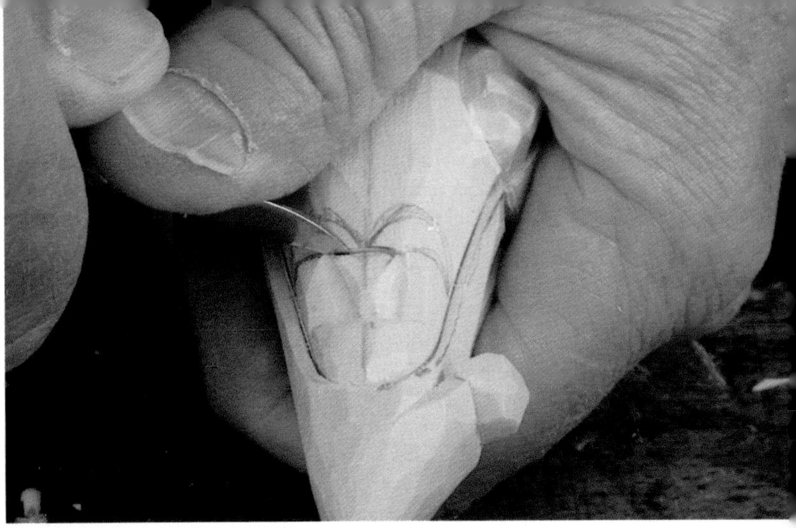

Incise the bottom of the nose ...

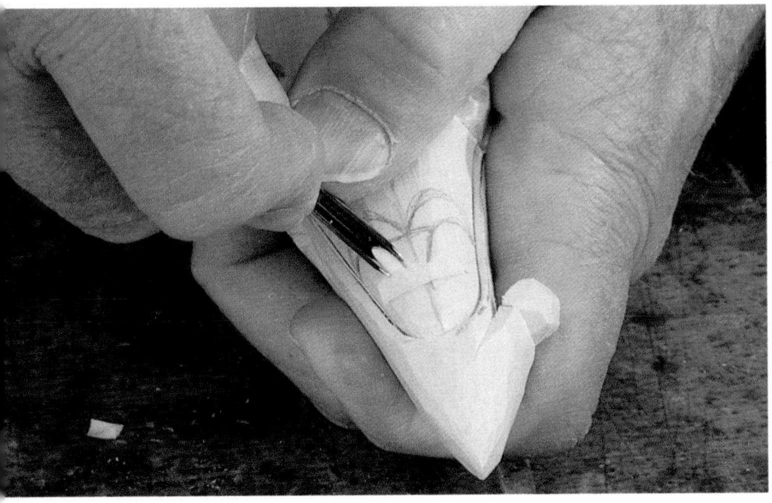

Use a gouge to come up each side of the nose to give it a little rounder transition from the cheek to the nose.

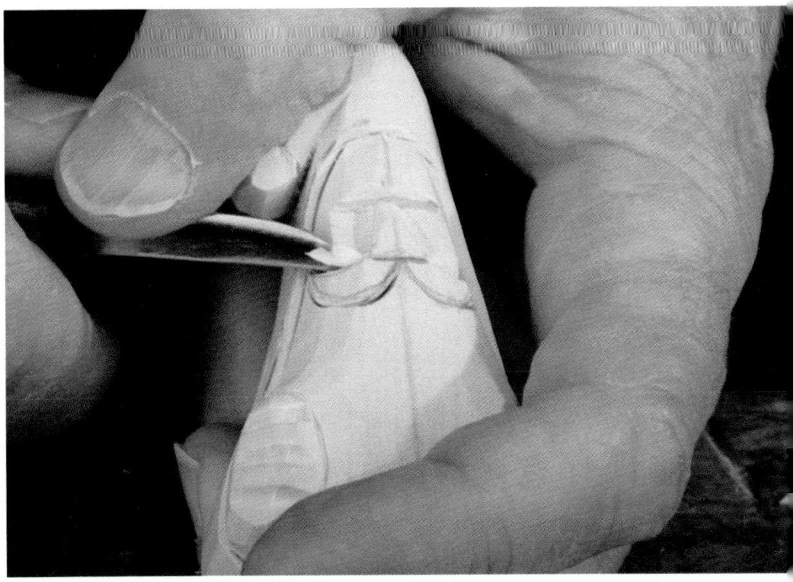

... and while you're there incise the cheek and mustache lines.

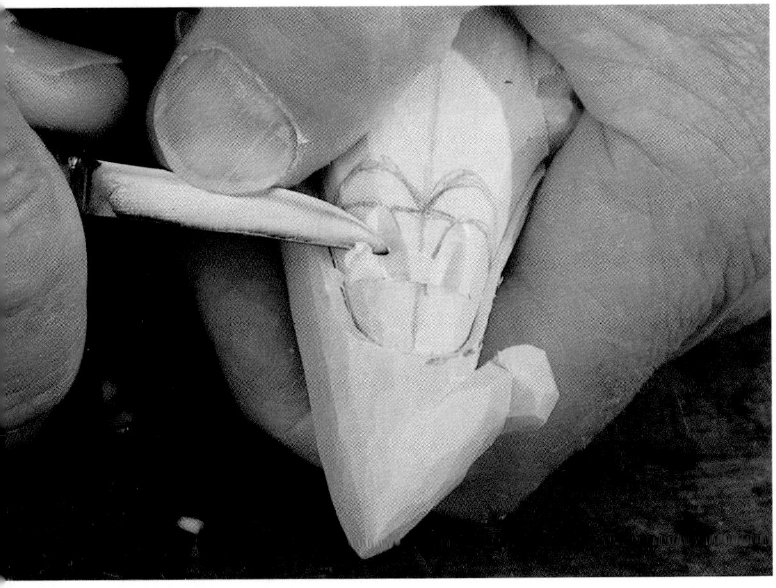

Trim down the line that goes out onto the cheek to make it nice and smooth.

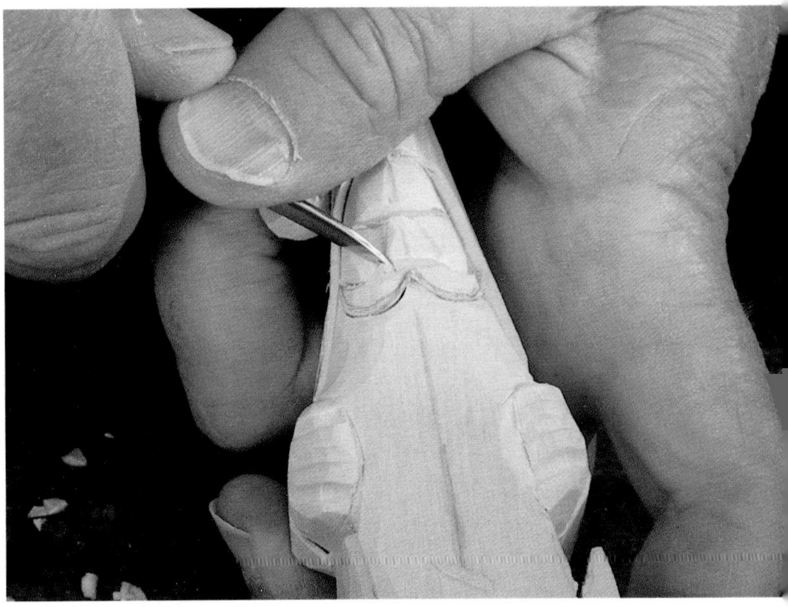

You need to clip off a little piece from each side of the nose for the nostrils.

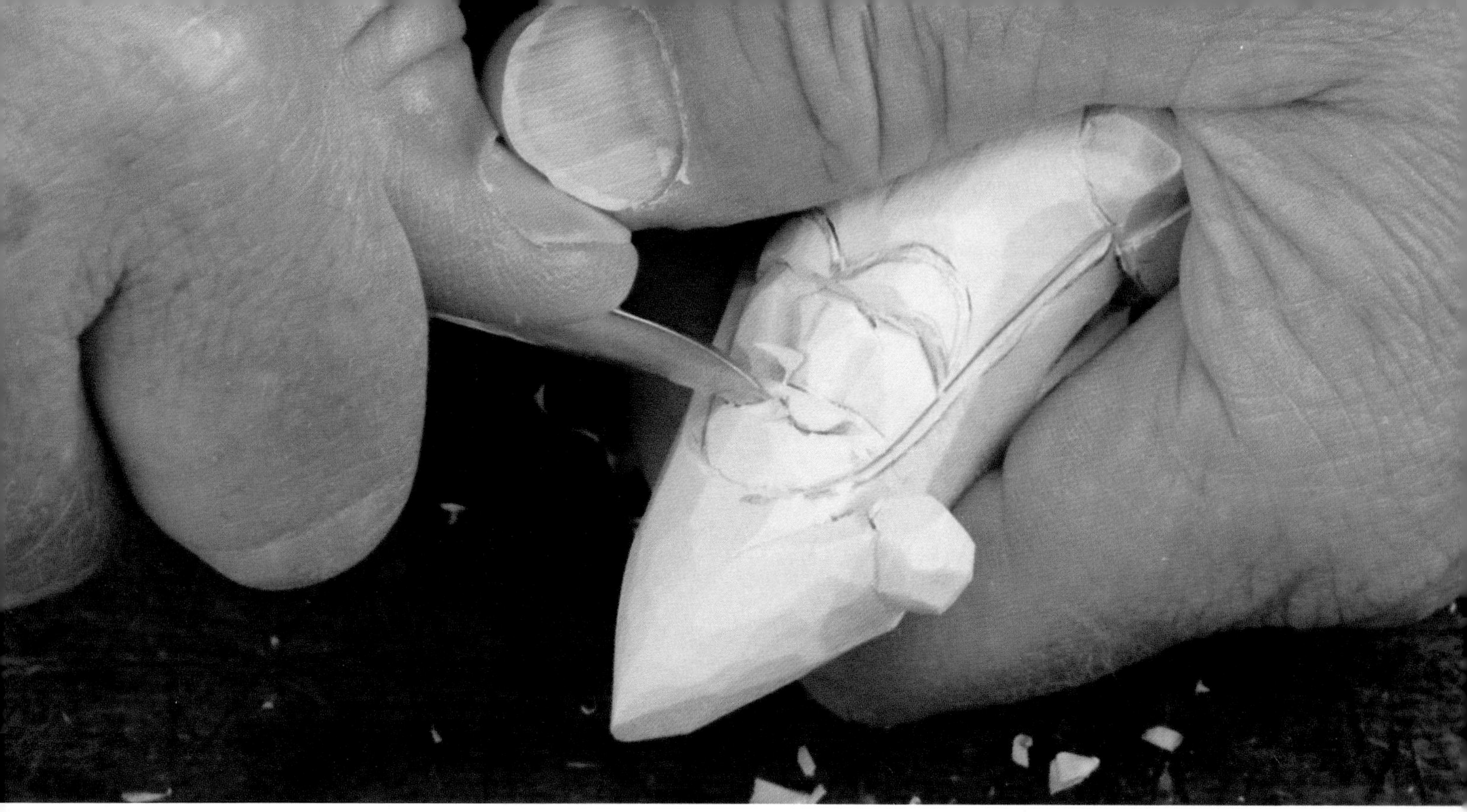

Carve in the eyebrows as before. Be very careful when you carve down or they will flip out.

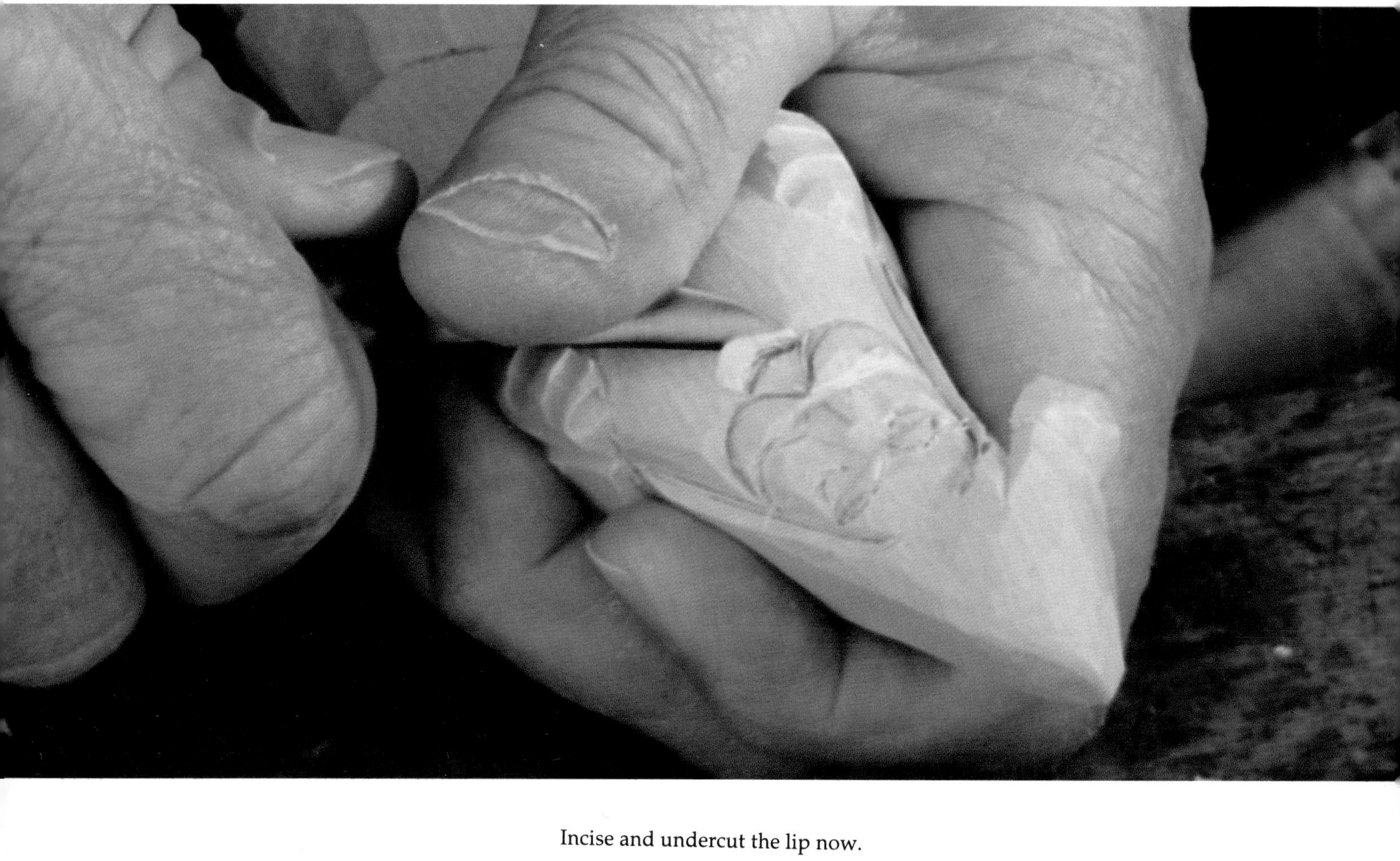

Incise and undercut the lip now.

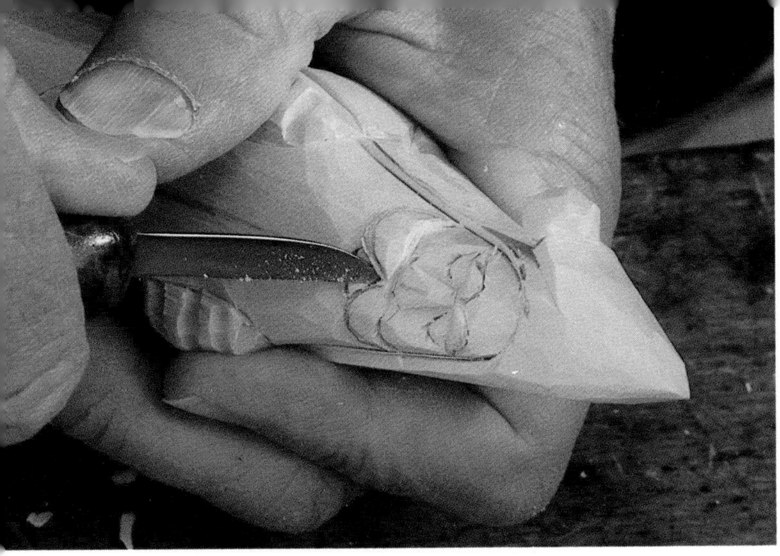

Carve out a small notch for the mouth just below the mustache.

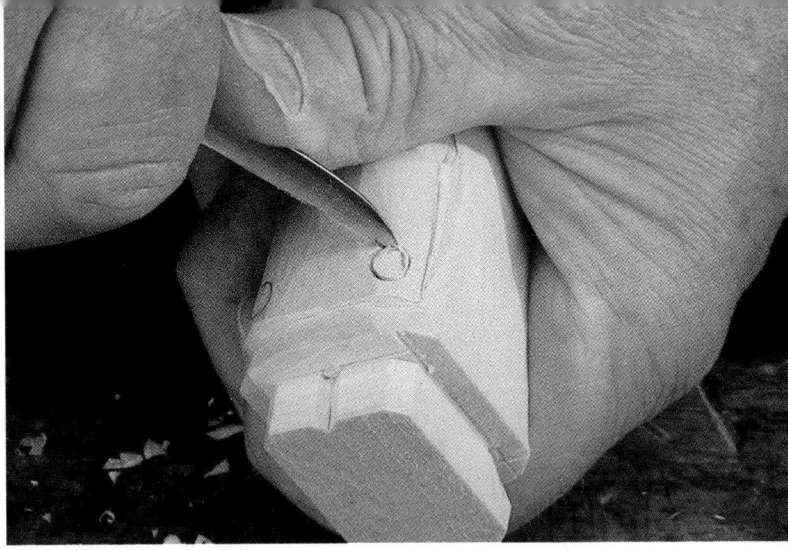

Cut in some buttons on the lowered back flap. Just draw two circles, incise and then use an angled cut around each. These can also be painted in. They are no big deal.

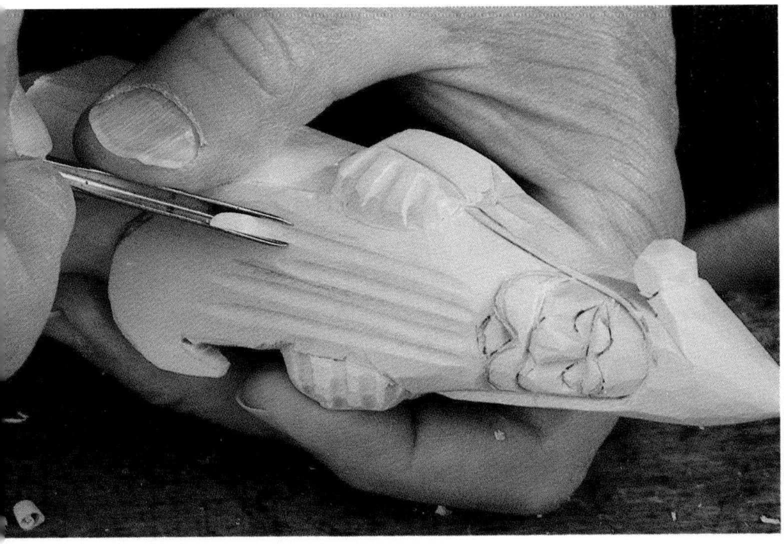

Use a small gouge to carve in the lines of the beard. A knife will work just as well.

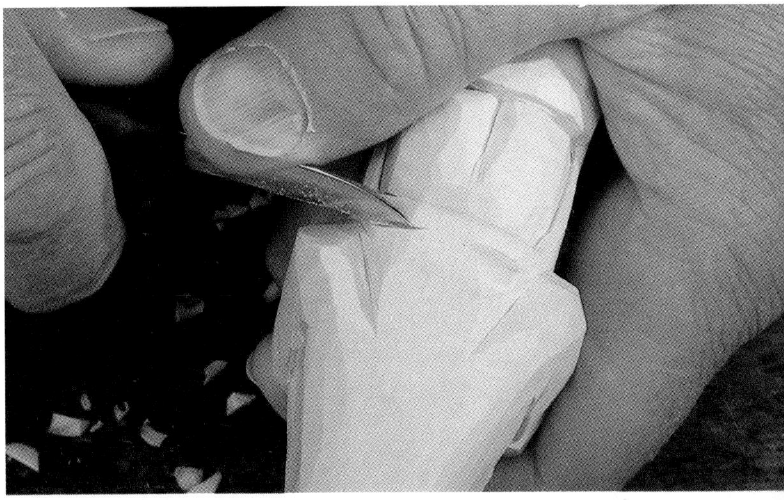

Cut in the button holes above.

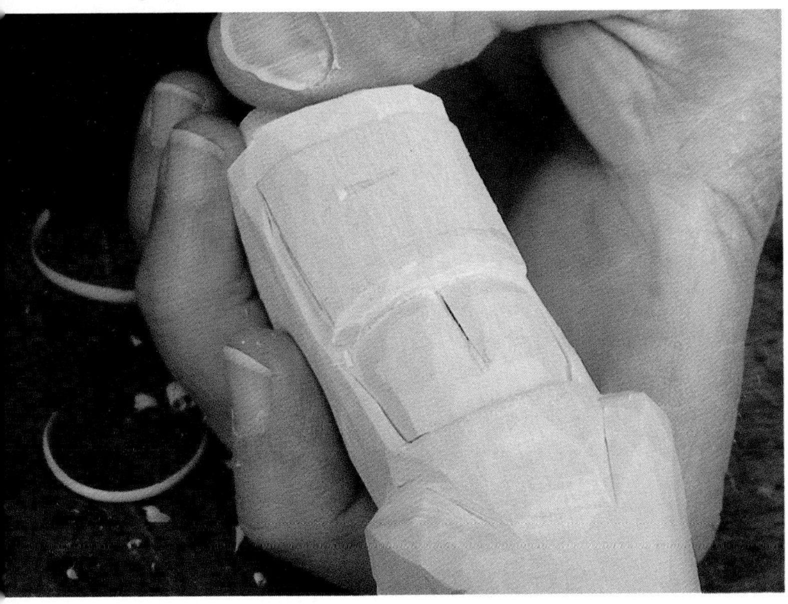

Go back and round around his backside if he needs it.

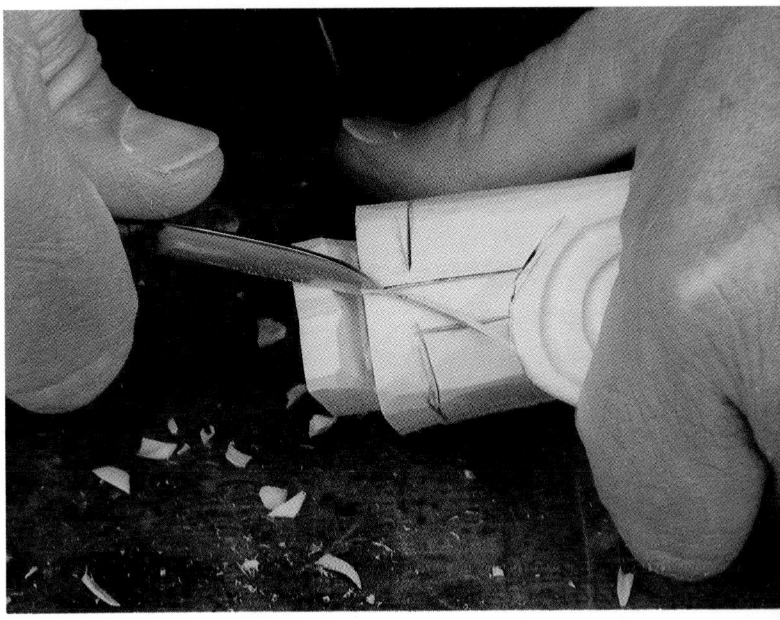

Add the fur lines and cut them in as before.

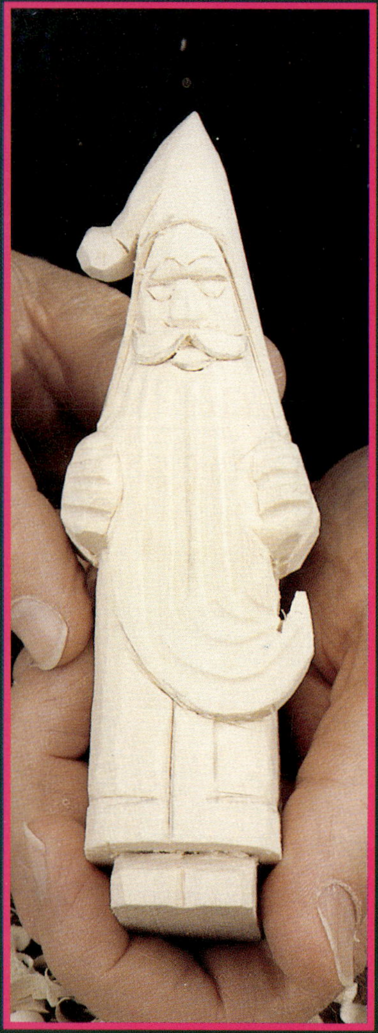

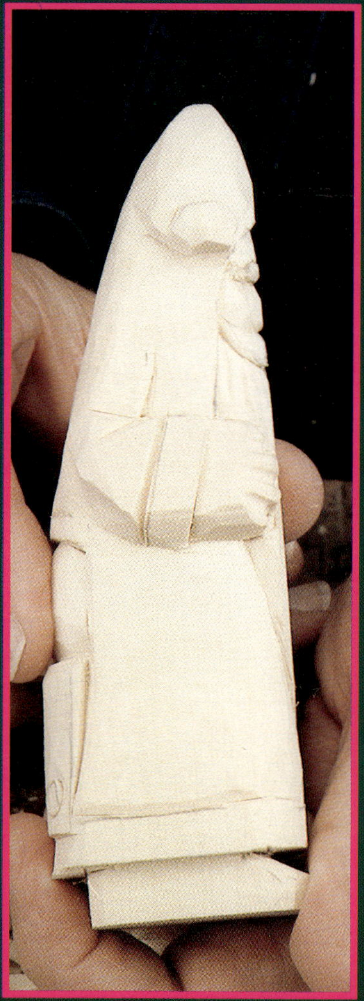

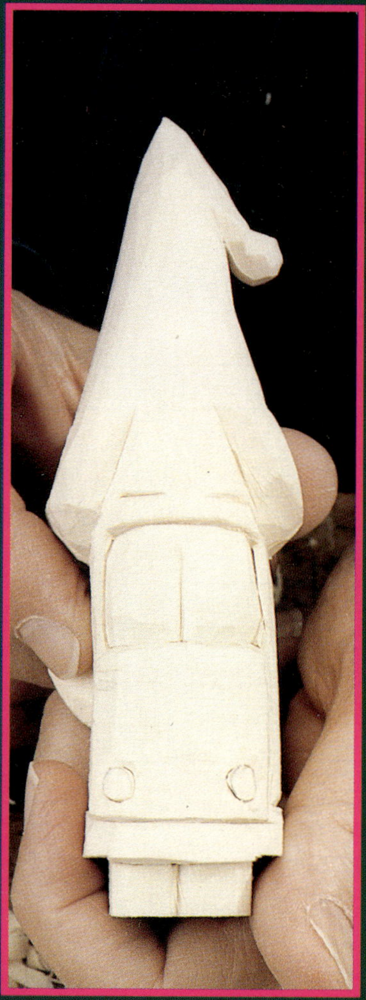

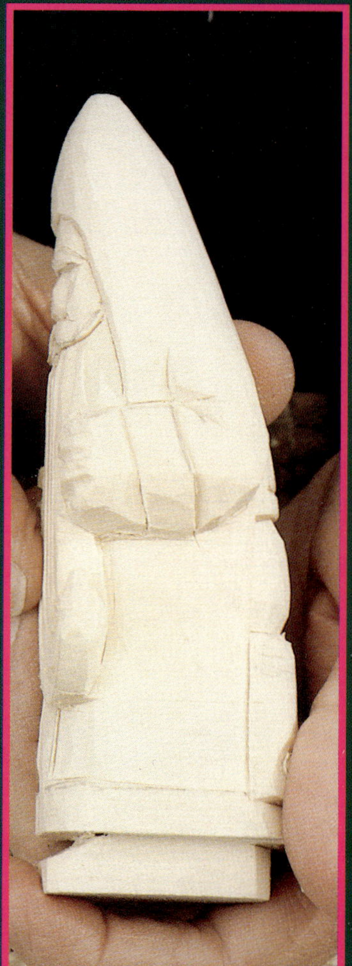

Go around and smooth one more time. Here's the finished carving.

PLACE
STAMP
HERE

SCHIFFER PUBLISHING LTD
77 LOWER VALLEY RD
ATGLEN PA 19310-9717

The Quilt Holding Santa

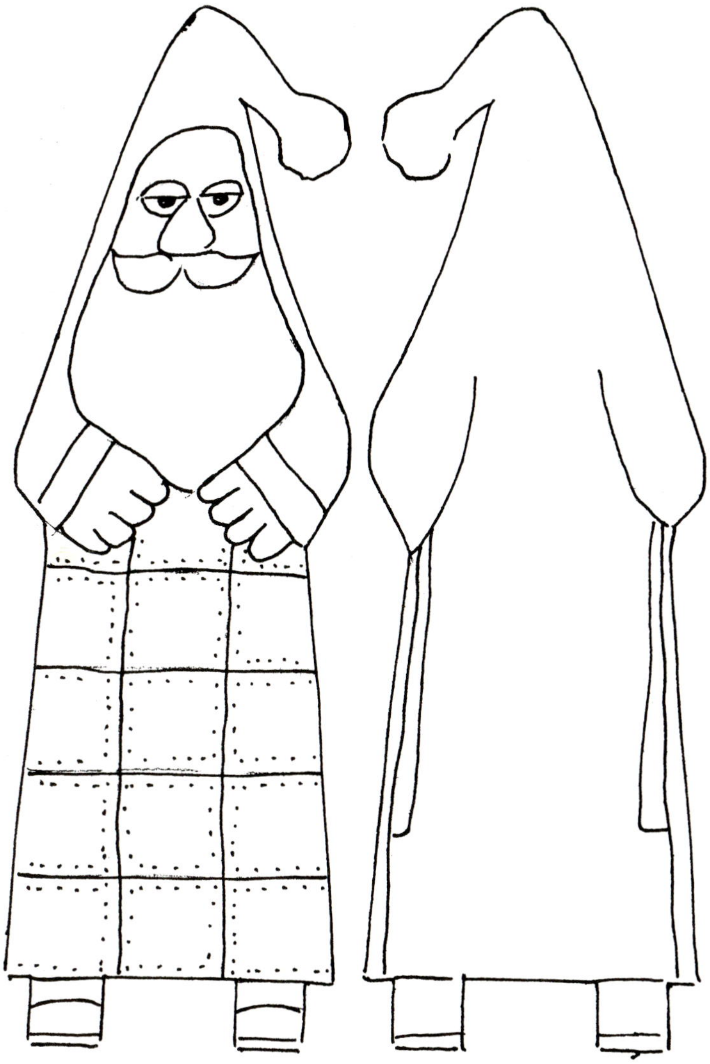

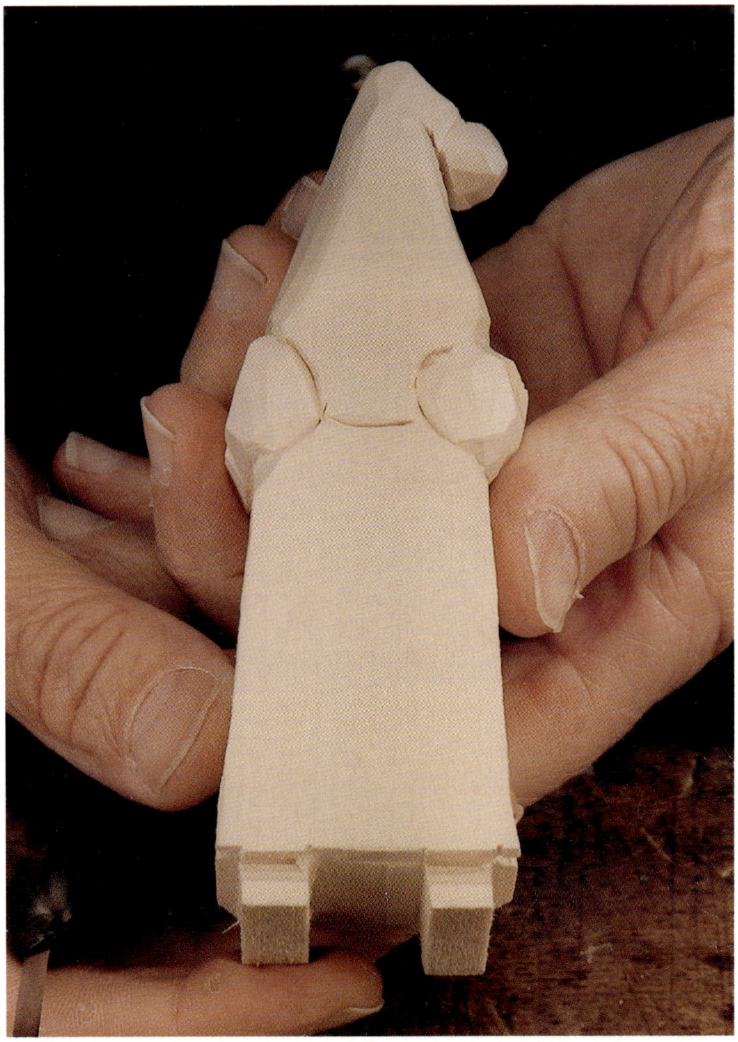

The next Santa is similar to the previous design. Round the pattern to start. I am going to show the differences you will encounter carving this design.

This Santa is going to be holding a quilt. I am cutting away to give the quilt its shape.

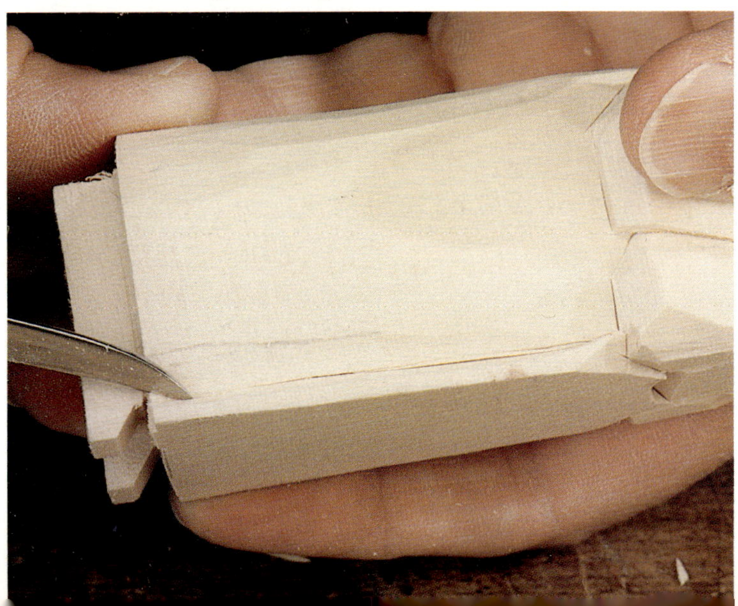

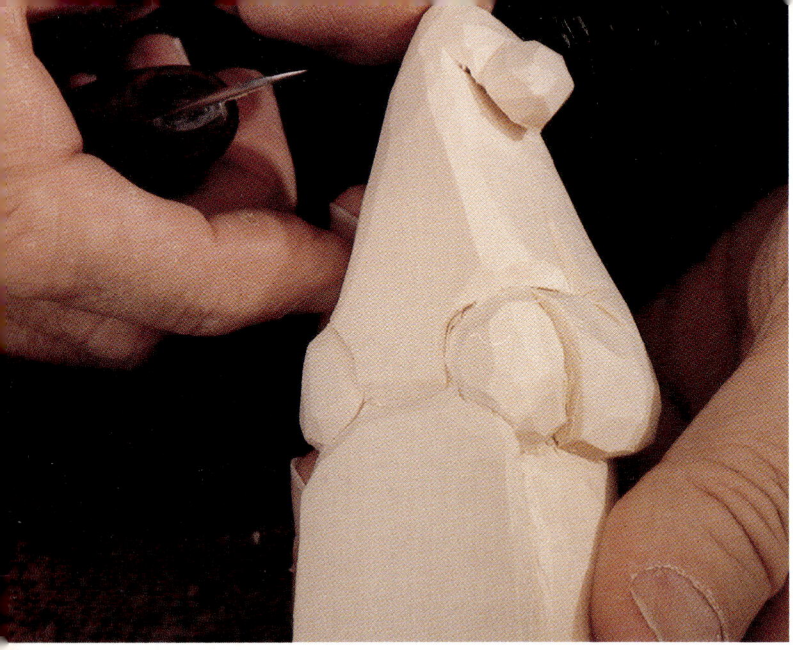

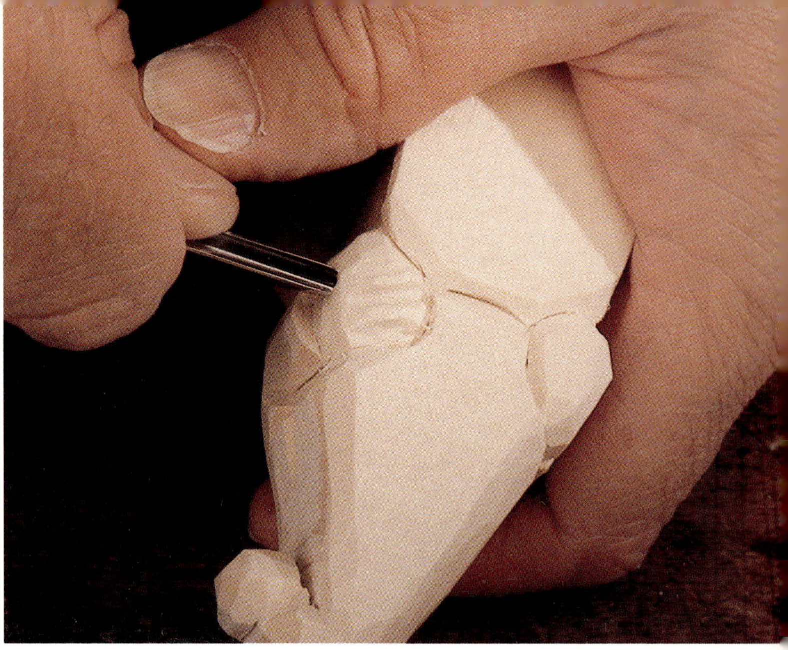

The hands are similar to the "night after" Santa, except that this Santa is holding onto the quilt. Round the hands into fists accordingly.

Cut in the fingers with a gouge, beginning with the middle finger and working out.

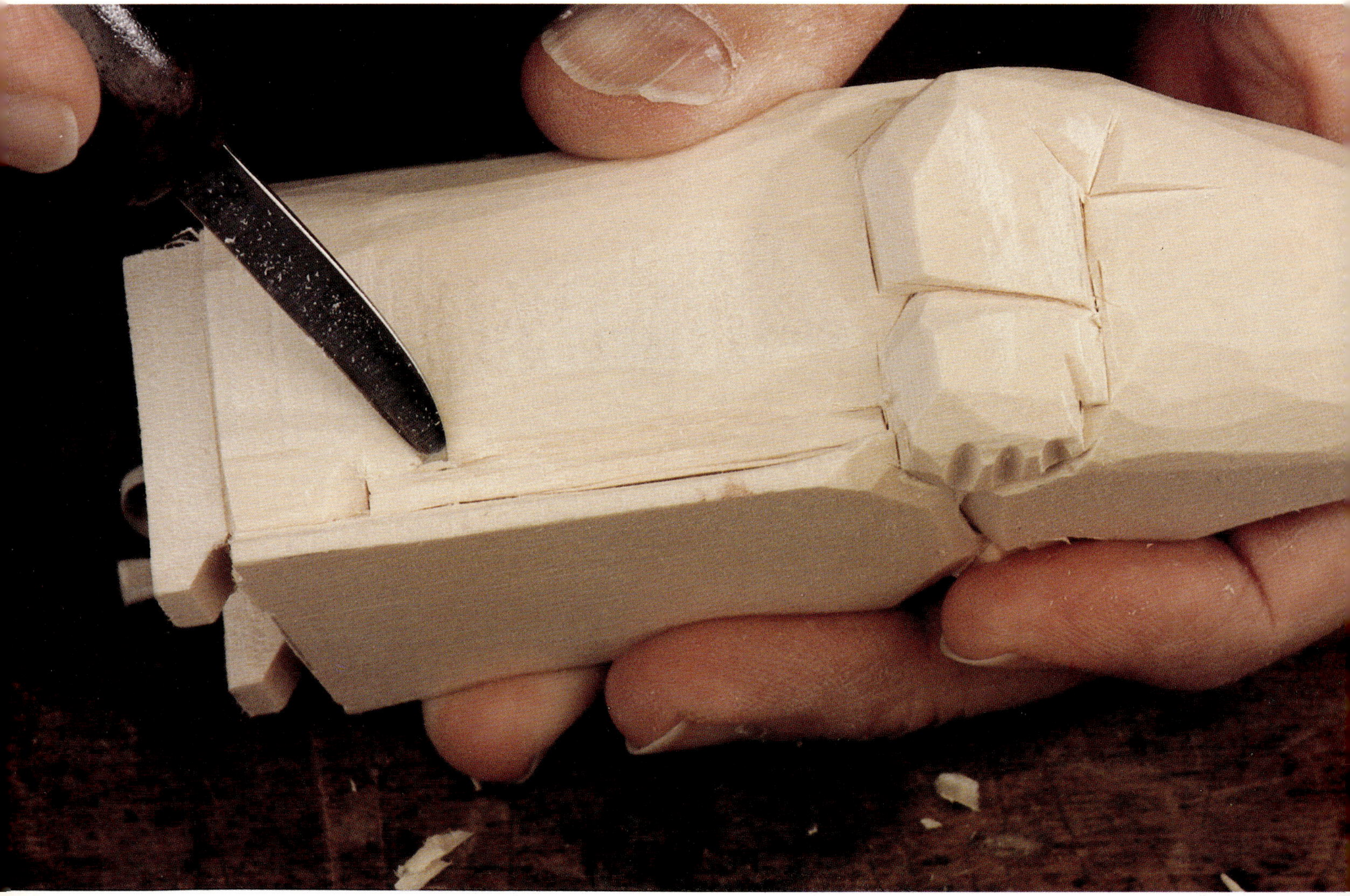

Carve in the fold at the back of the quilt. Incise inside and cut back to the line.

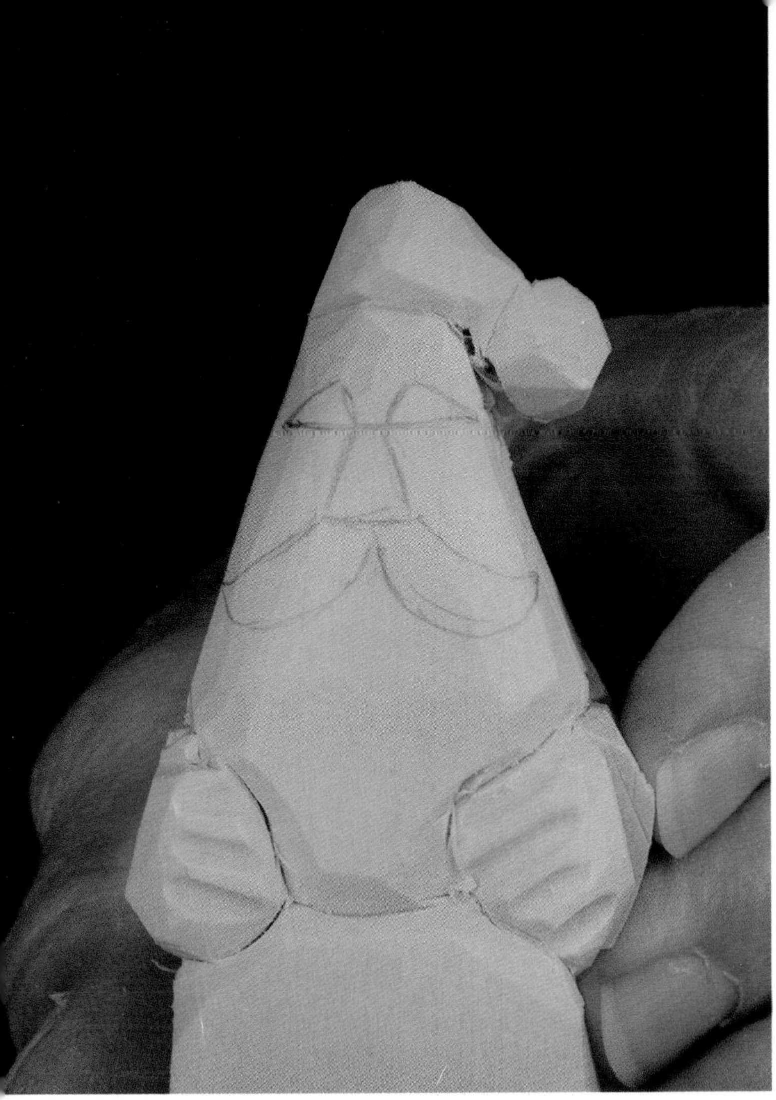

As you will notice, this is a fatter and wider face than before. We will carve it the same way as before, however.

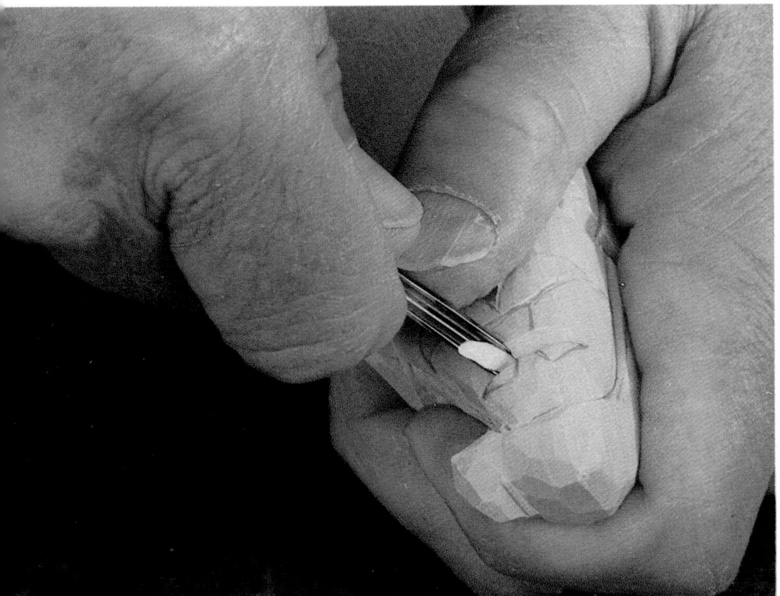

Use the gouge again around the nose. I'm going to cut deeper than I usually do.

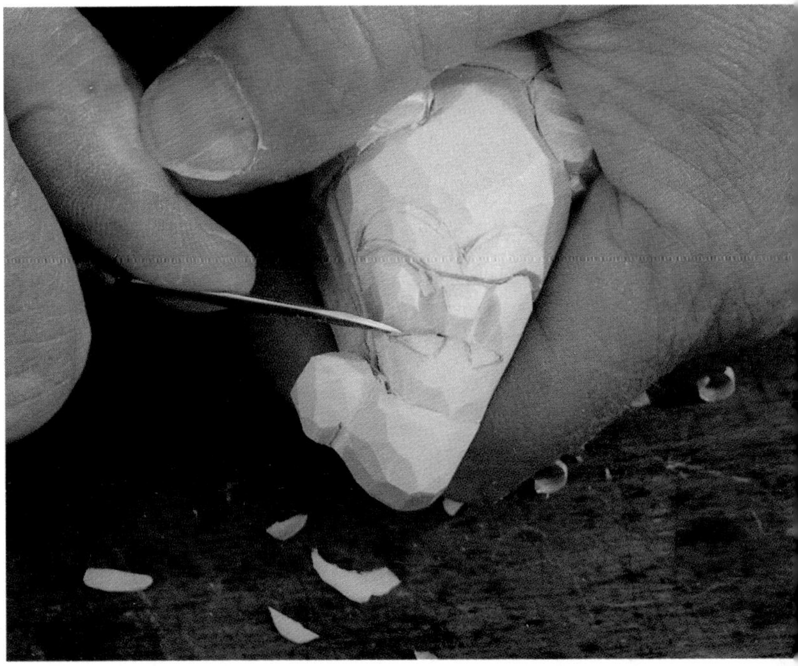

Notice that I am going deeper into the eye channels as well.

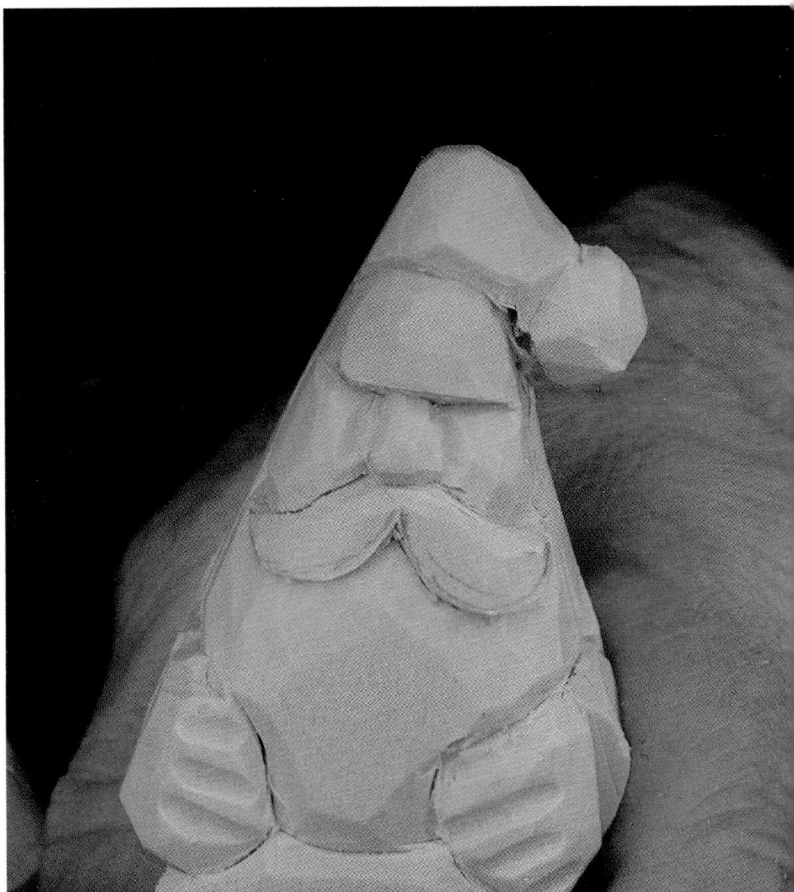

Now you can see how far back the eyes are carved in.

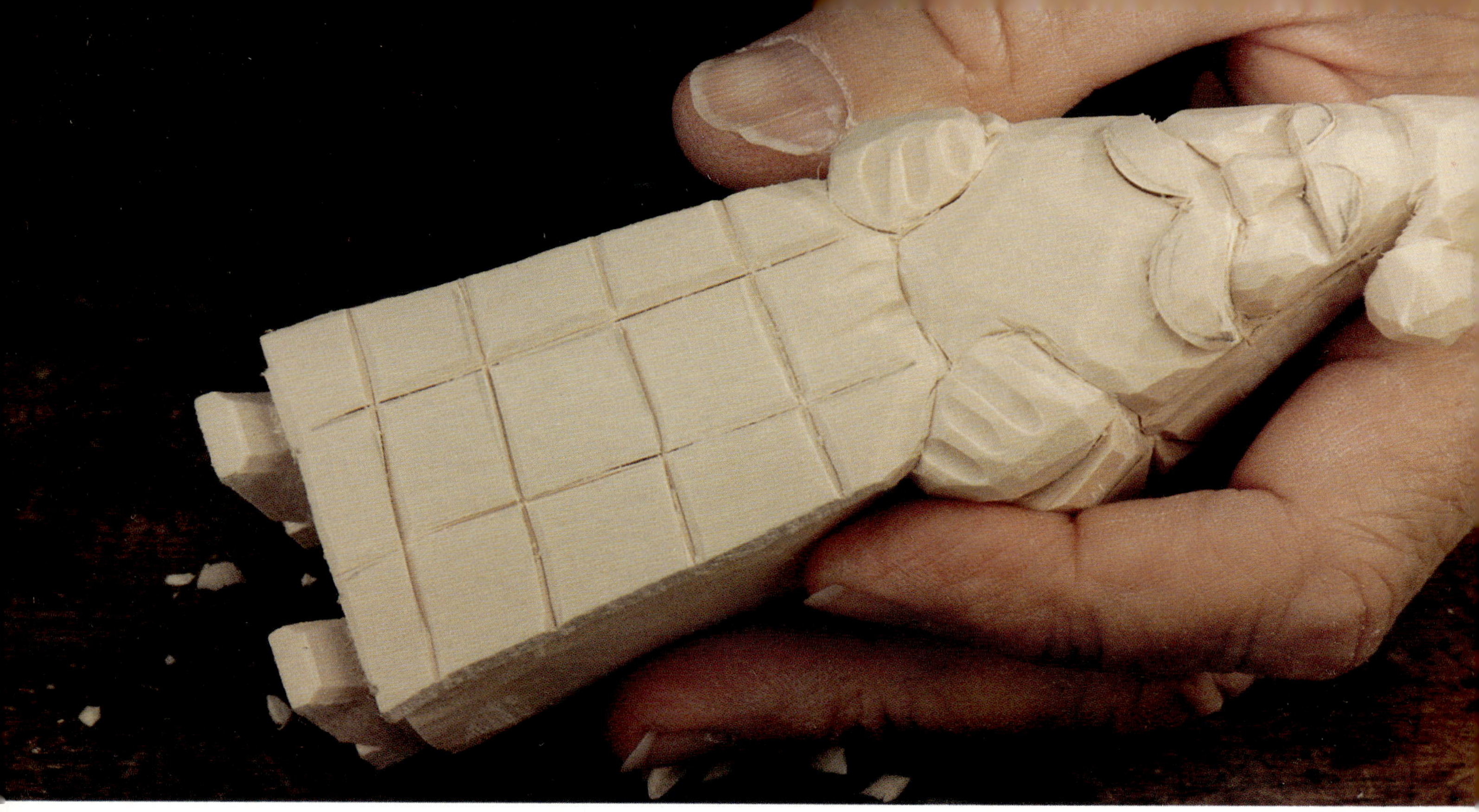

Add the lines for the quilt by incising them and then making little V cuts to separate the pieces.

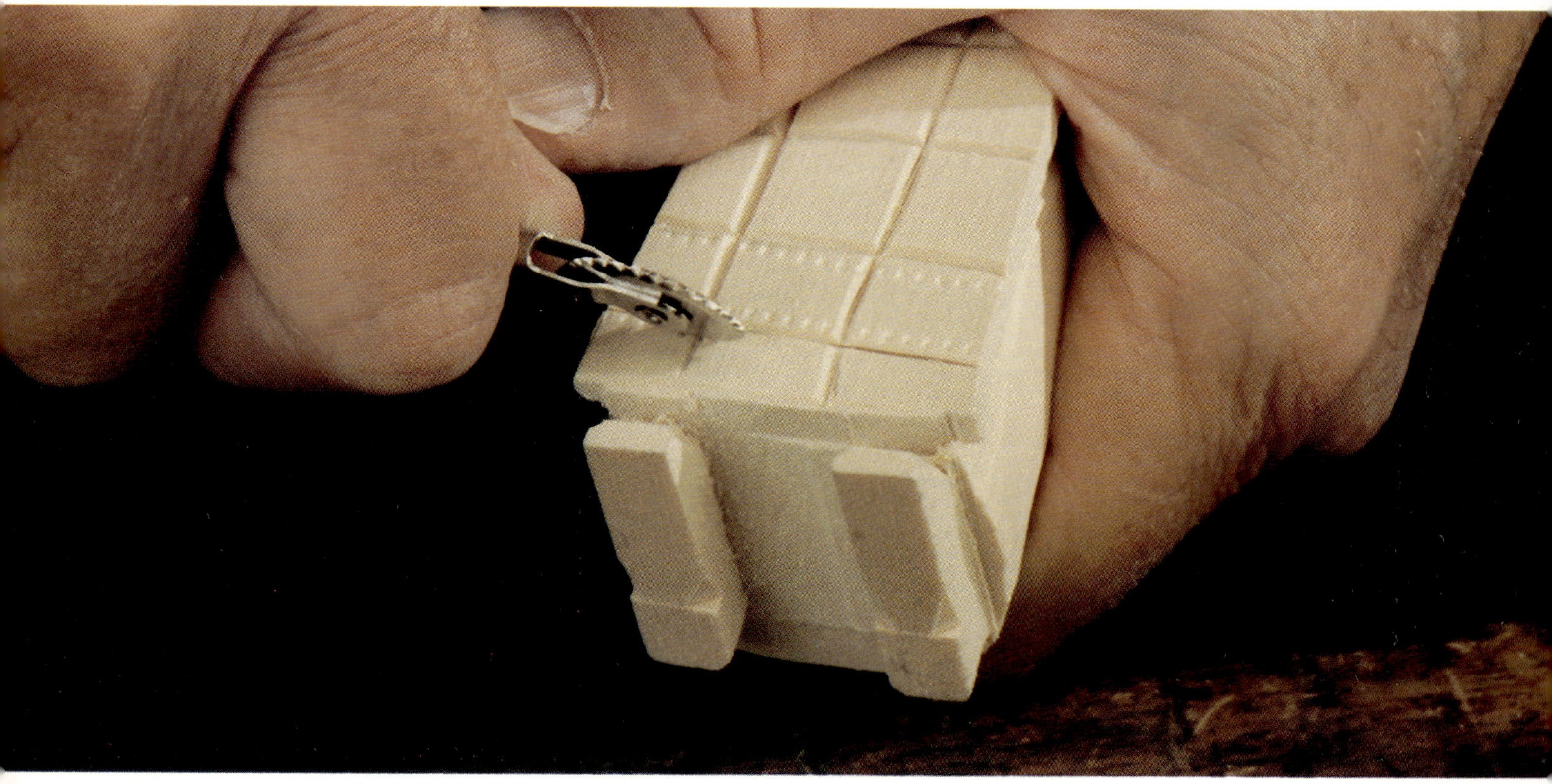

This is a Tom Wolfe idea from his golfer book. This is a tracing wheel. This makes the little stitches of the quilt. Nobody in my carving group ever takes my tracing wheel because of the pink handle. Instead of a quilt, you can make this a sandwich board with little messages for Christmas.

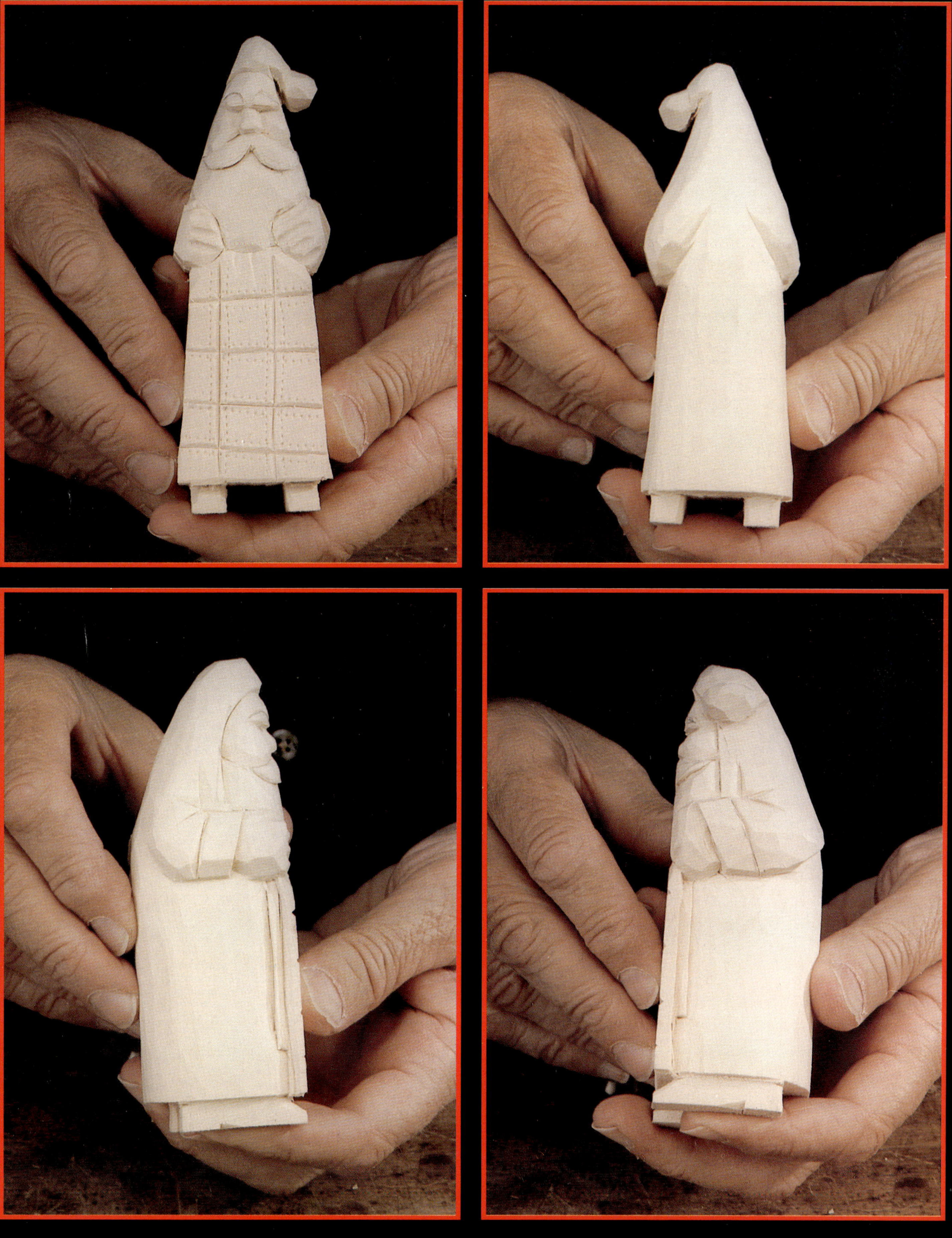

The finished quilt-holding Santa.

Santa Holding Snowman

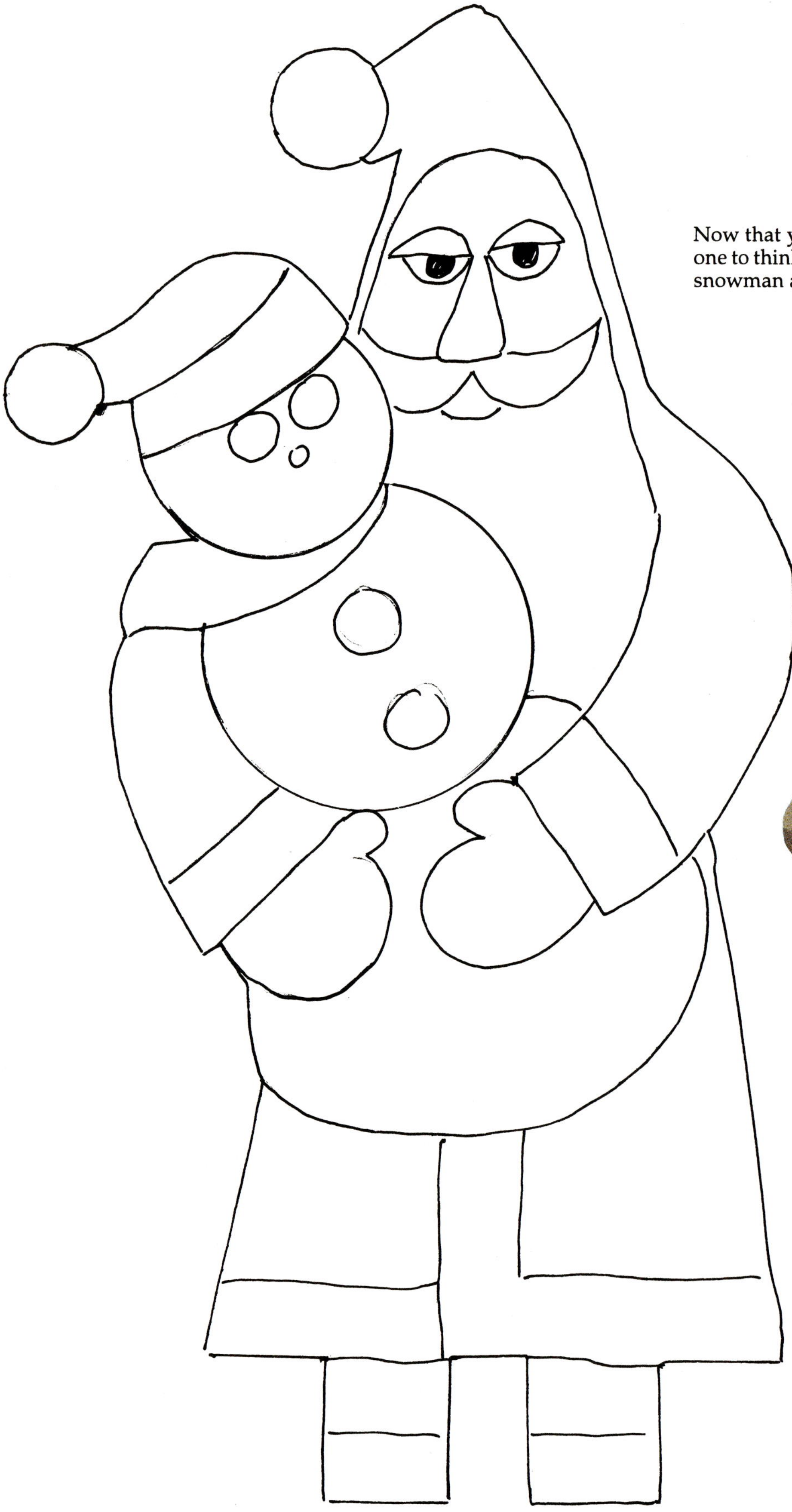

Now that you've mastered the little Santa's, I'll give you a big one to think about. Draw in the pattern for this Santa holding a snowman and cut out your block.

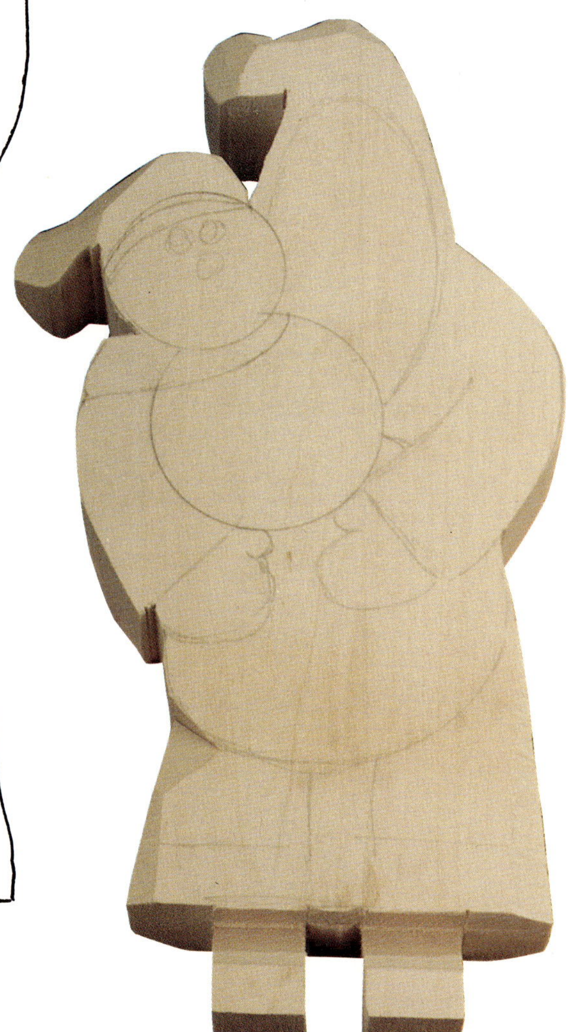

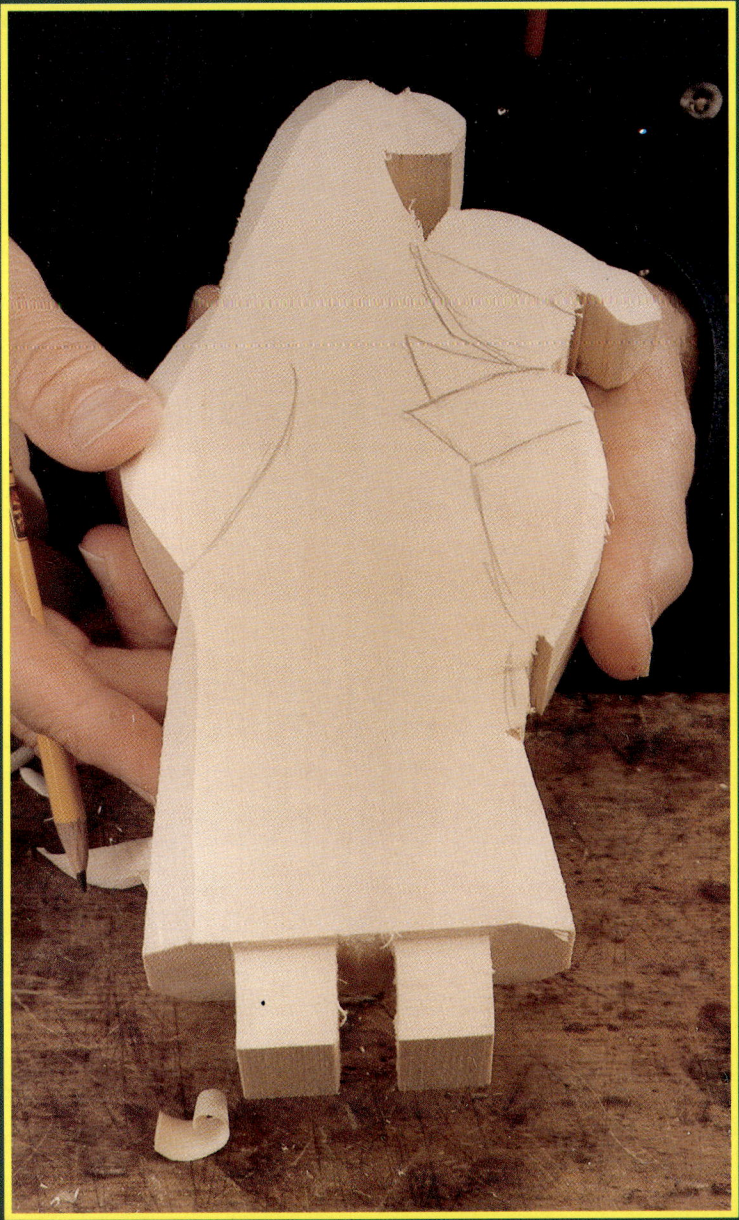

I'm showing the backside with the lines drawn in so that you will see that you need to leave some wood for the scarf you are going to carve in later.

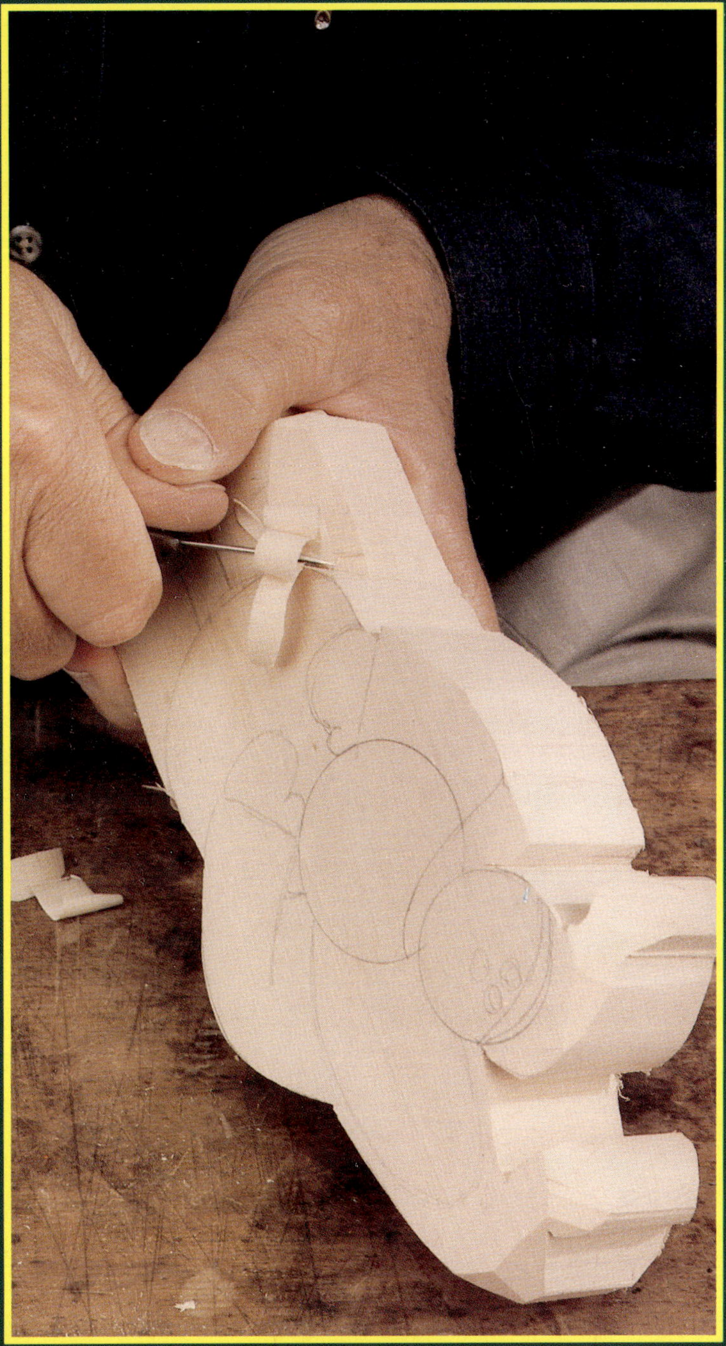

Start rounding with your knife.

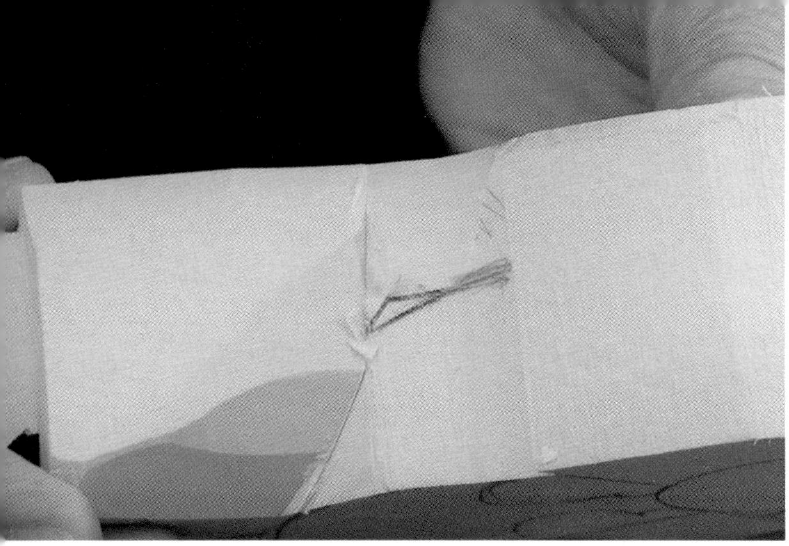

It's a good idea to draw in the snow man on the side. If you want a wider snow man, you need to use a 4" thick piece of basswood.

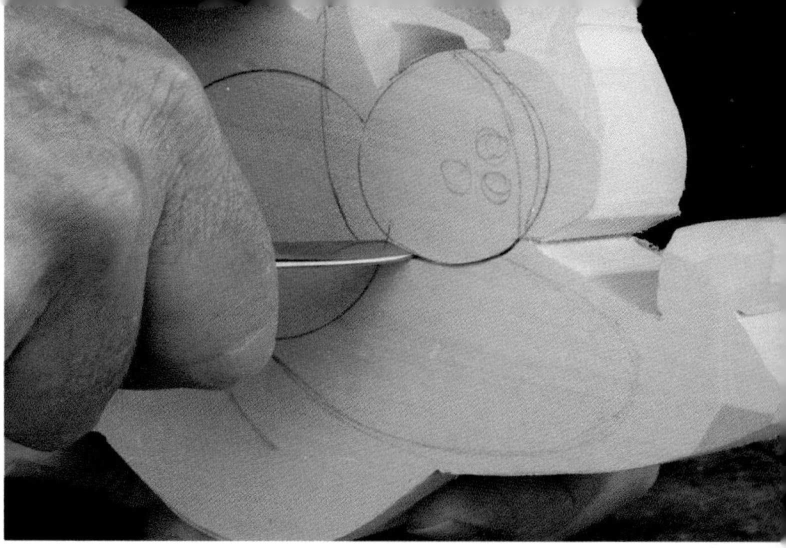

Start incising the snowman's body. Notice that it is cut very deep.

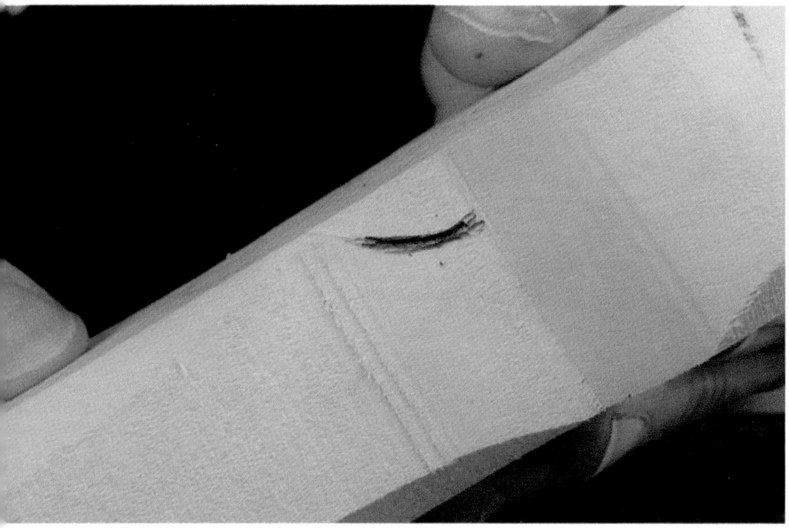

Here is the other side of the snowman. Be careful not to cut this away or you will lose the snowman's roundness.

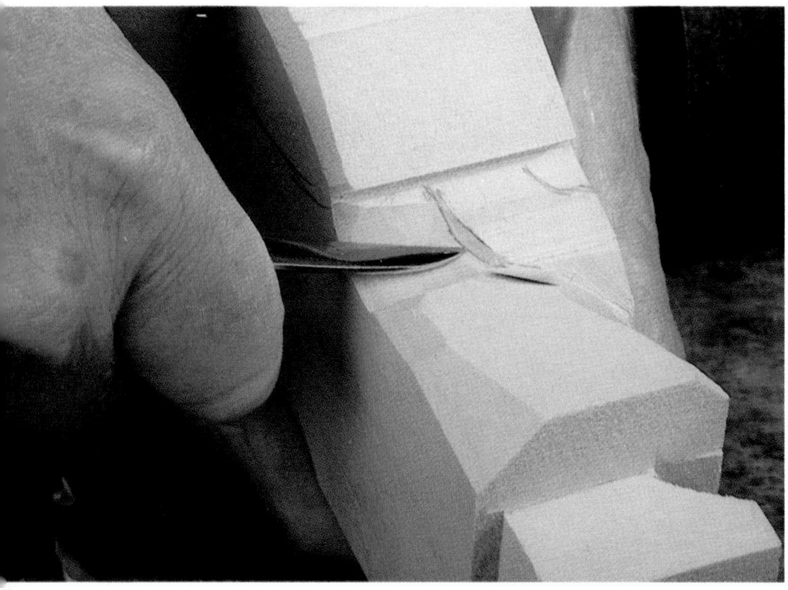

I've started defining the snowman on both sides. I've also drawn in where I want the right hand to go.

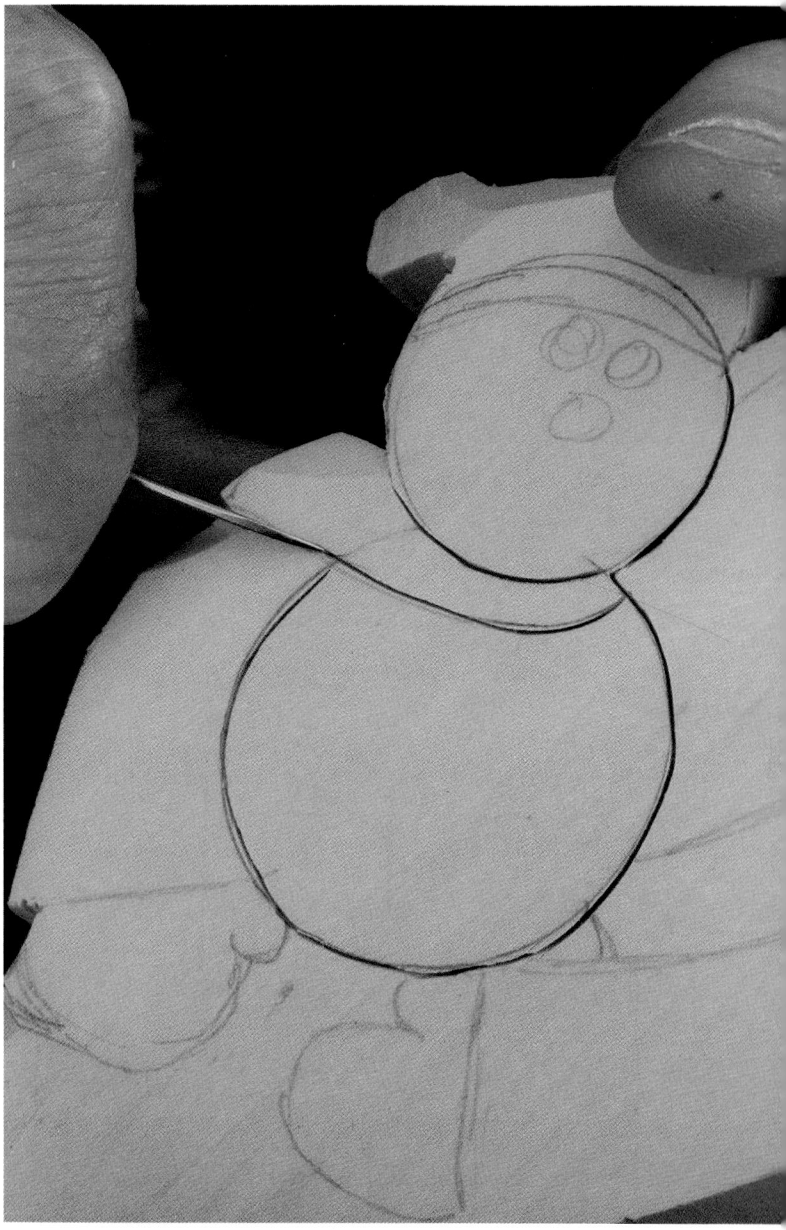

Continue to score around the snowman. Put in the scarf now.

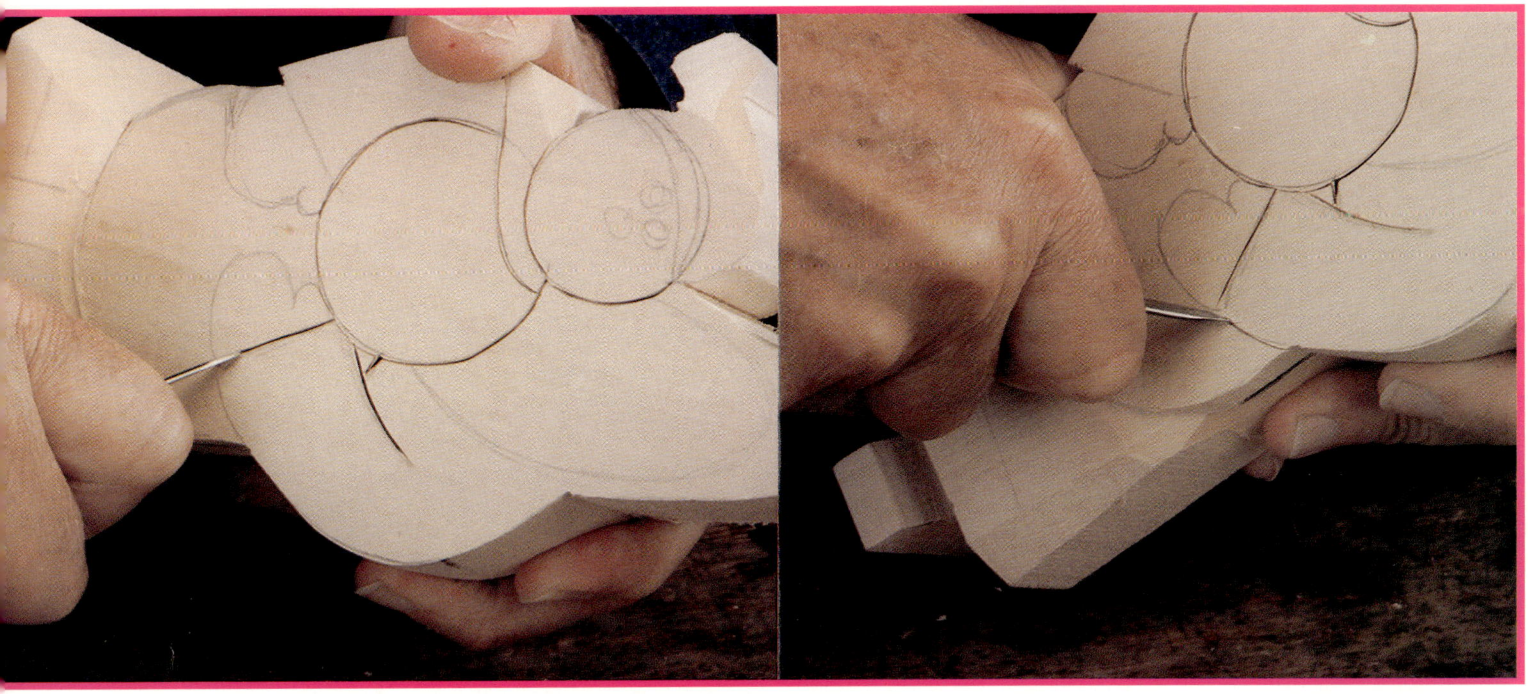

Incise the arms and the hands as these are important to the look of the snowman.

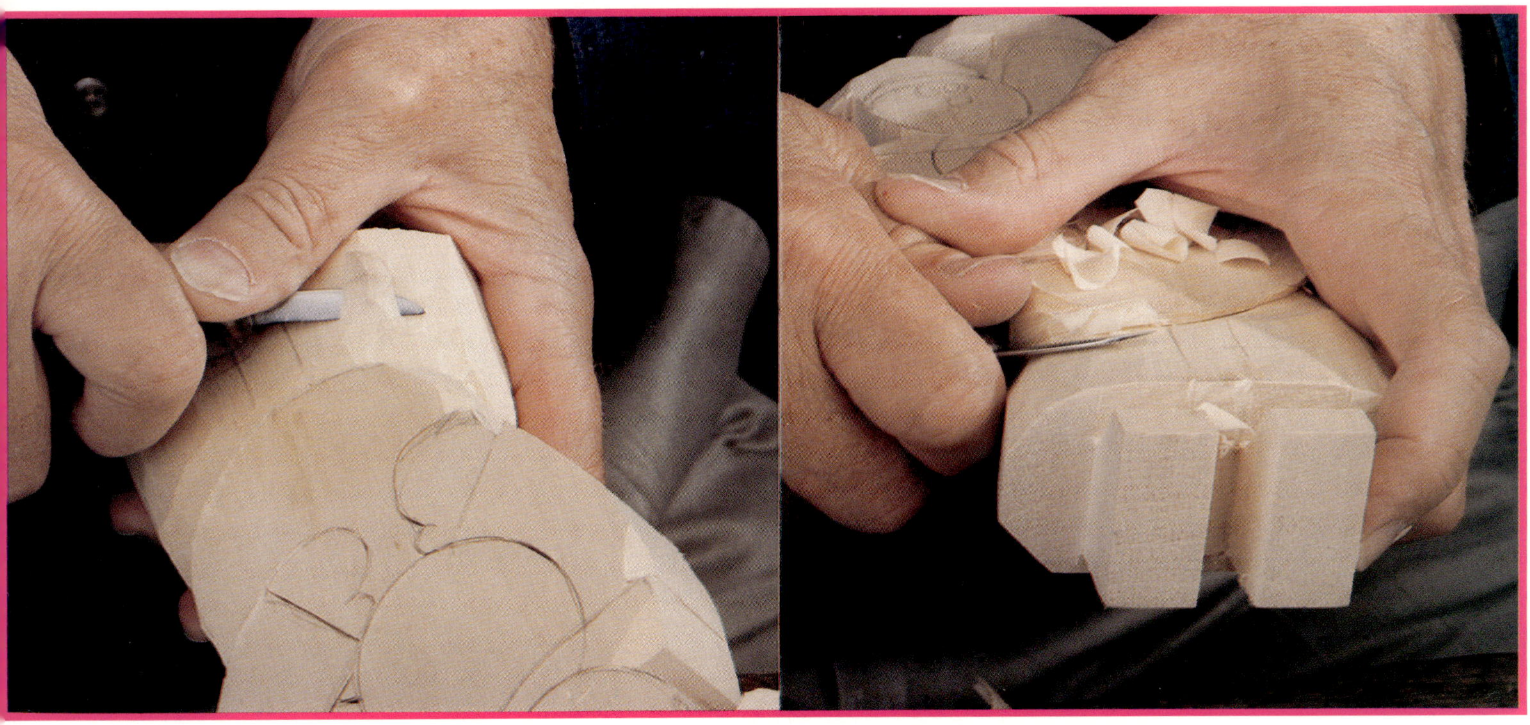

Start carving up into the bottom of the snowman to begin to give it some definition.

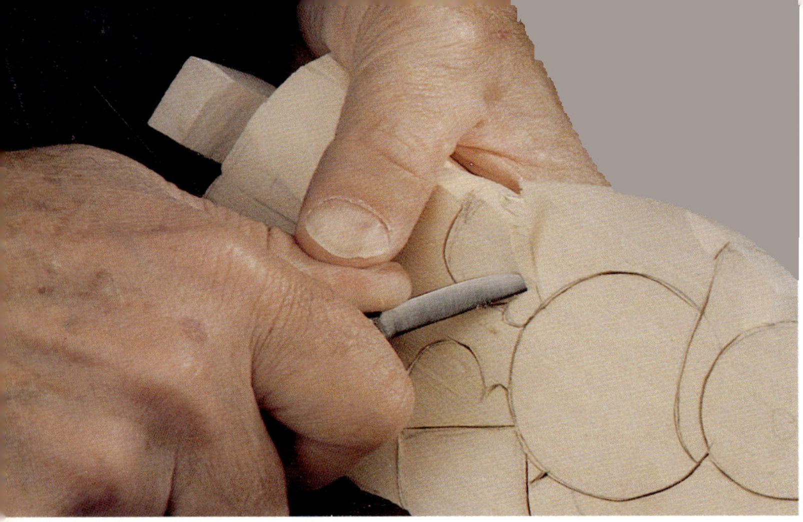

Start to define the hands ...

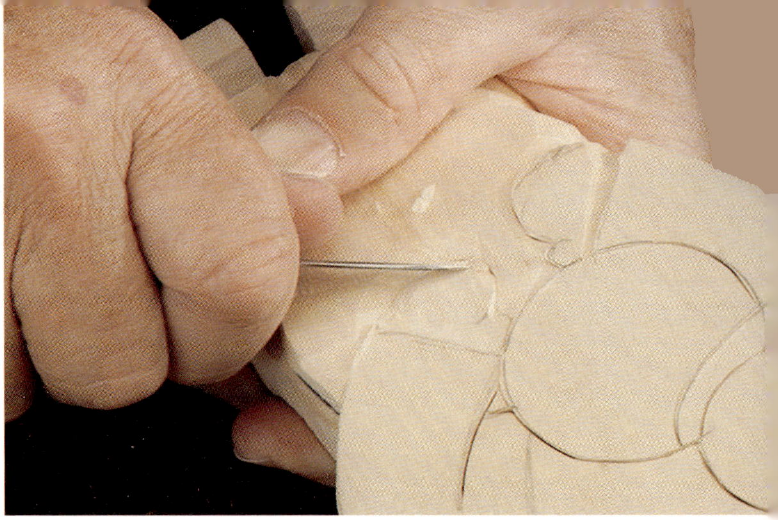

Further rounding the hands.

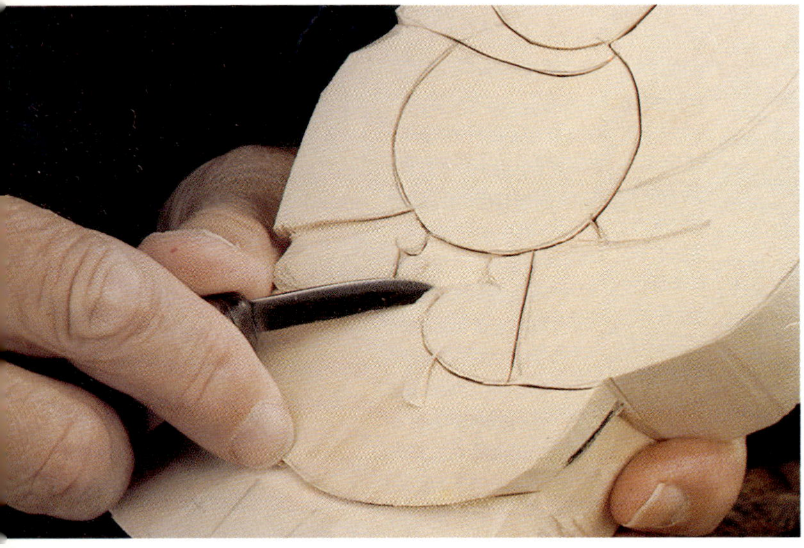

... and the snowman around the hands.

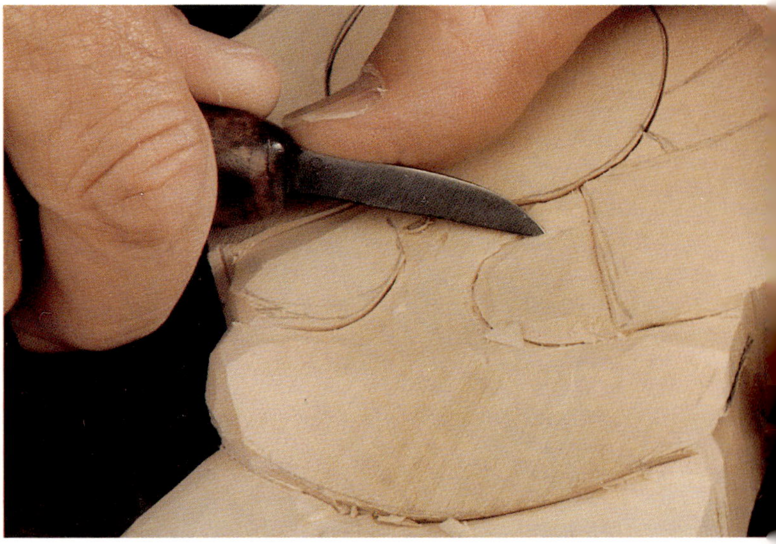

Recess the thumb from the rest of the hand as shown.

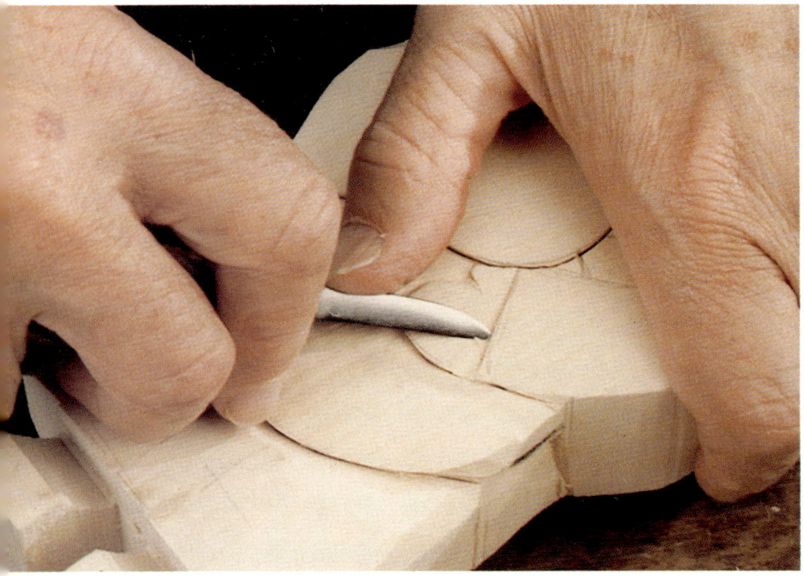

For some reason, some of my students have trouble understanding that the hand goes into the sleeve and will recess the sleeve instead of the hand. This cut shows the hand being recessed into the sleeve.

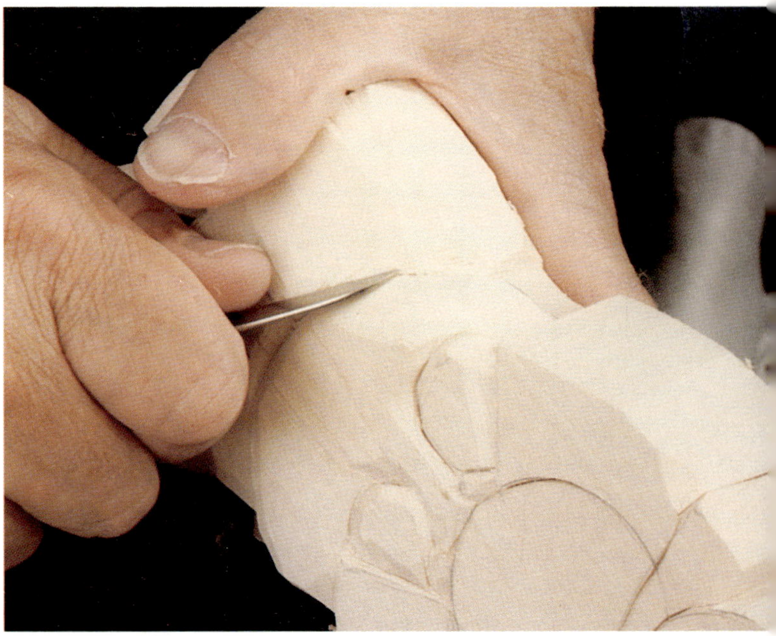

Rounding the lower body of the snowman.

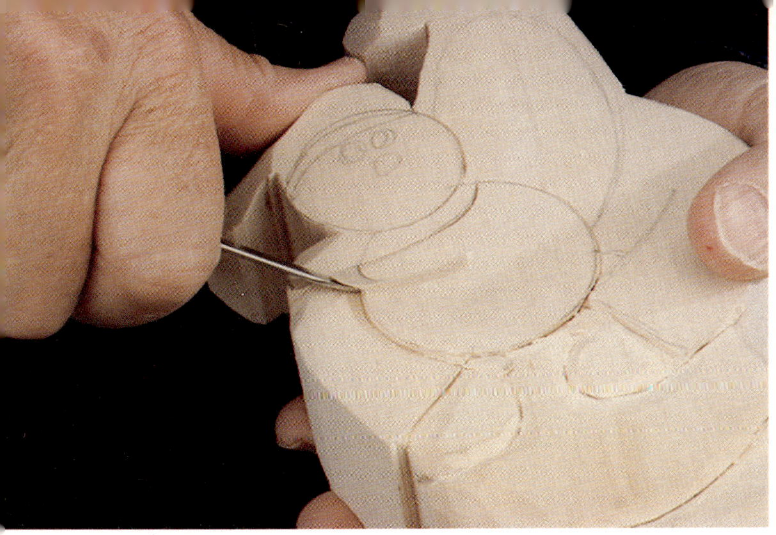

I'm starting to round Santa's arm and the snowman's chest.

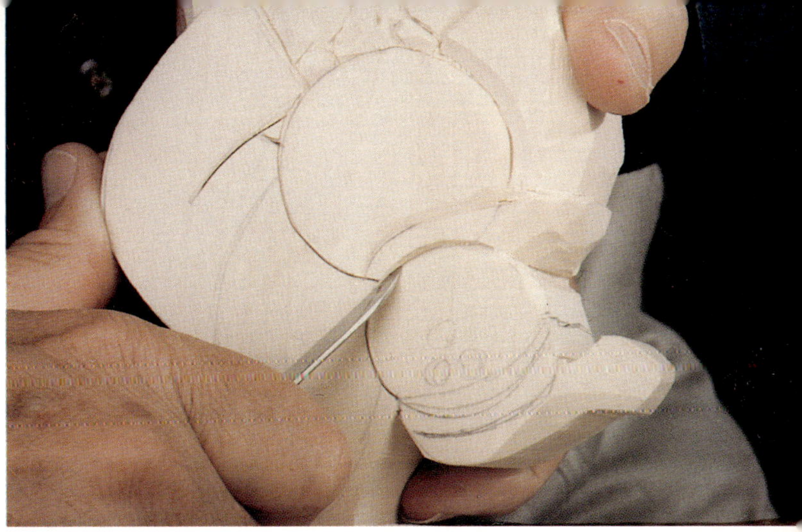

Start rounding the snowman's head.

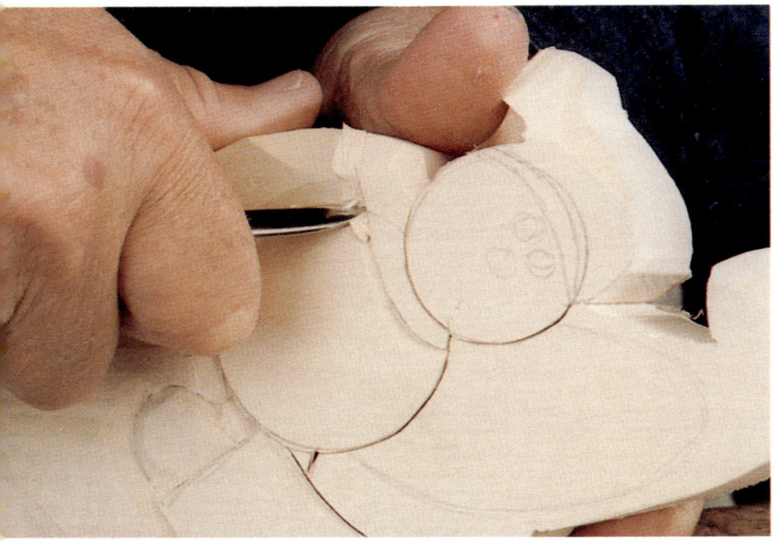

Undercut the scarf and begin to work it into the arm.

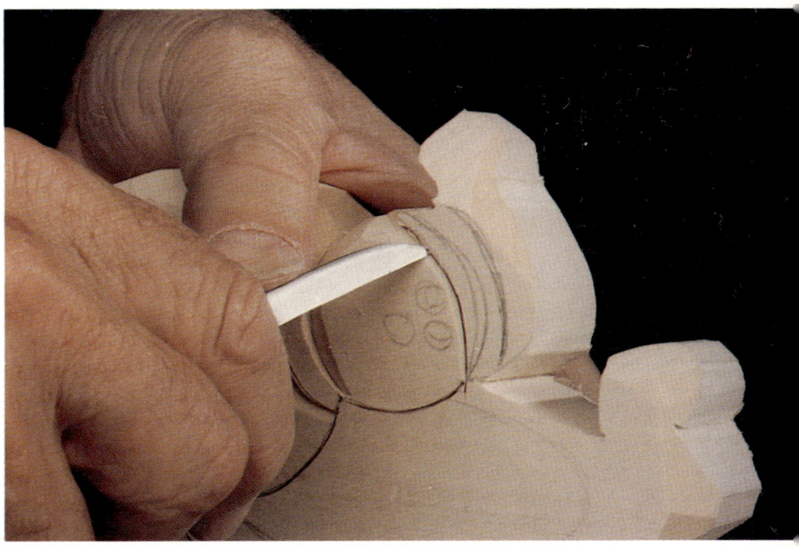

Cut the bottom of the toboggan into the snowman's head.

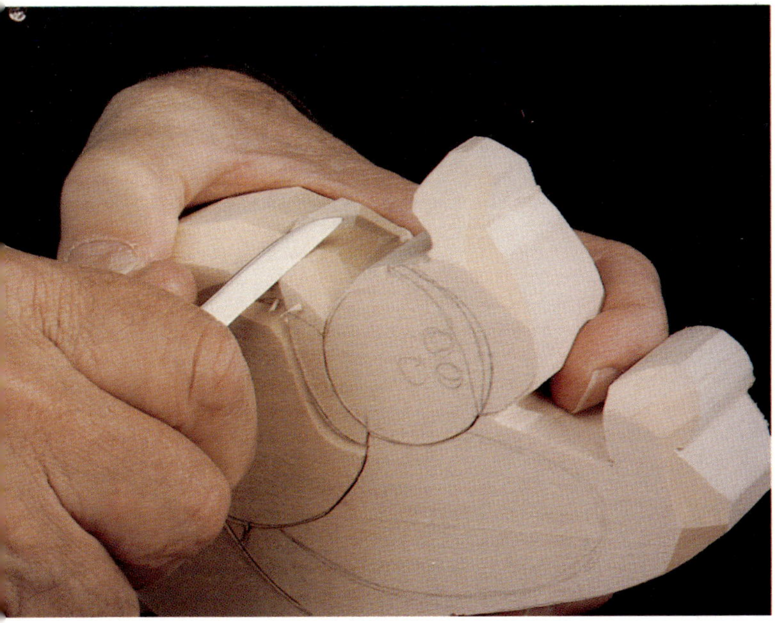

Start rounding the scarf and the upper arm of the Santa. Blend the scarf of the snowman.

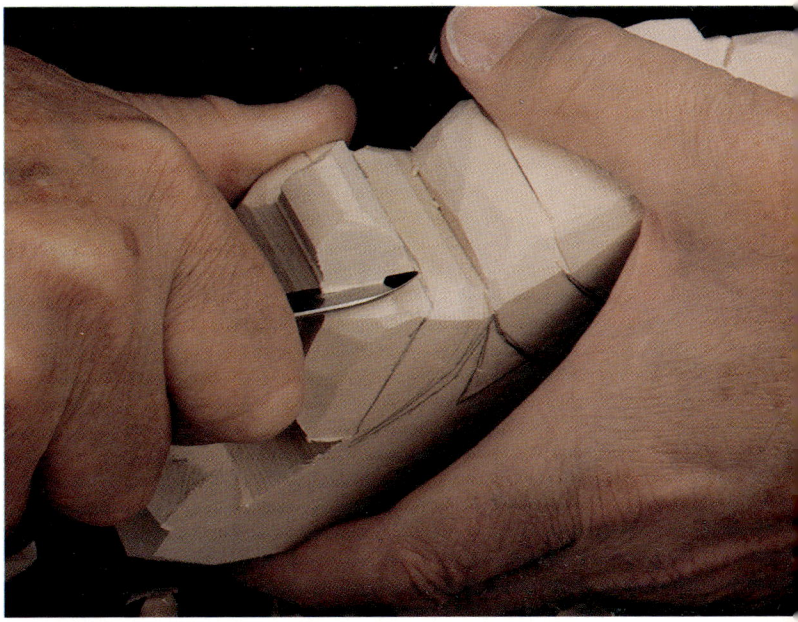

I've found a good way to make these balls is to make a stop cut at the base ...

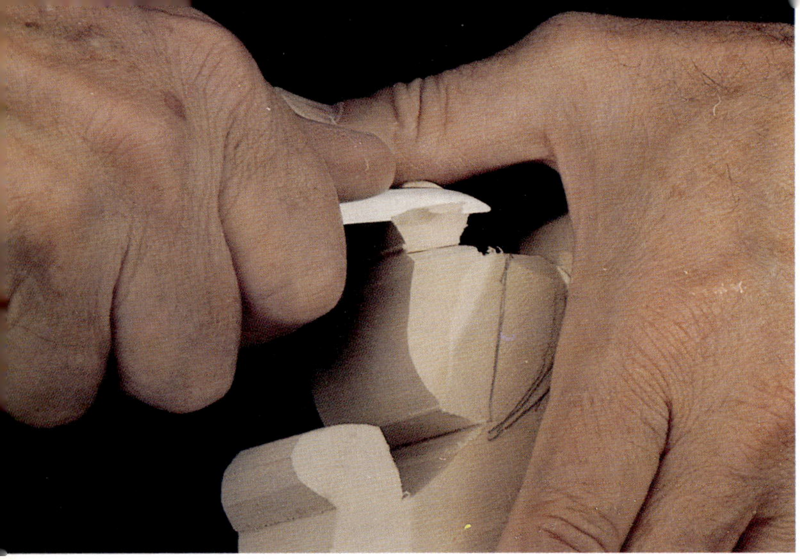

... and then to come back from the top to where you made your cut.

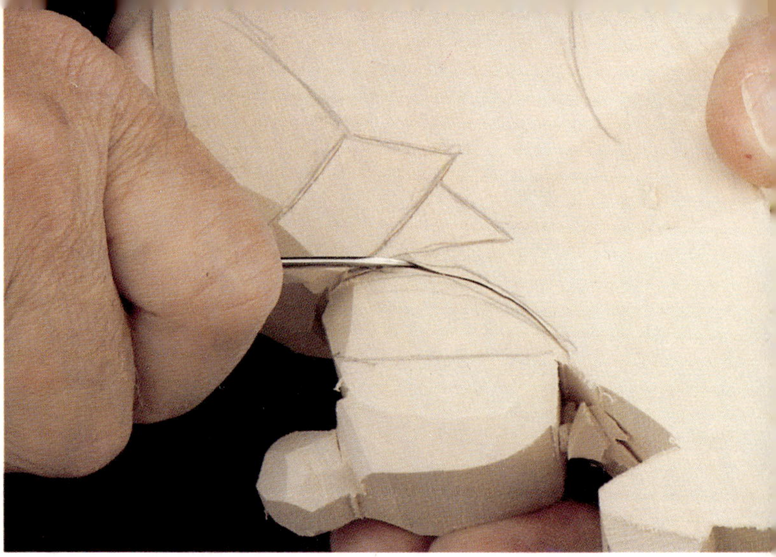

Incise the line where the snowman's head fits into Santa's shoulder.

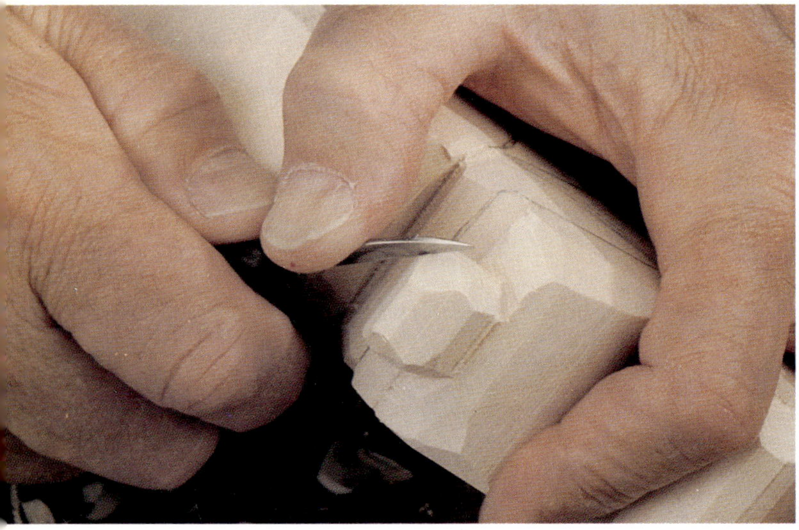

Keep doing that, alternating until you get the roundness that you want.

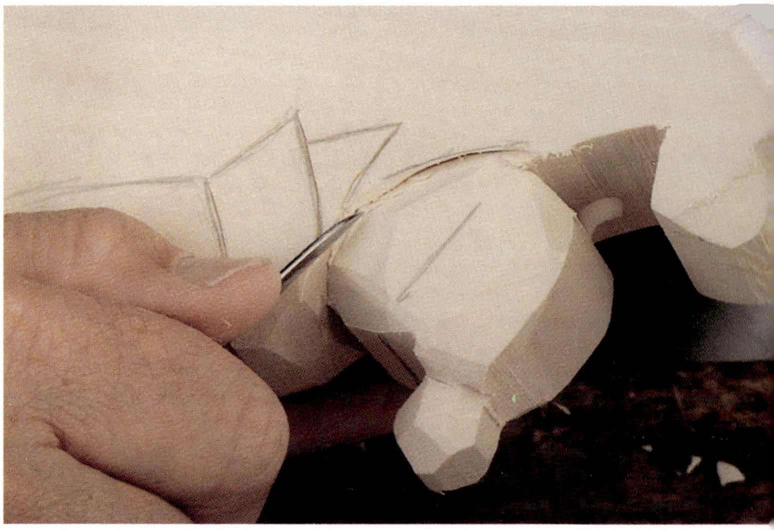

Start rounding his head into the cut you have made.

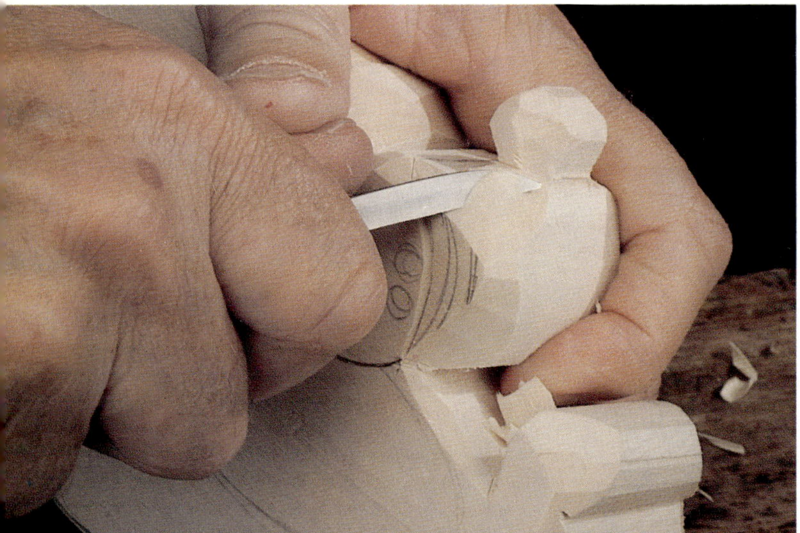

Round the toboggan.

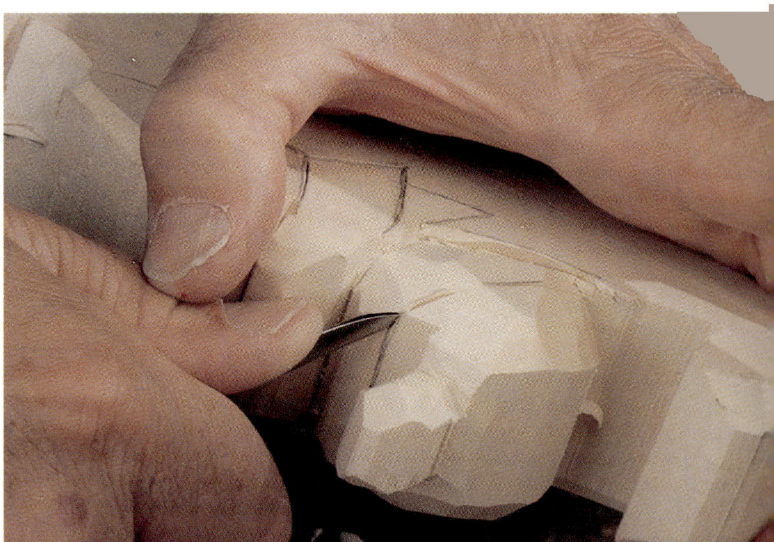

Incise the line all the way around where the snowman's head and the toboggan come together.

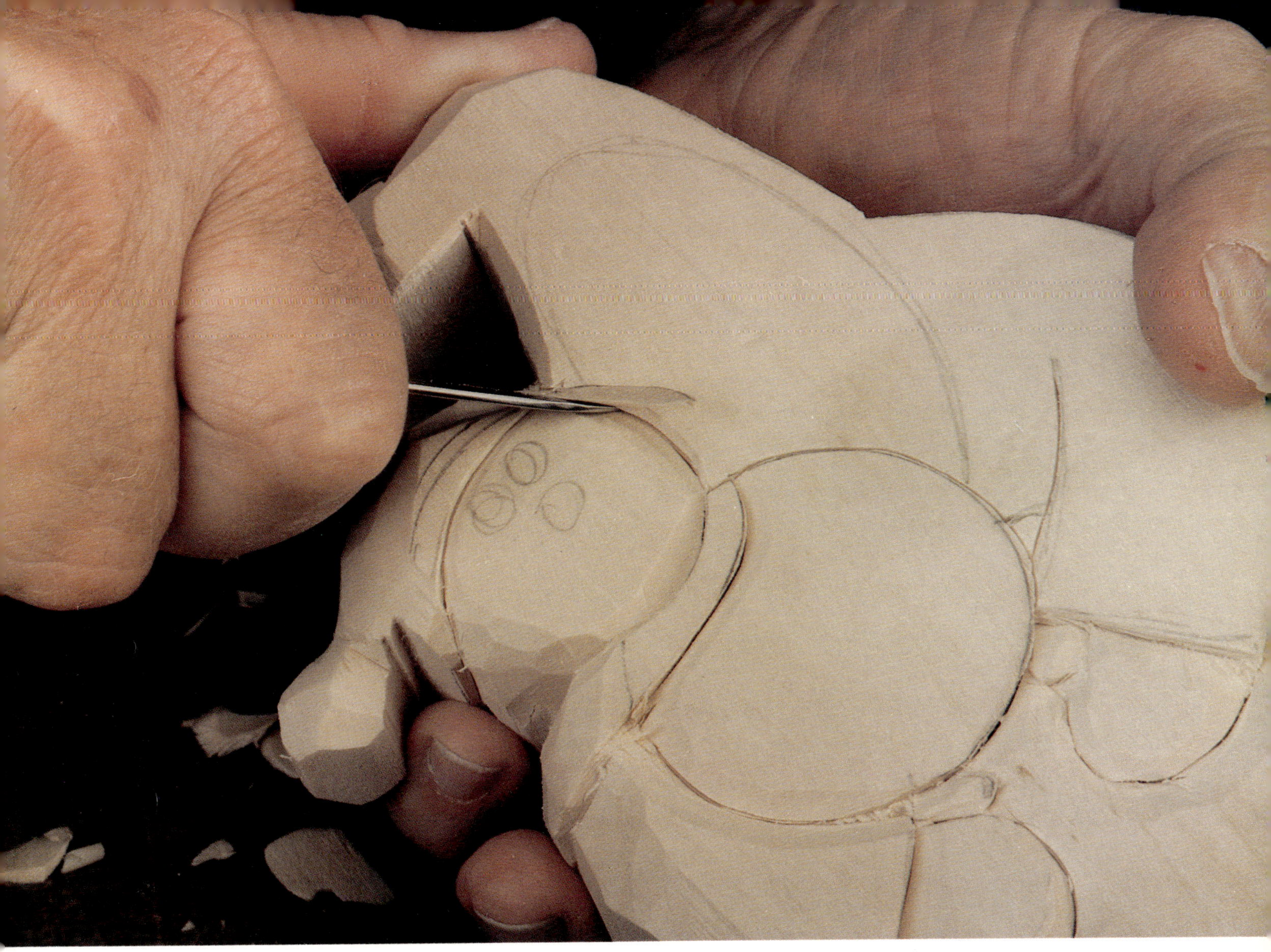

Round in the snowman's head where it meets Santa's face.

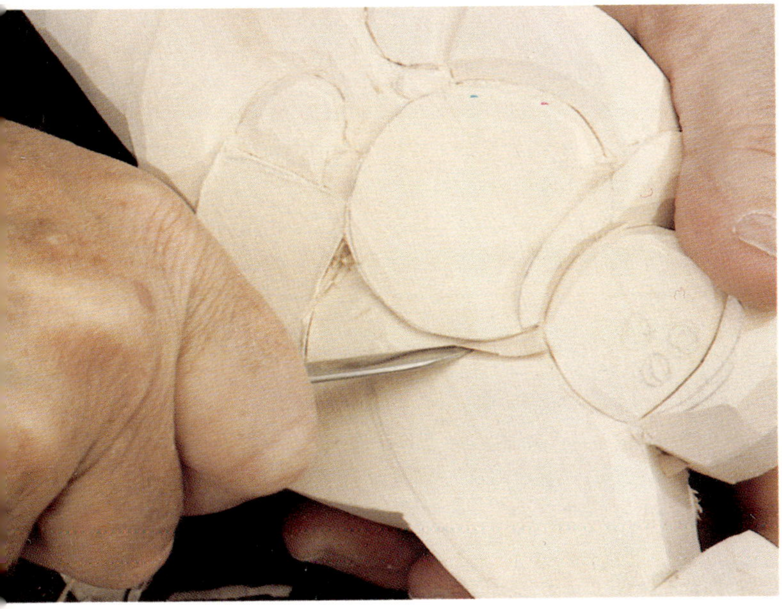

Start to cut in from the beard into the snowman.

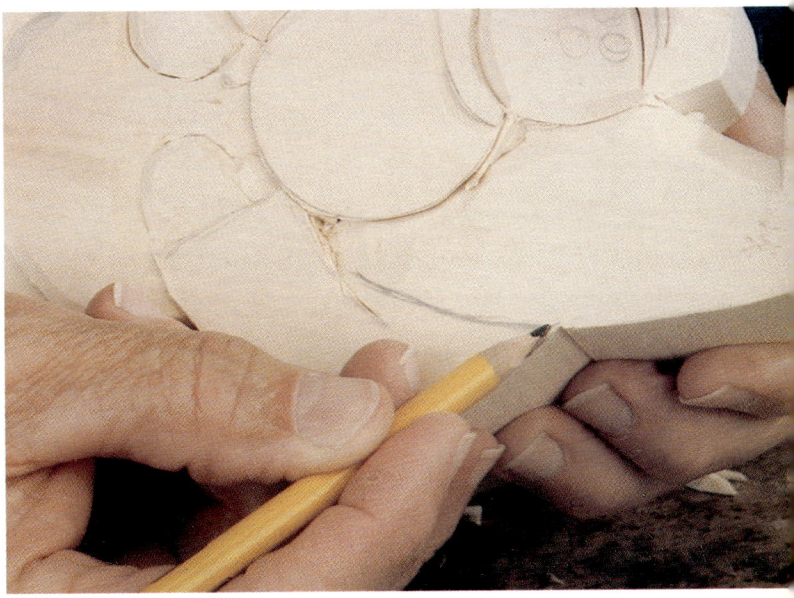

At this point, I've decided to change the line for the bottom of the beard like so.

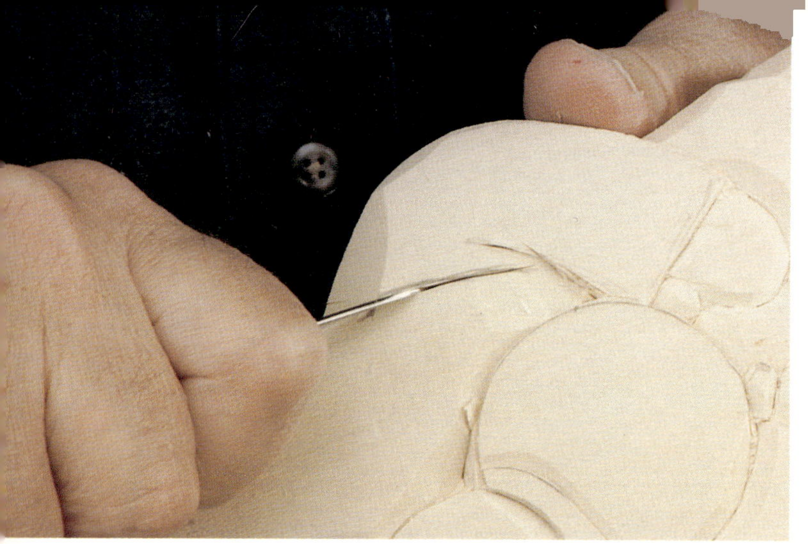

Incising the new beard line.

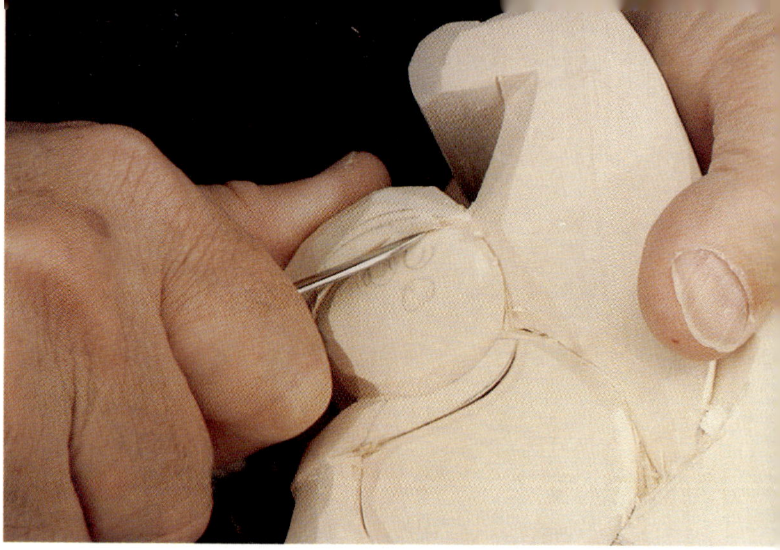

Round the snowman's little fat head some more.

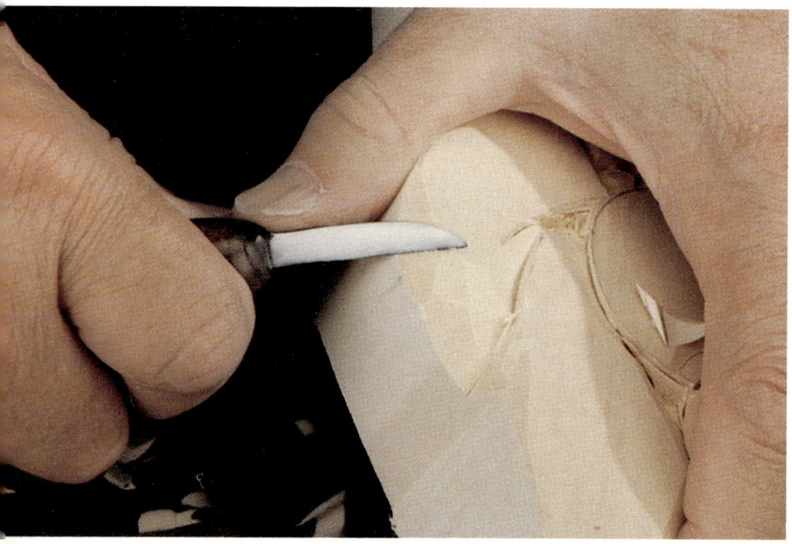

Start rounding the shoulder away from the beard.

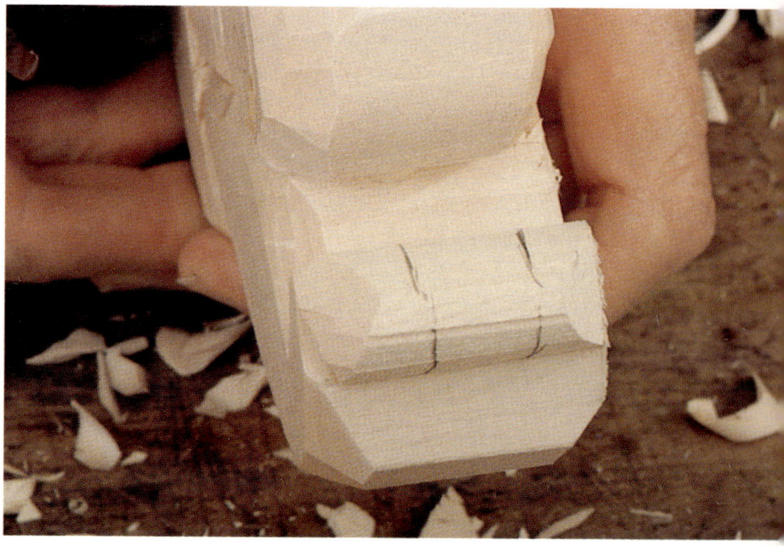

At this point draw in the ball on Santa's cap.

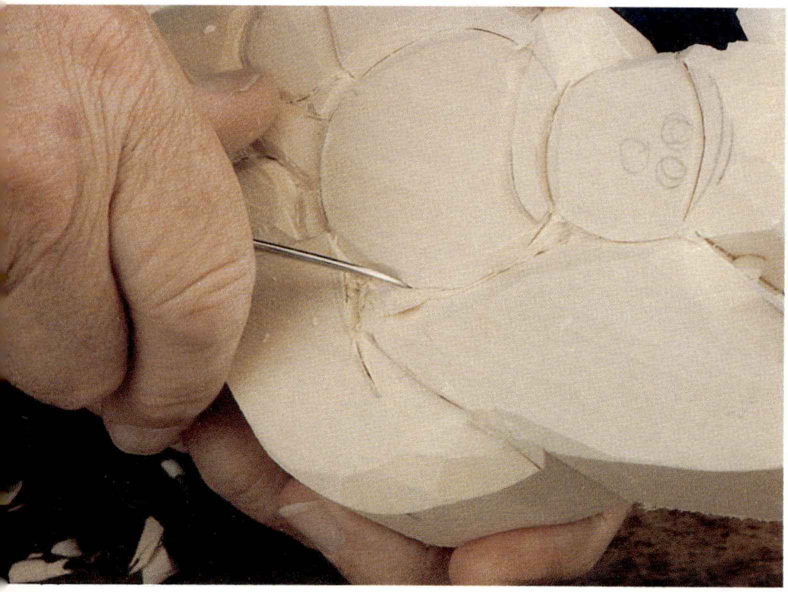

Now I can see where I need to start rounding in the area of the chest of the snowman.

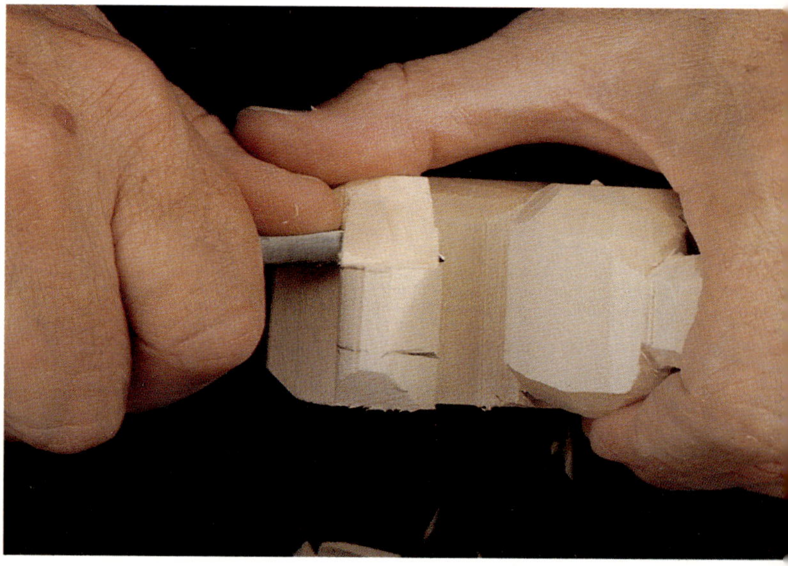

The same technique applies here as with the little ball on the snowman. Make a series of stop cuts and downward strokes to reduce the ball to it's proper size.

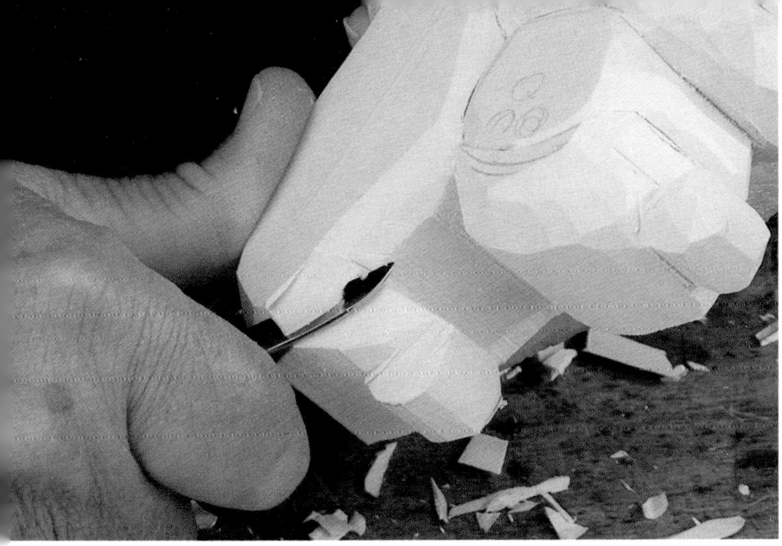

I've rounded away from the ball. You're not having a race. Take your time with the ball. You can glue it back on if you slip but it's better if you don't have to.

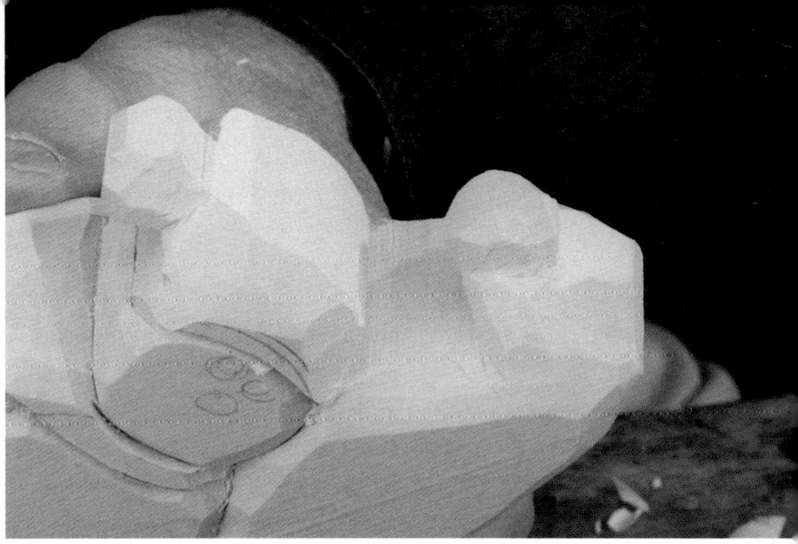

Both finished balls.

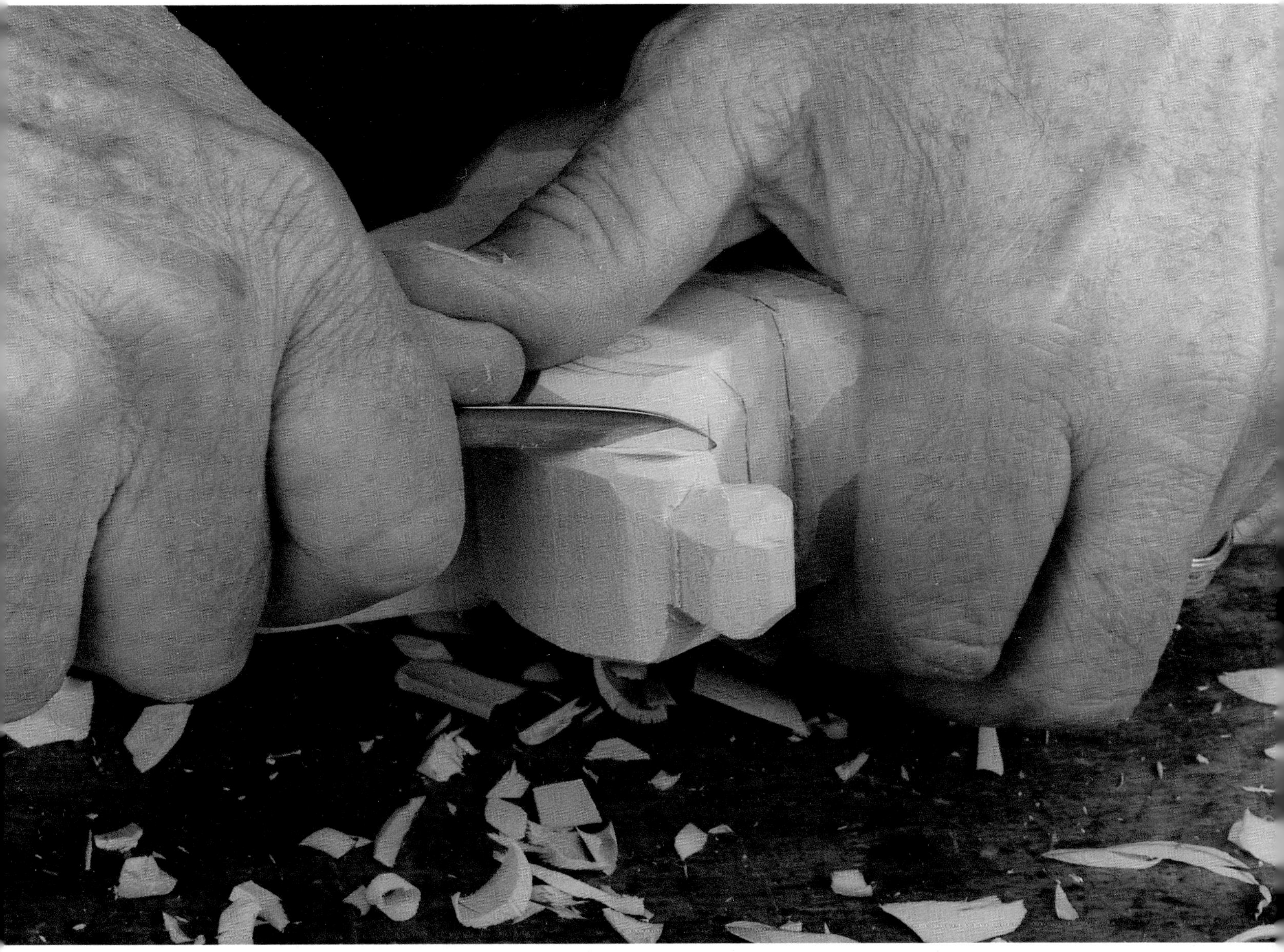

Make a series of V cuts to give the flapped over portion of the toboggan a little more natural look.

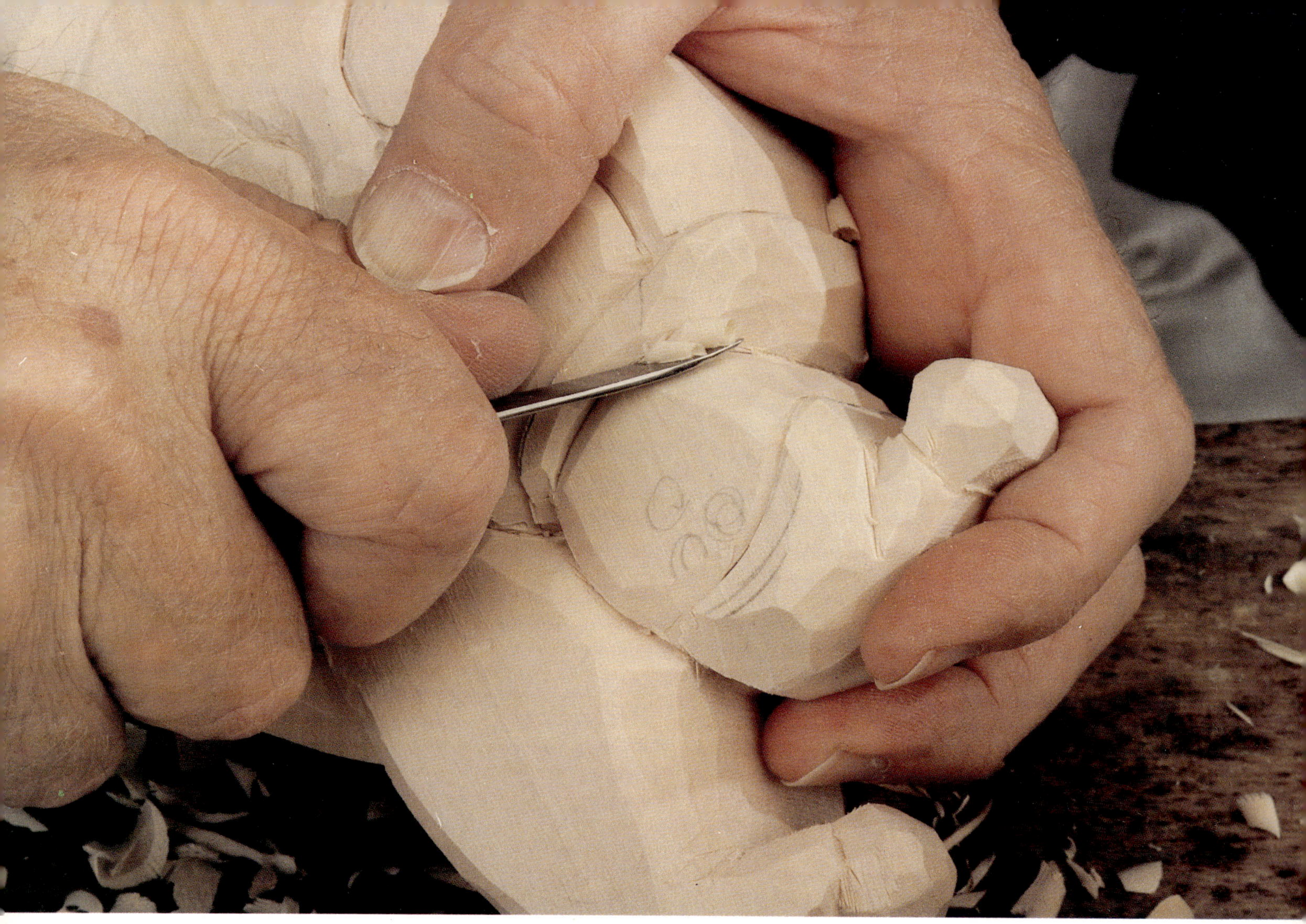

Continue to round the snowman's head.

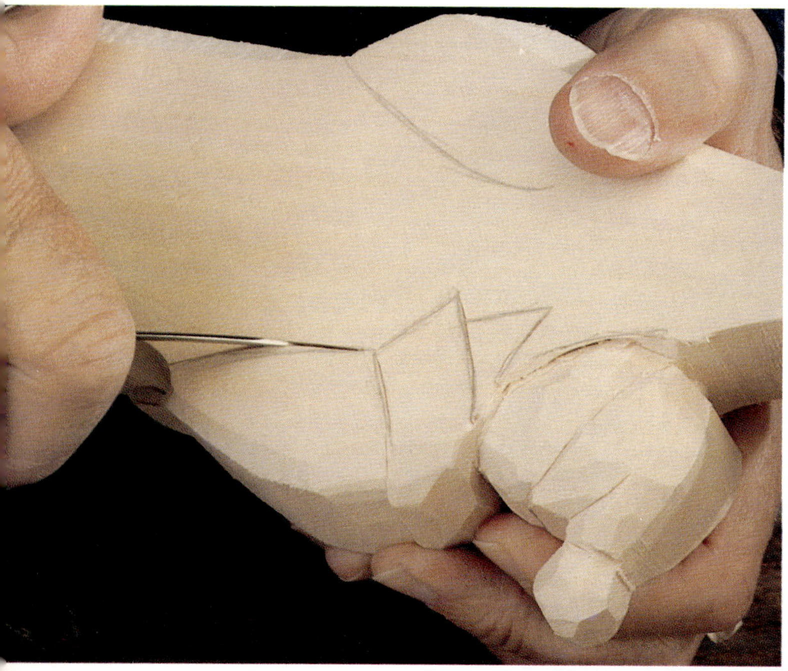

Incise and begin defining the back of the snowman.

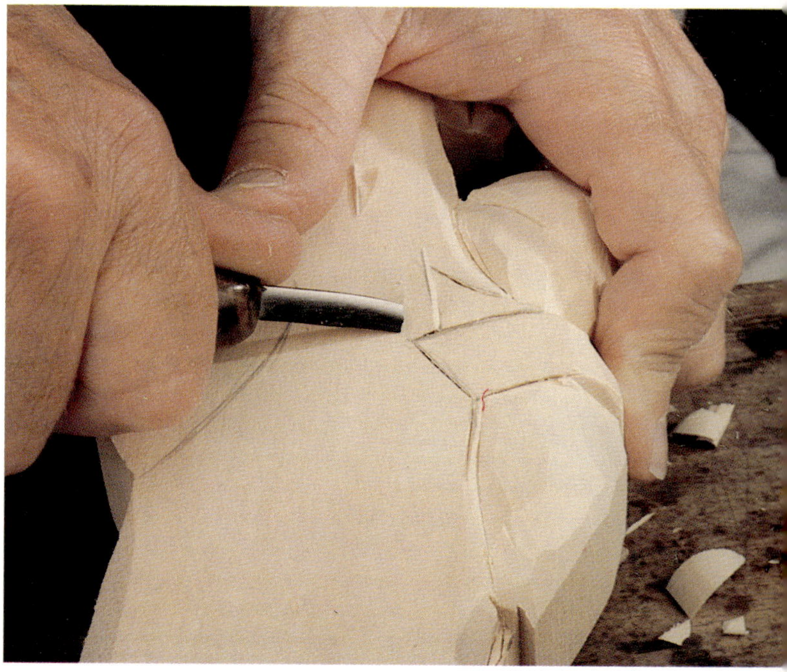

Define the rest of the scarf in the back now.

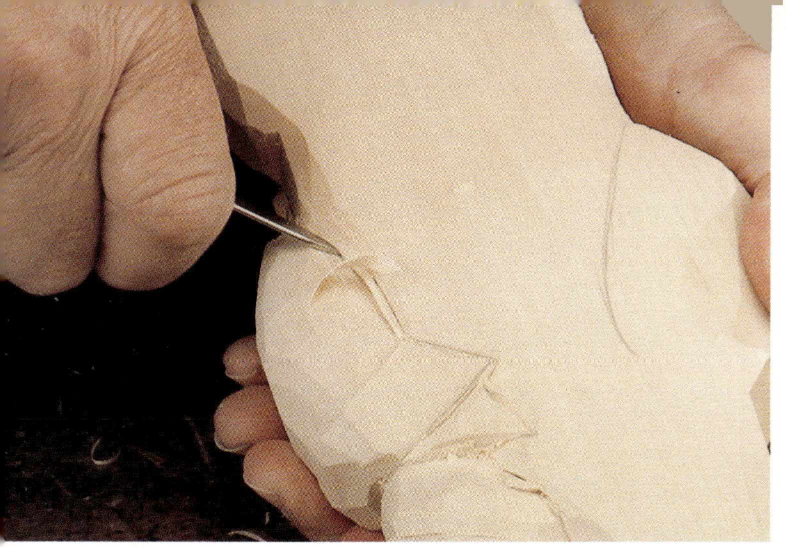

To define the back of the arm, make a series of little V cuts.

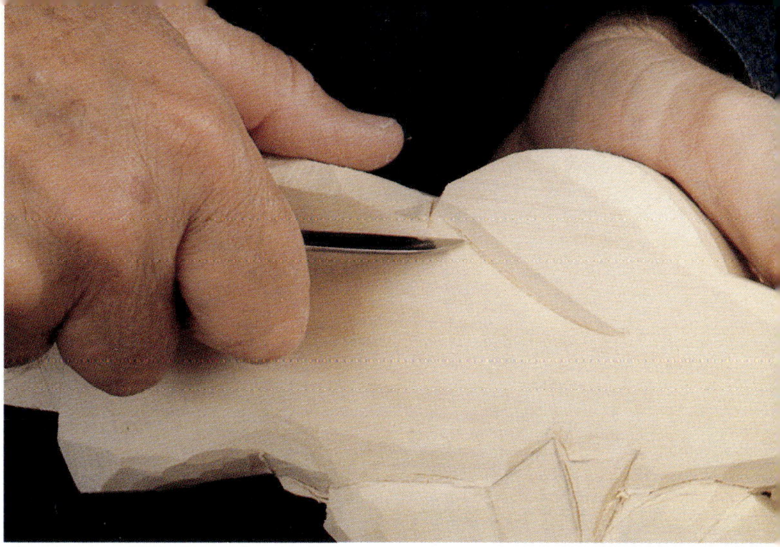

Make another V cut along the other side to complete the back of the arm.

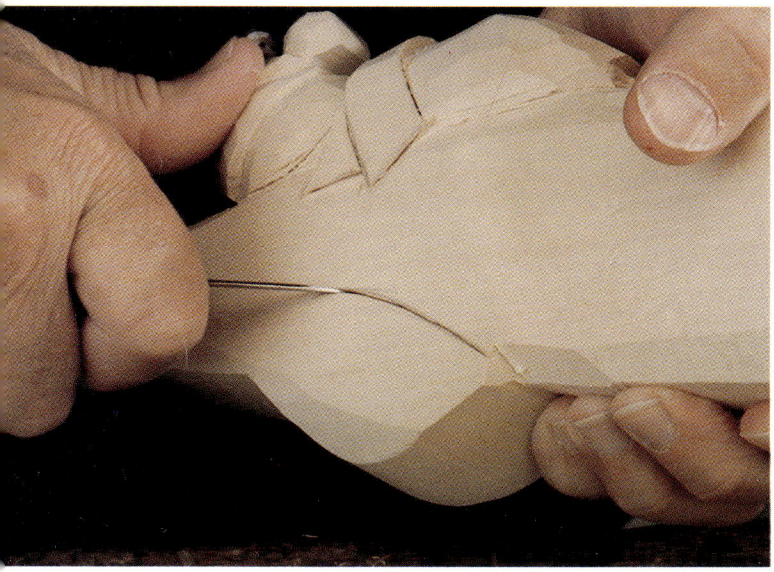

To carve the other arm, first incise along the line ...

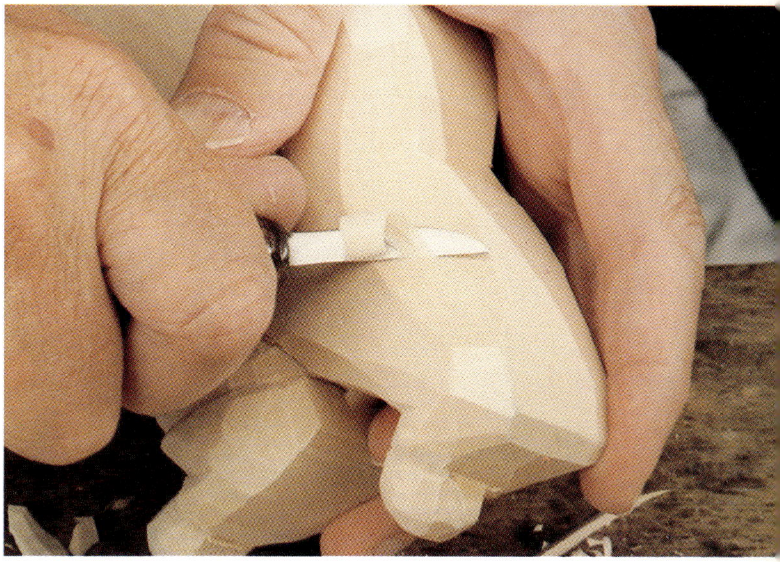

Blend the hood to fit.

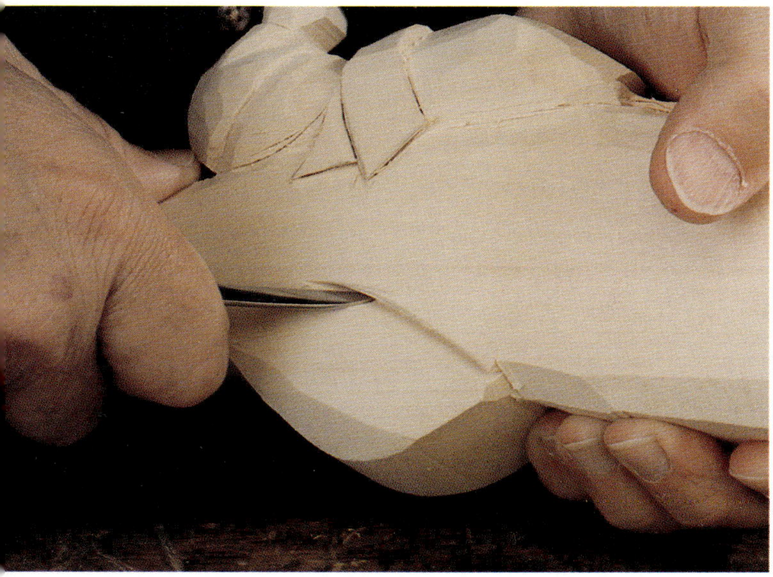

... and then make a V cut along one side of the line.

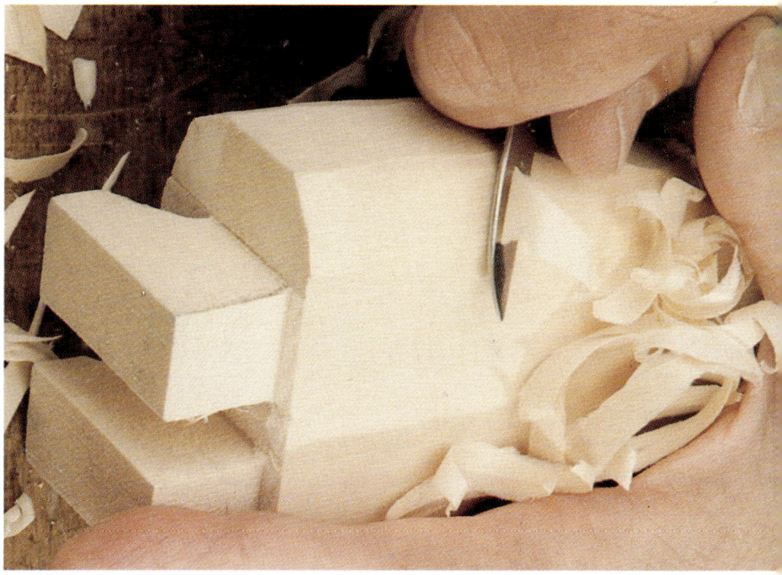

Continue rounding down the robe.

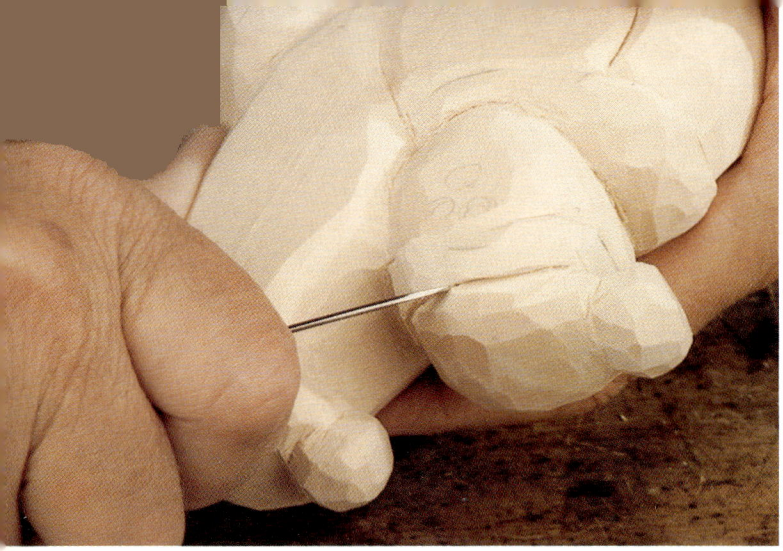

Cut in the toboggan roll.

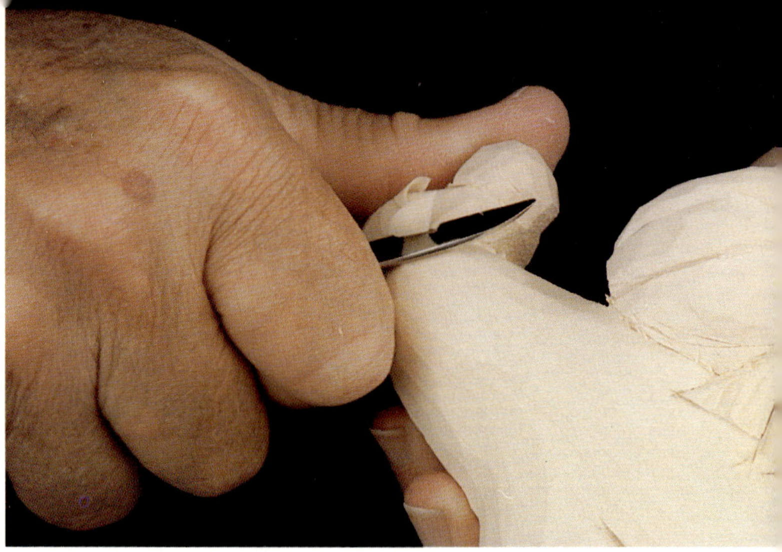

We're doing some clean up before we move on to the face.

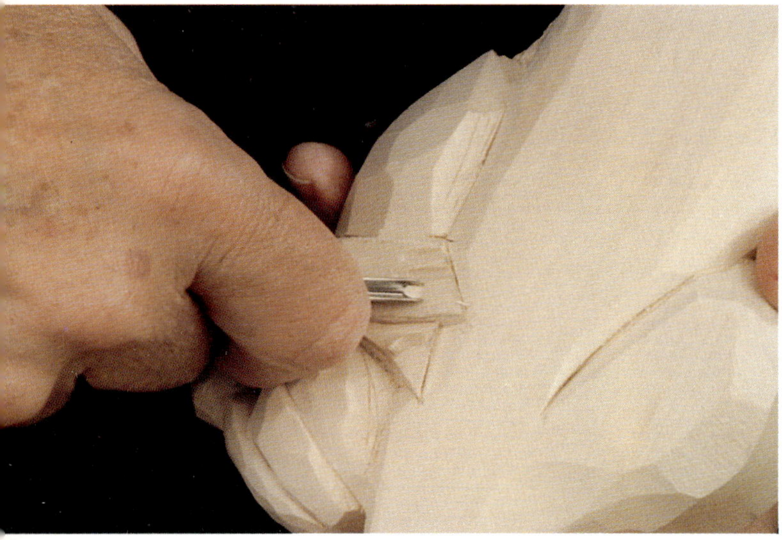

I want my scarf to have a fringe so I'll take my trusty gouge and make one.

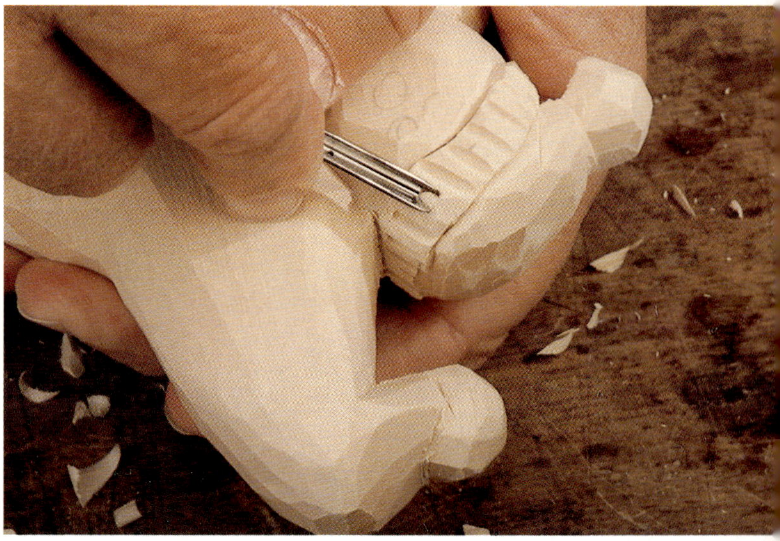

Cut in some fluting in the roll of the toboggan with the gouge.

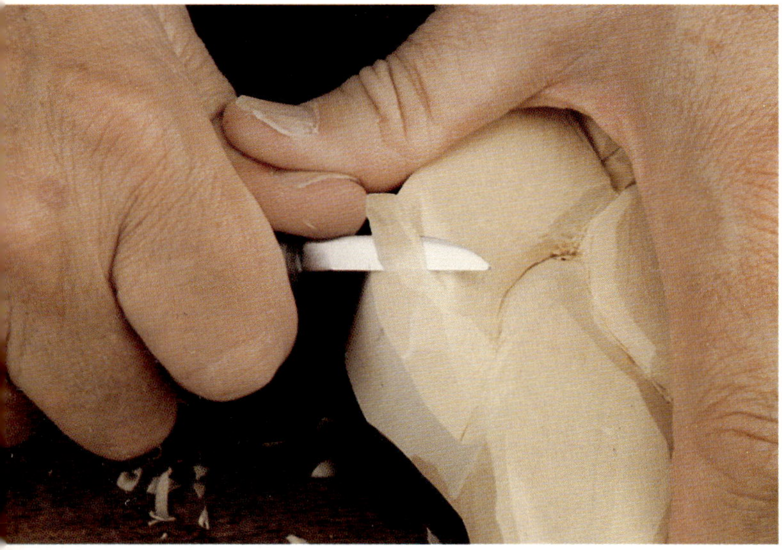

Cut back the left arm a little further to get it to blend with the rest of the body. On these bigger figures you can always go back and see what needs to be removed.

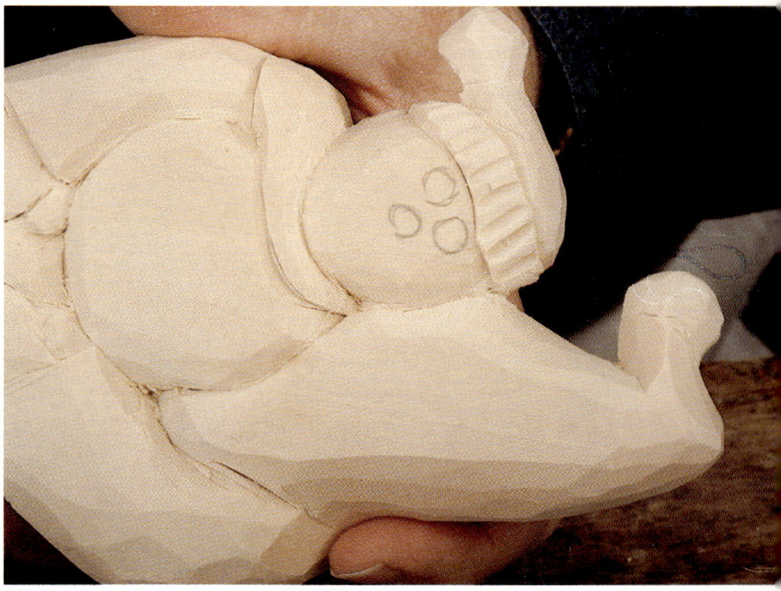

I have drawn in the eyes and the location of the hole I will drill in for the dowel that will become the carrot nose.

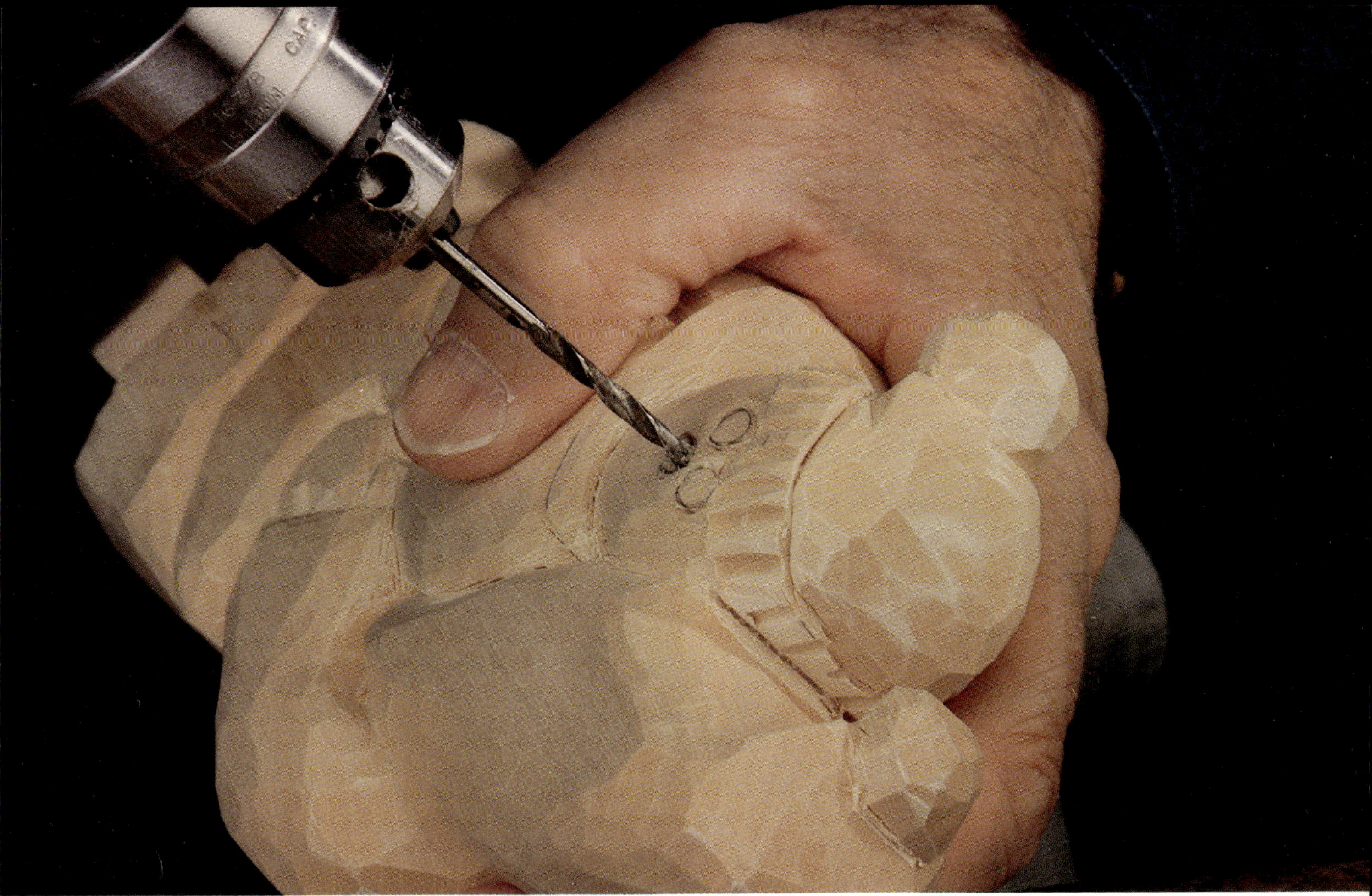

Drill a hole for the nose. Some of the "early" snowmen had eyes made from small pieces of coal. Some of you younger carvers may need to get your granddads to explain to you what a piece of coal is.

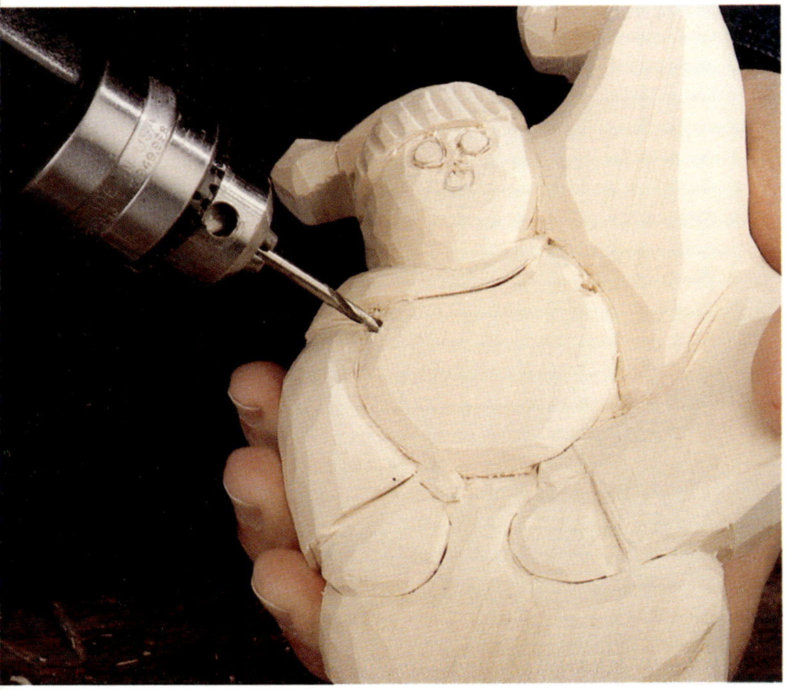

Drill holes for the limbs we will use as arms too. This is the angle you will want.

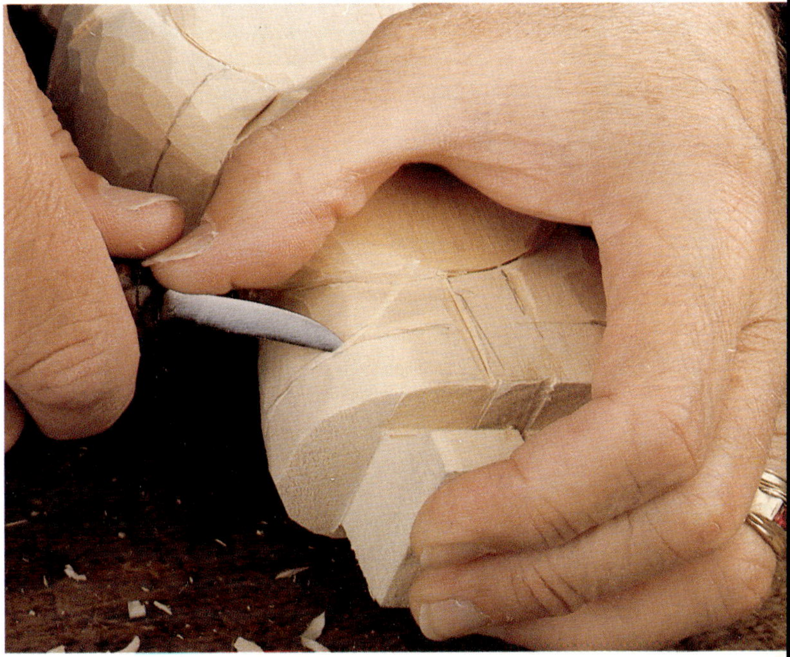

We're ready now to put in some fur around Santa's robe. Draw in and incise the lines of the fur trim as before. Undercut to the incised line to raise the fur off the robe a little.

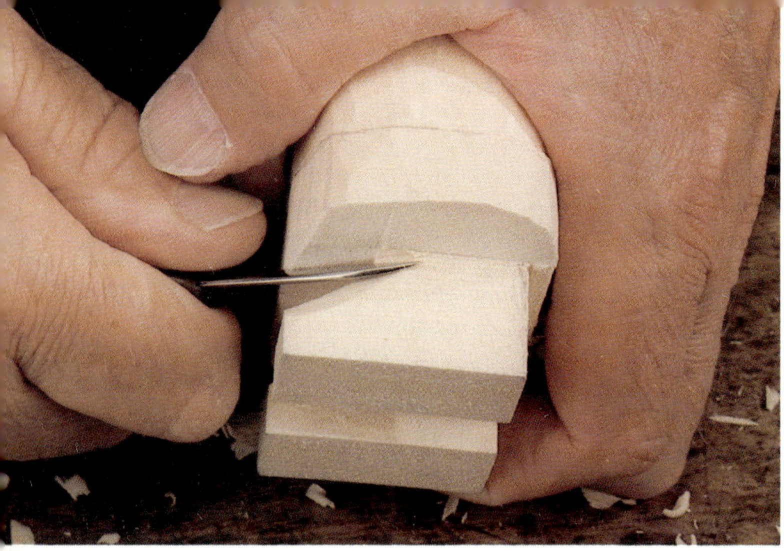

The feet are important on these larger carvings. Round off the sharp edges.

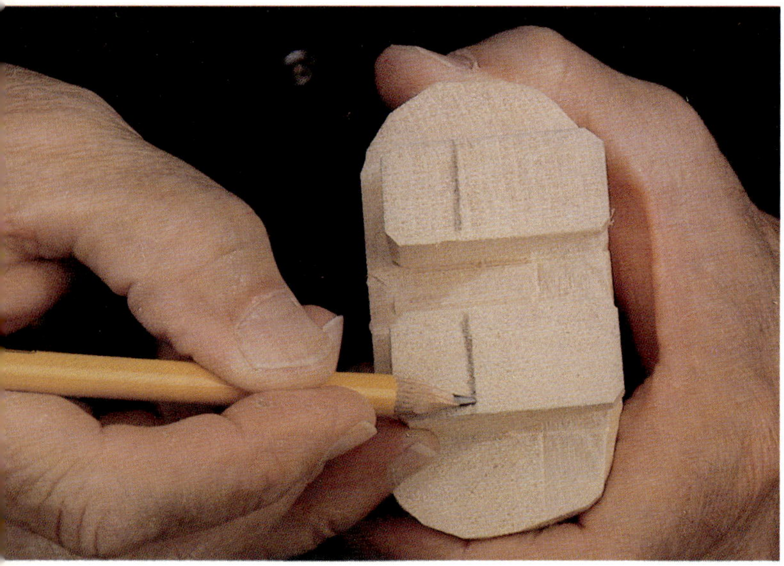

Draw in the heels.

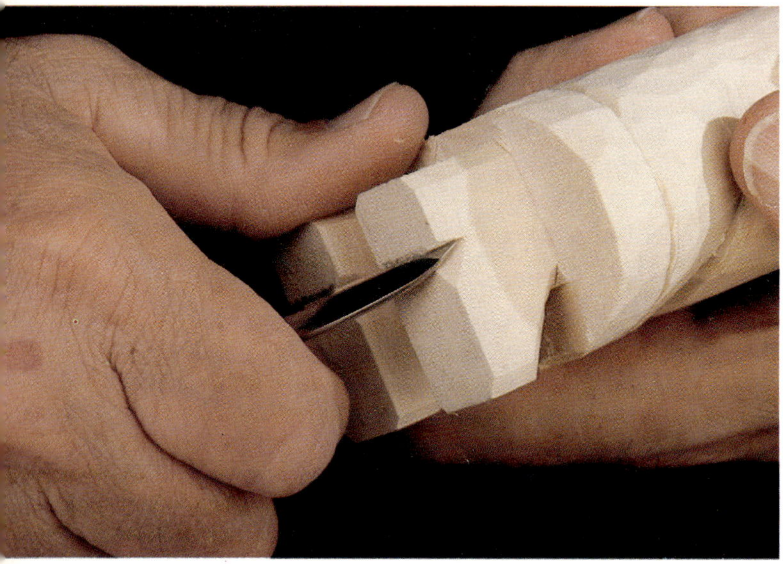

Notch the corners of the heels. You don't have to cut all the way in as the bottom of the shoe won't show.

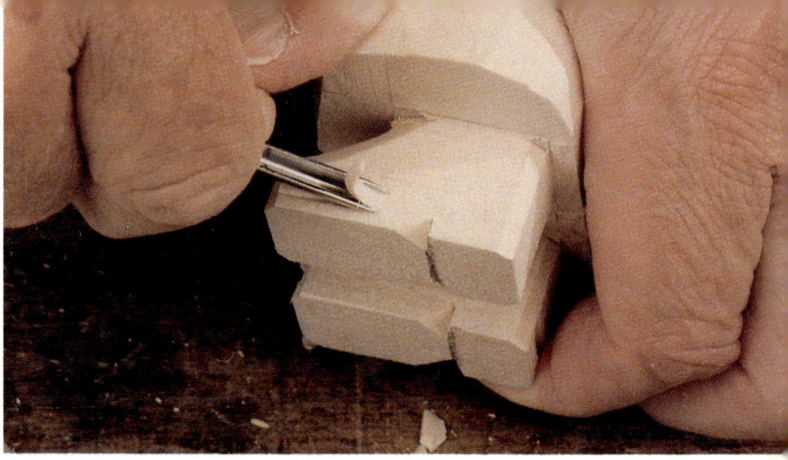

Use a gouge to put in the soles of the shoes ...

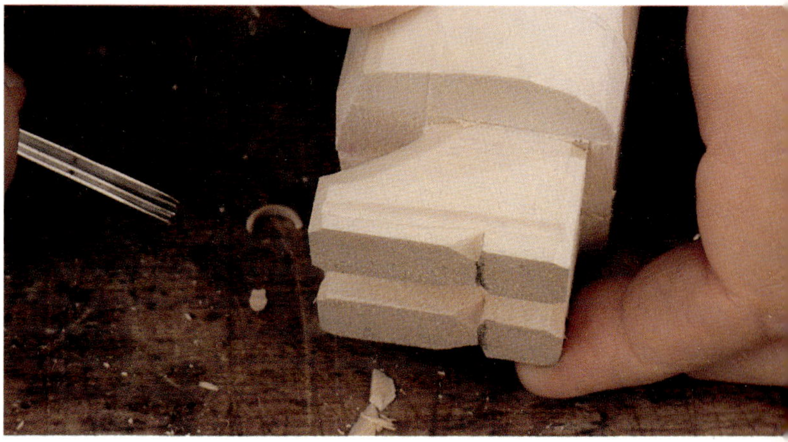

... like so.

Draw in the area of the face from shoulder to shoulder.

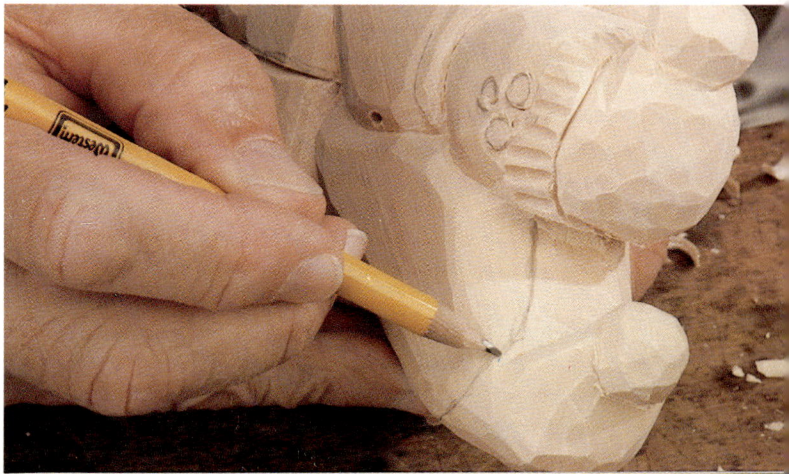

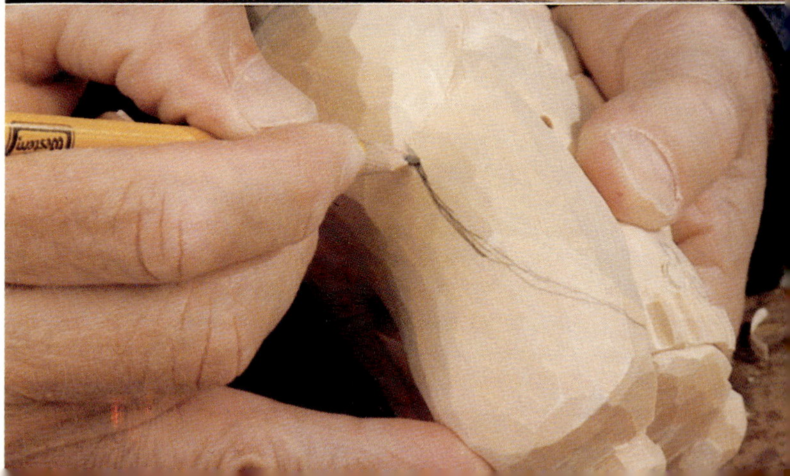

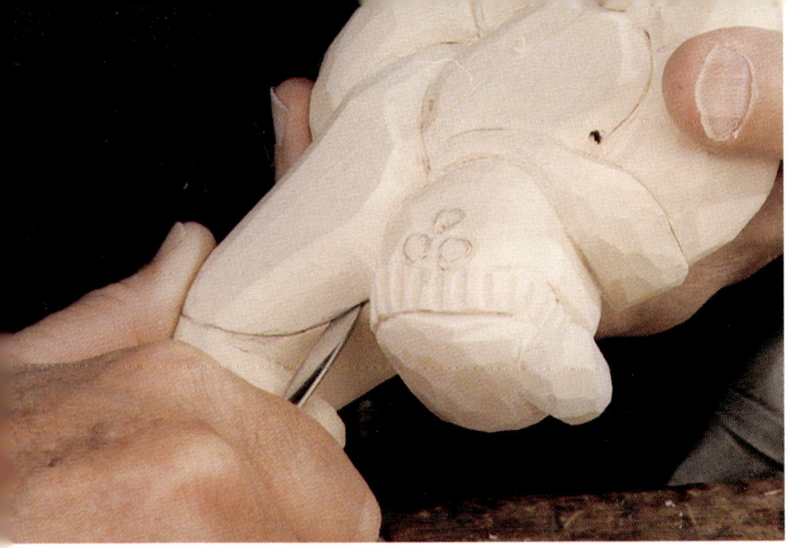

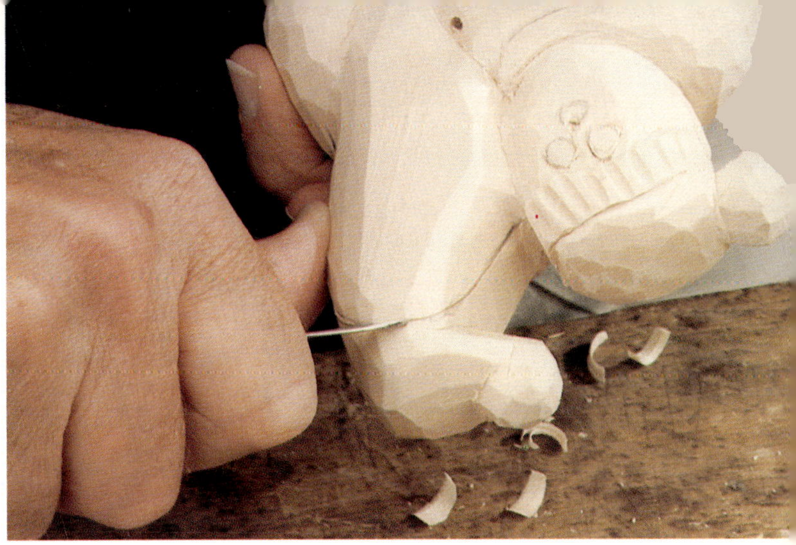

Incise the line of the face as deeply as you can on the sides and to a lesser depth on the front.

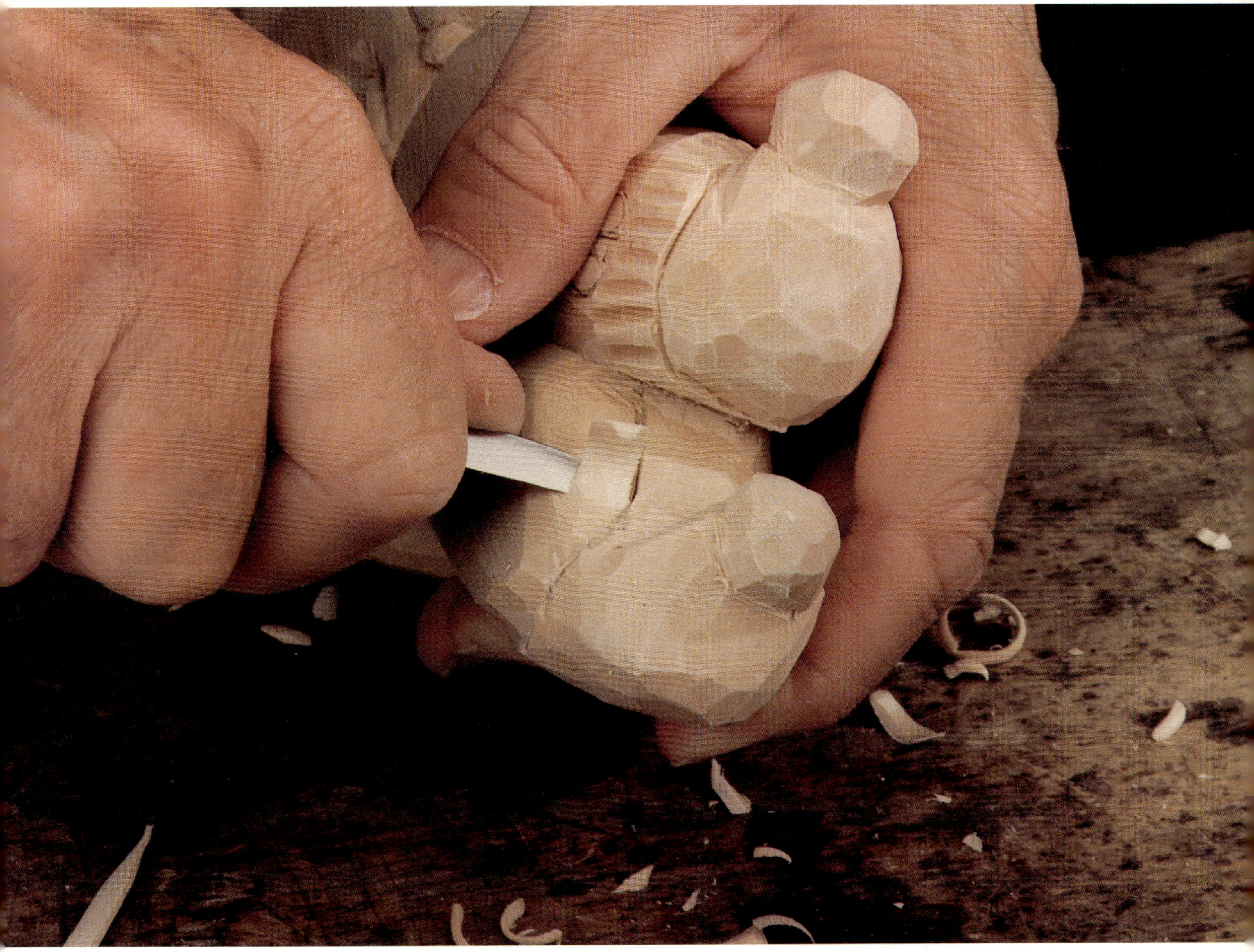

Begin to cut away from the incised area, rounding the face.

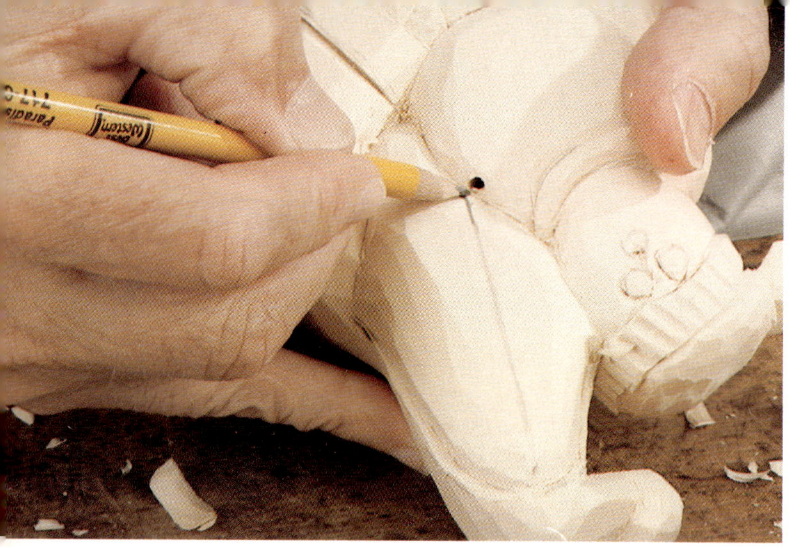

Draw in your center line and keep the head roughly egg shaped.

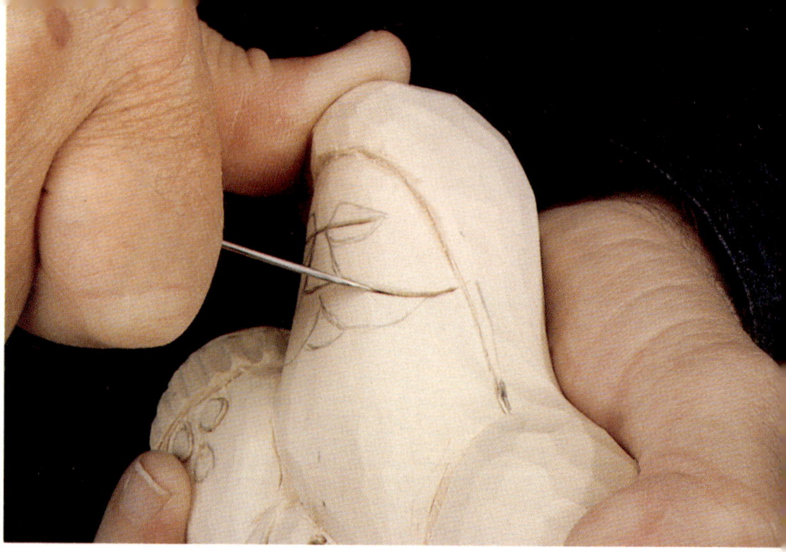

Cut in nice and deep along this line to make fat cheeks.

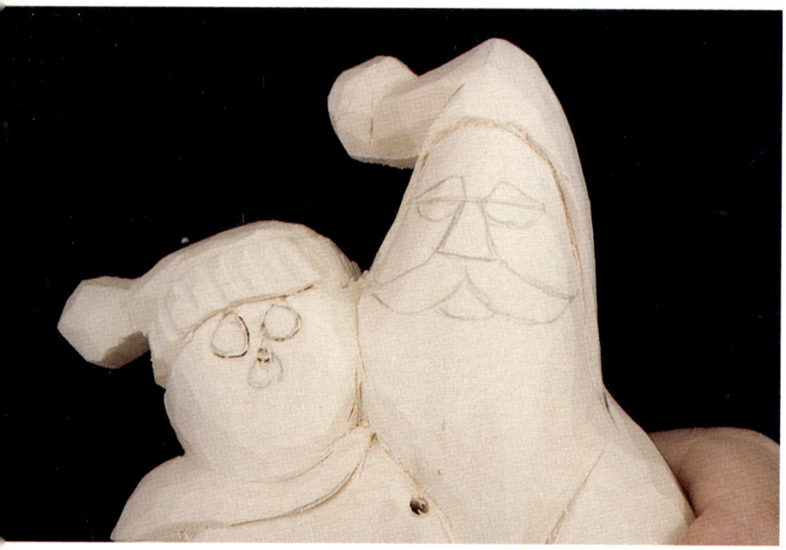

It's the same deal with the face again. Draw it in and make sure the nose is wide enough. Covering a larger area, this Santa's face will be a little easier to carve.

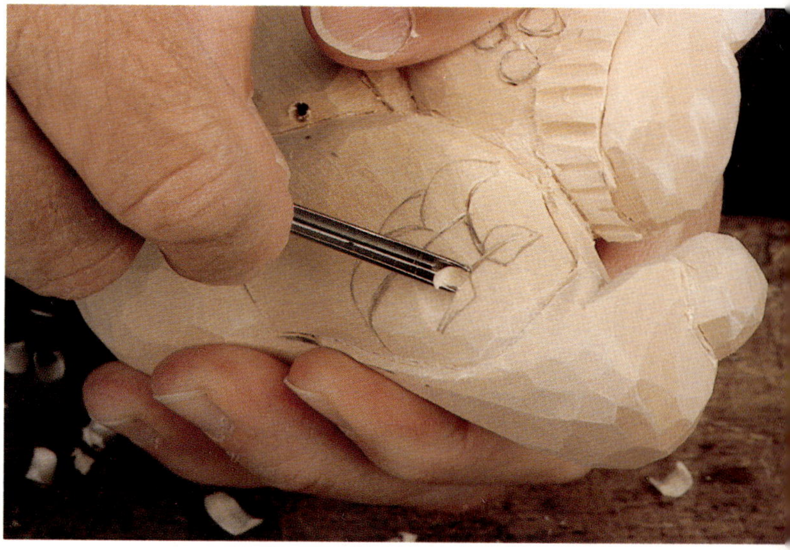

Use a gouge to define the sides of the nose and the eyes.

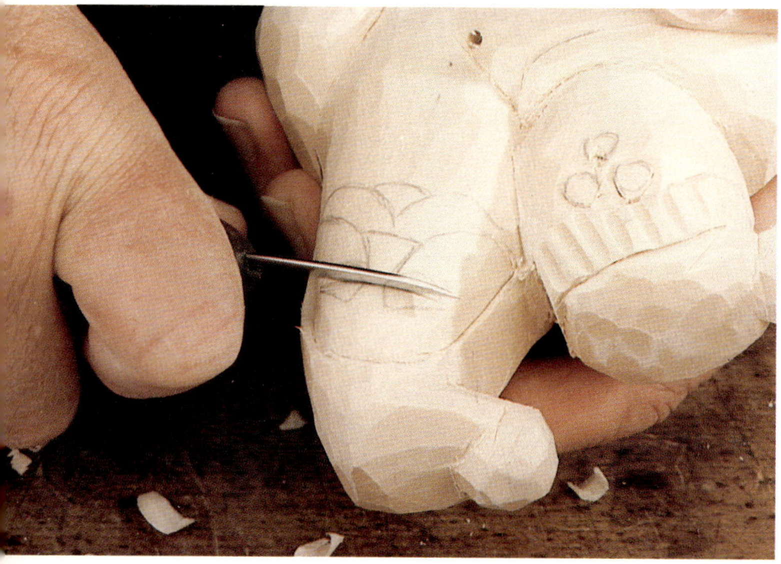

Cut in the eye channel.

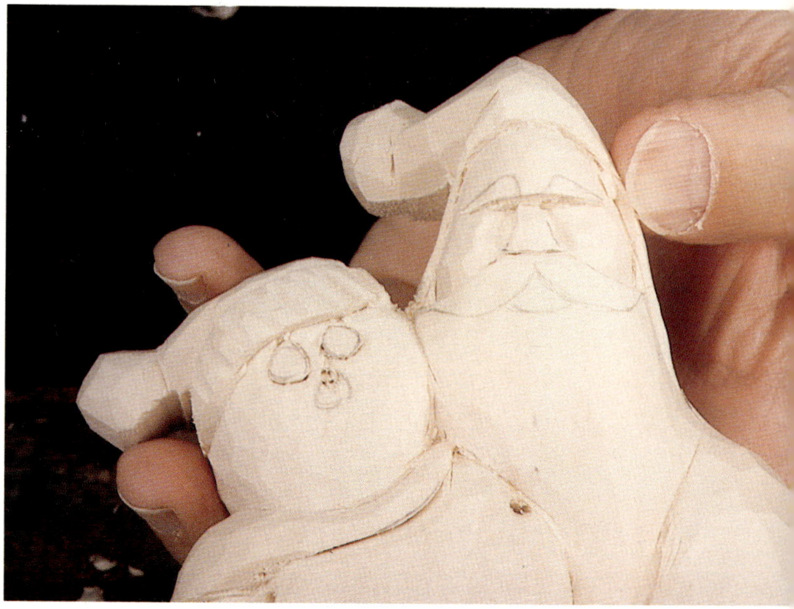

Round off the cheeks to the mustache line.

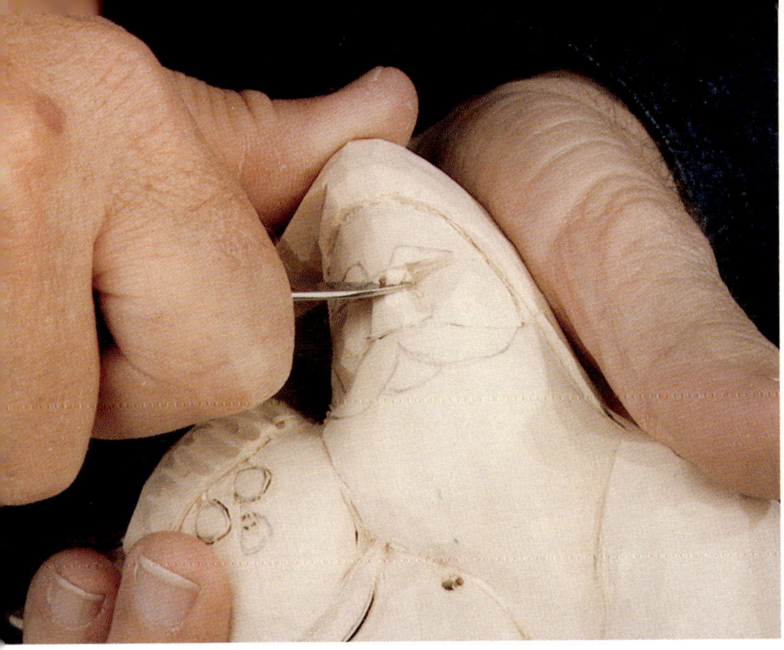

Clip off the corners of the nose to make the sides of the nostrils and thin down the nose if you like. If you wonder why Santa has this pained expression, have you ever tried to hug a snowman for any length of time?

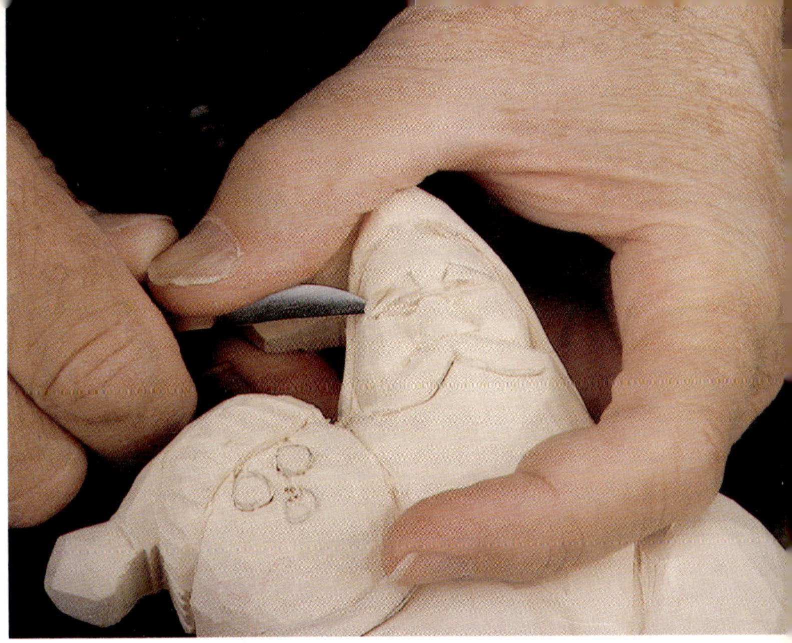

Incise and remove wood around the eyebrows. I always remind you to be careful around the eyebrows or they will pop out.

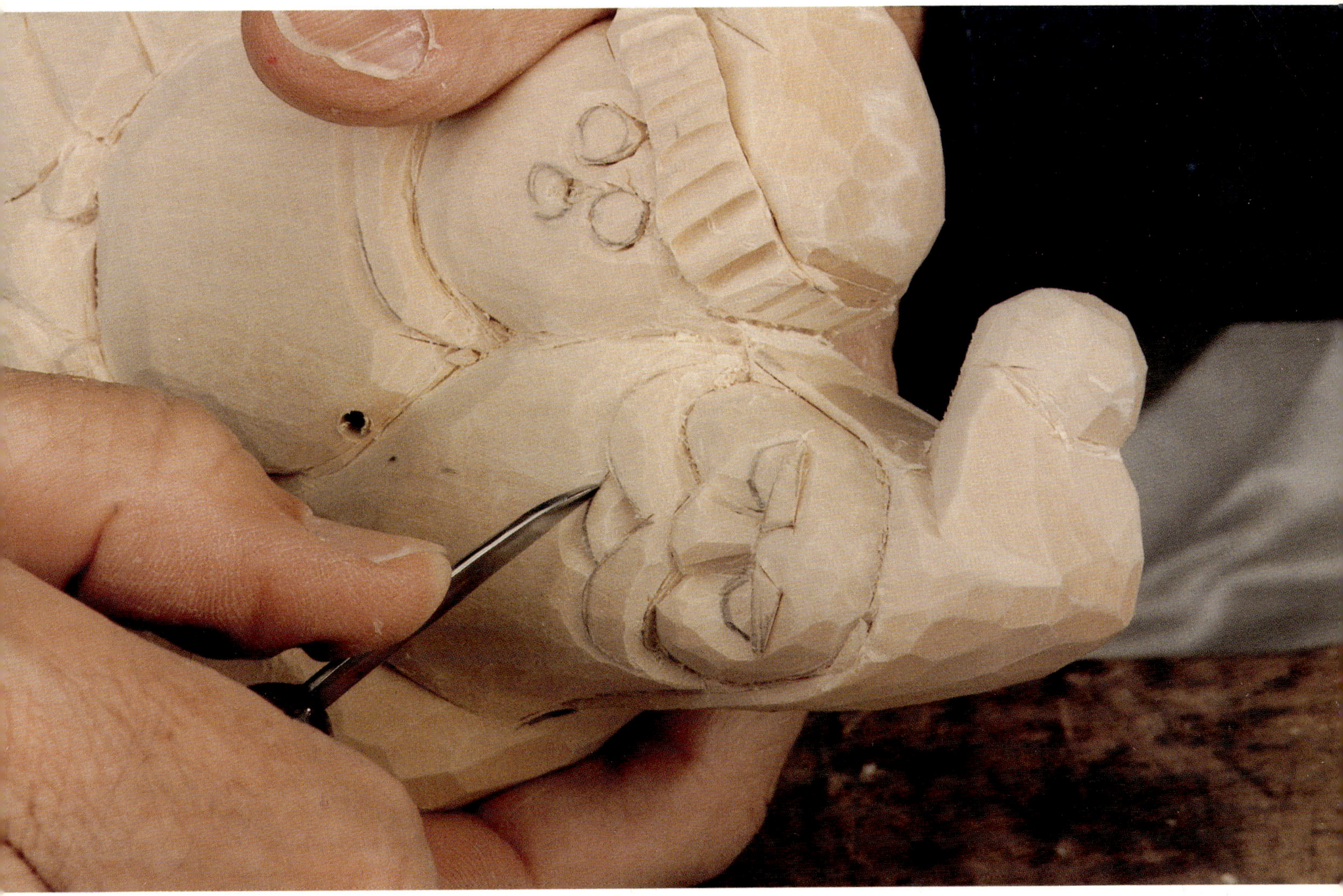

Cut in the lower lip, making a little curve for the lip shape. Trim around it.

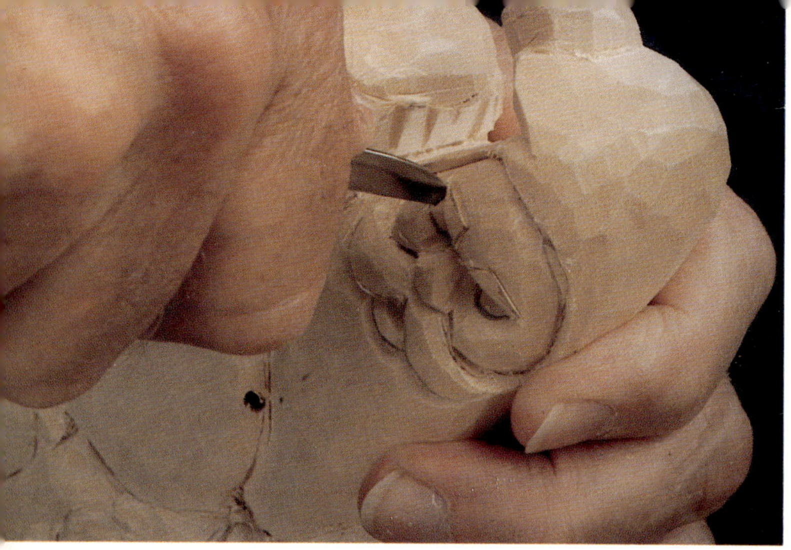

Next we'll do the eyes. Cut deeply into the side of each eye and incise the eyes.

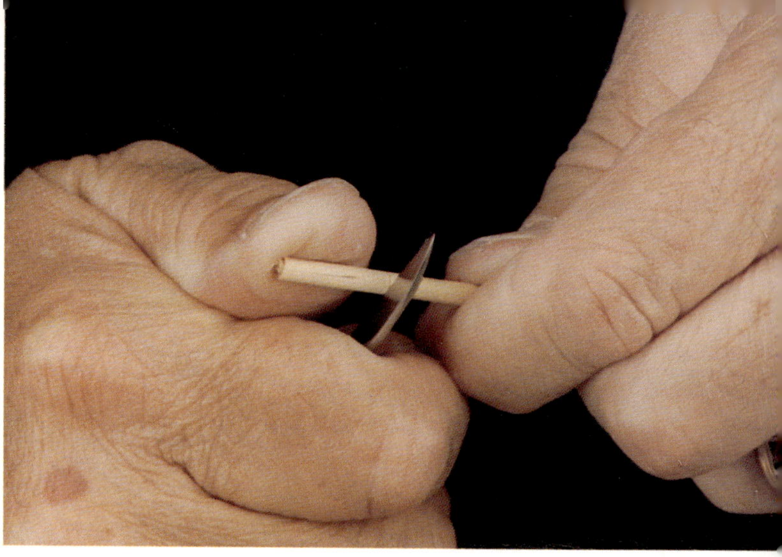

This is the old carrot trick. Cut off a length of small diameter dowel ...

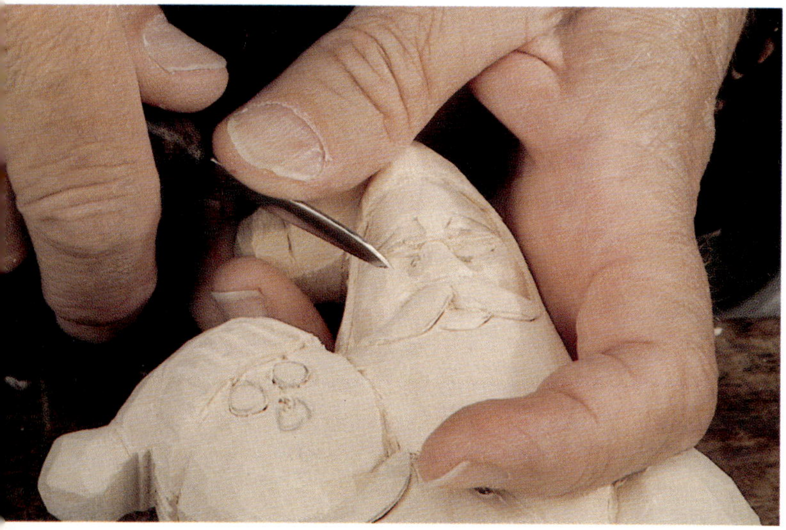

Then round carefully down into where you have cut.

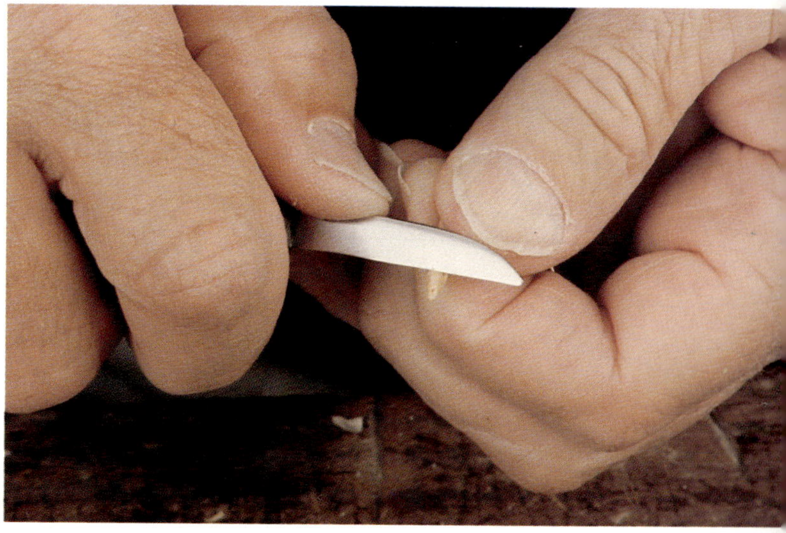

... sharpen one end of it ...

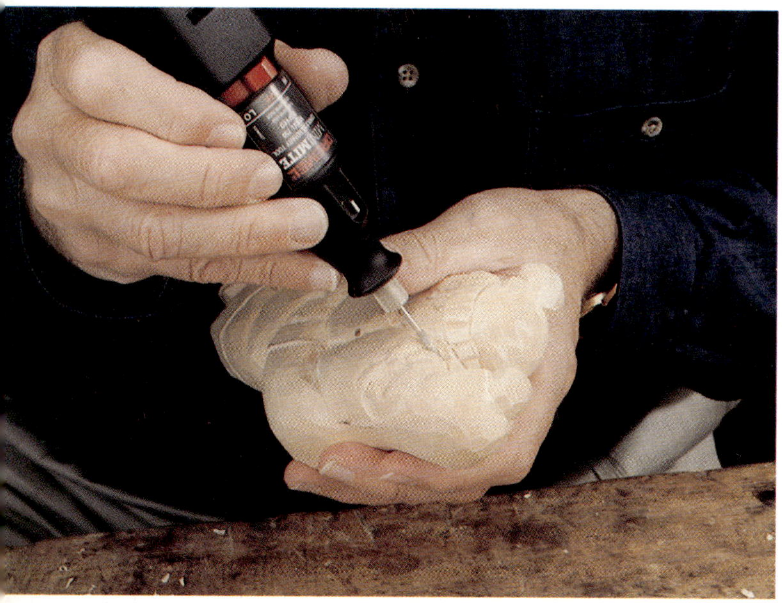

This Dremel MINIMITE is very helpful for getting into tight areas.

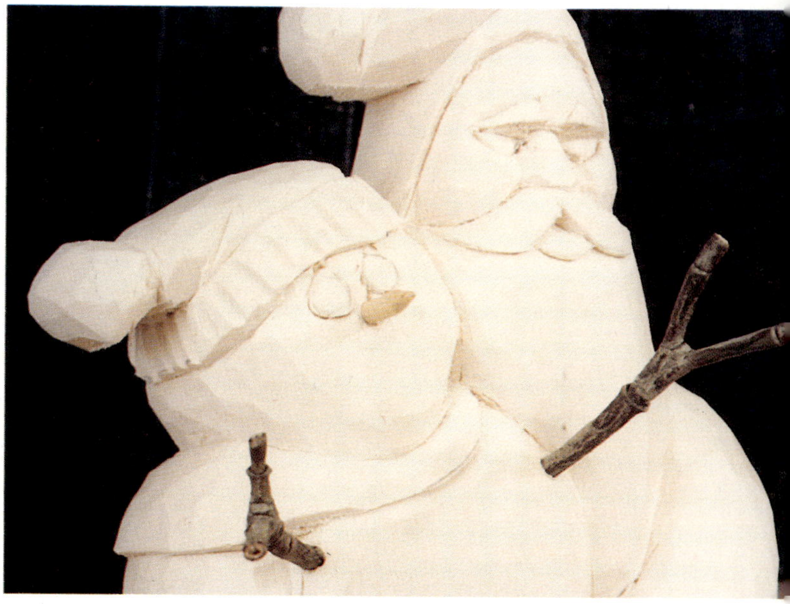

... and stick the dowel in for the nose. Two twigs give the snowman arms.

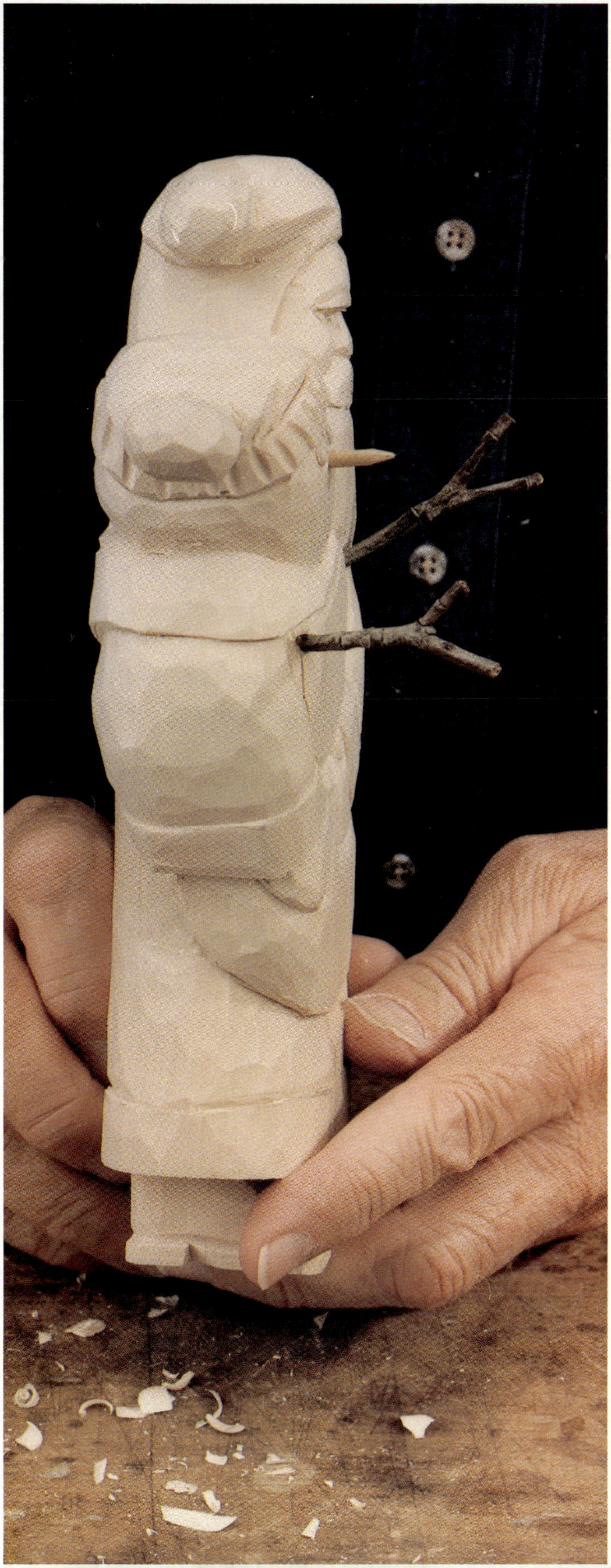
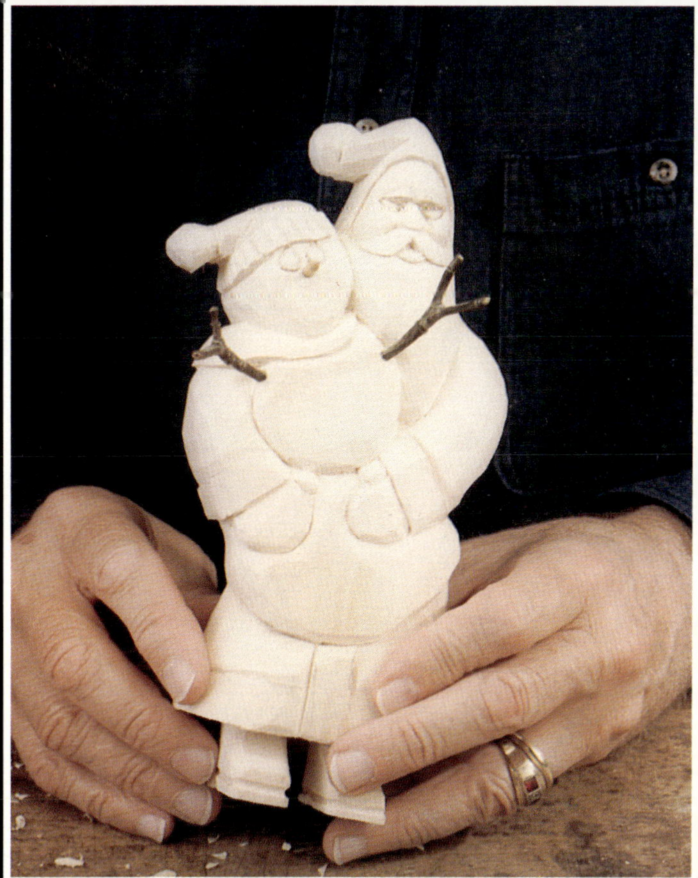
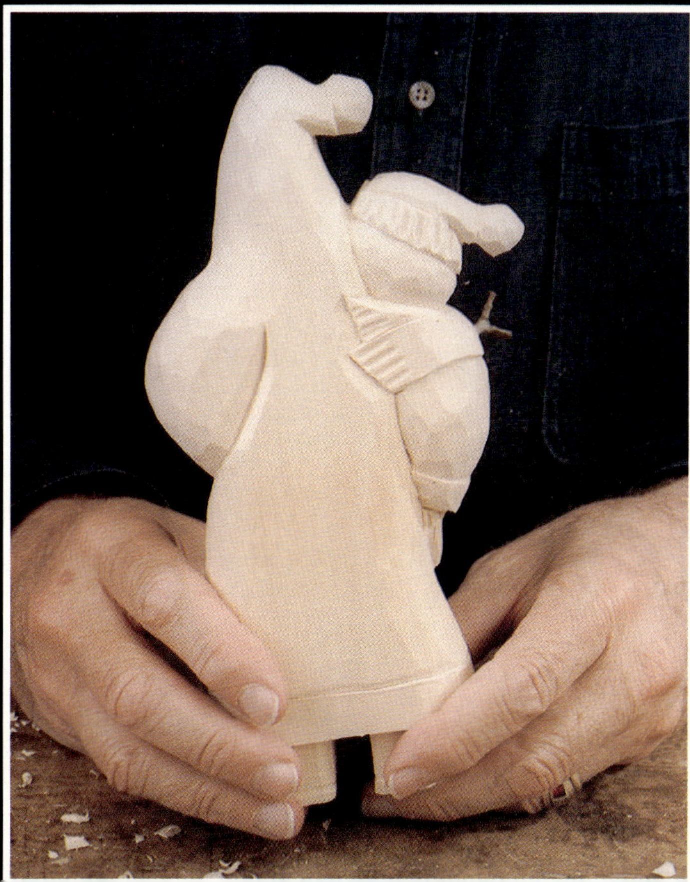

Painting

I have been using Ceramcoat from Delta Coatings for as long as I have been painting my carvings. I've found the quality and color to be consistent and the Tompte Red I use on my Santas matches the blood I sometimes leave on an unpainted piece. If you're happy with your colors, continue to use them.

Santa Holding Snowman

The colors I'm using on the Snowman Santa are Tompte Red, Christmas Green, Santa's Flesh, White, Black, Antique White for the snowman and Pumpkin for the carrot nose. The scarf and toboggan are Christmas Green with White stripes. The limbs are from a dogwood tree I pruned.

The Tall Santa

Tompte Red, White, Black, Santa's Flesh, and a mixture of Santa's Flesh and Tompte Red for all cheeks, front and back.

The Quilt Holding Santa

Tompte Red, White, Black, Santa's Flesh, Green, Navy Blue and Christmas Green.

The Generic Santa

Tompte Red, White, Black, Christmas Green and Santa's Flesh.

Painting the Santa Holding Snowman

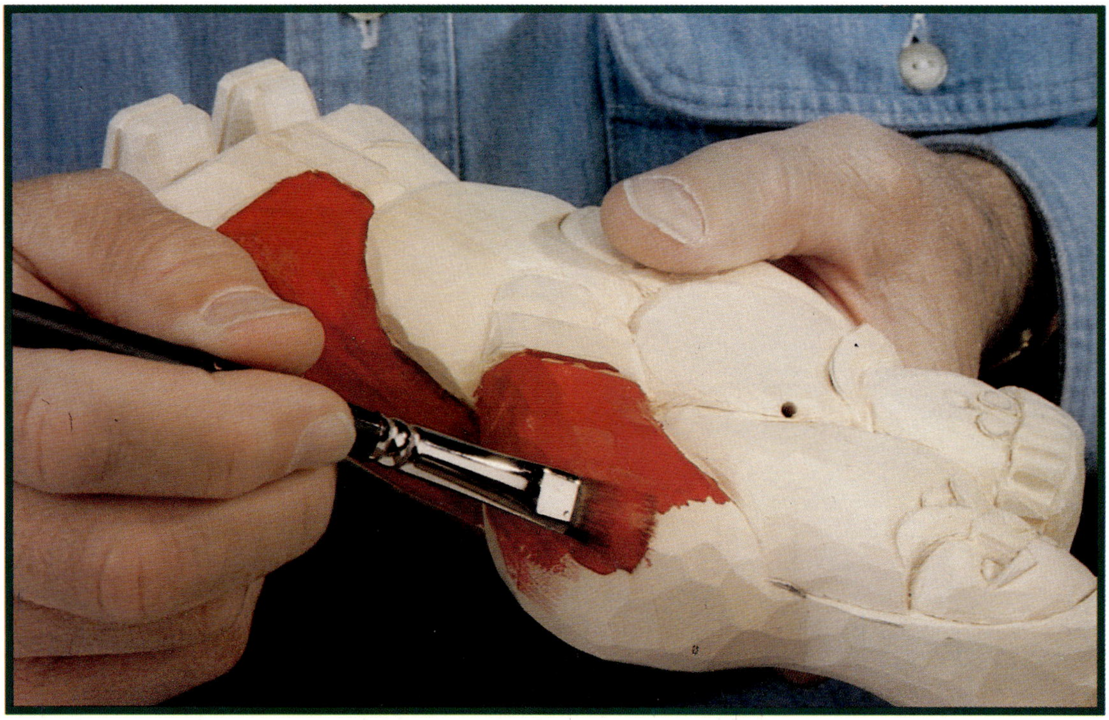

I put on the Tompte Red of the robe first since the red covers the largest area. I am using a #12 shader. To clean my brushes I use two cups of water. One for the dark colors and one for light colors. Don't leave your brushes in the water. Sectioned paper plates work just fine as a palette.

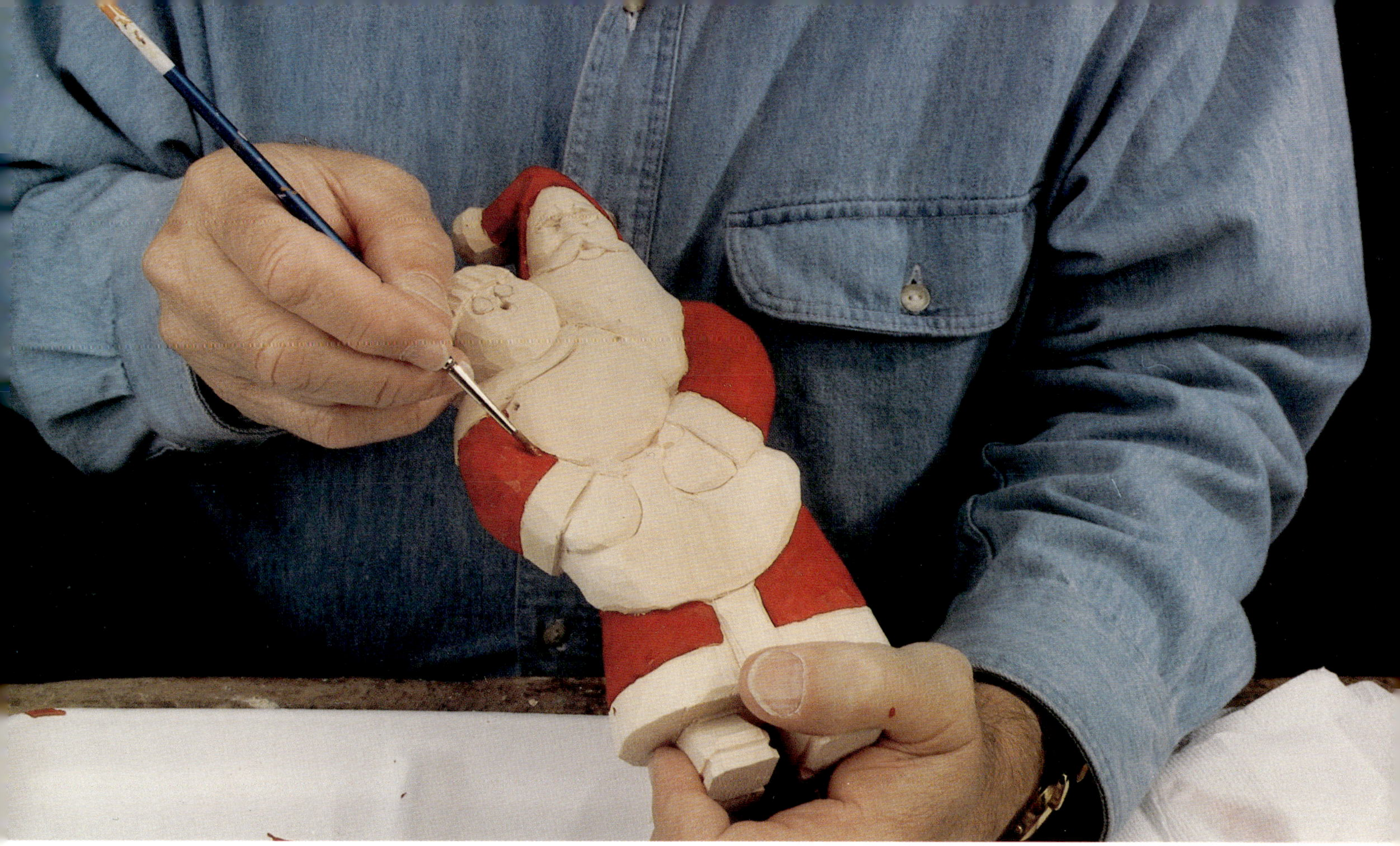

Use a smaller #3 brush to get into the tight spots.

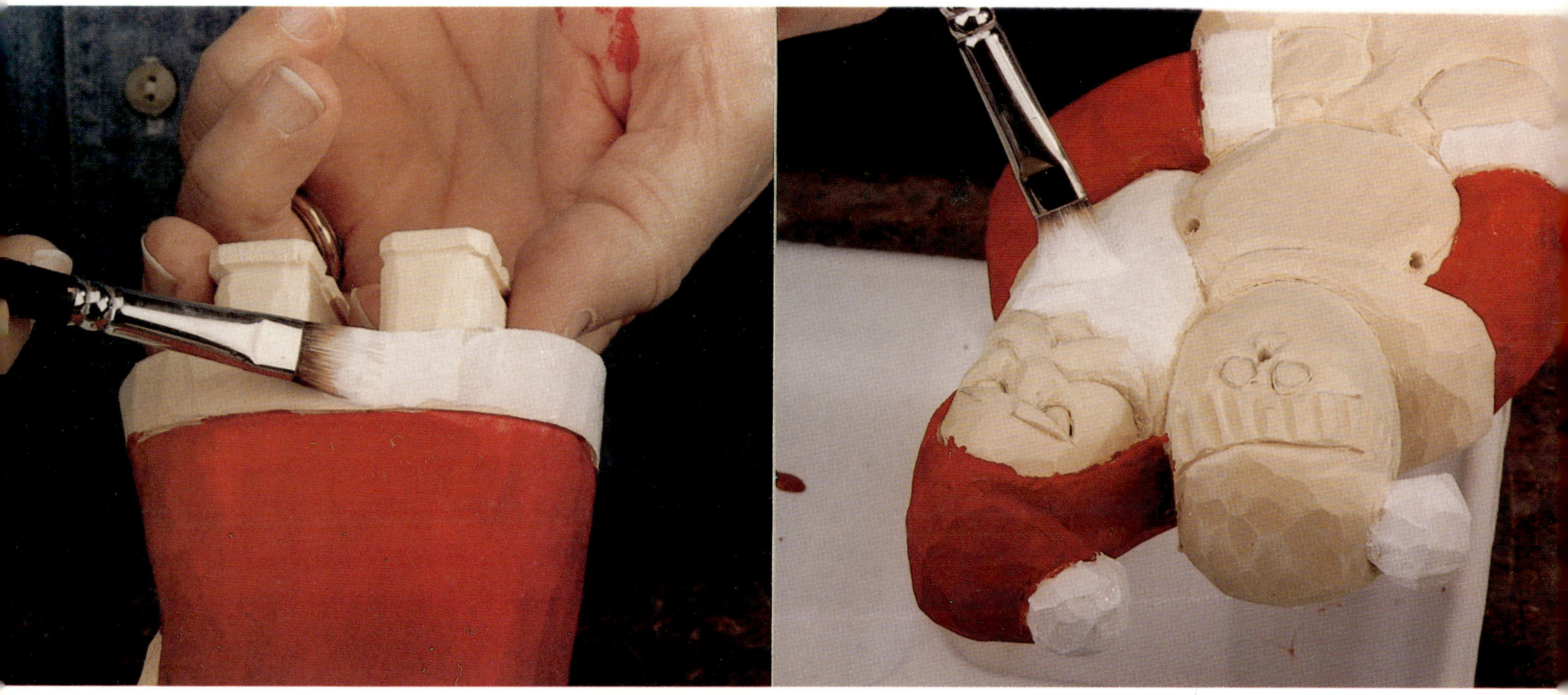

The next color I'm going to use is white, which covers the second largest amount of area on the carving. Use a paper towel to insure the previous color is out of your brush before using the brush again. Paint the fur trim, the balls of both caps, Santa's beard, his eyebrows, and his eyes white. Obviously I never get any paint on myself.

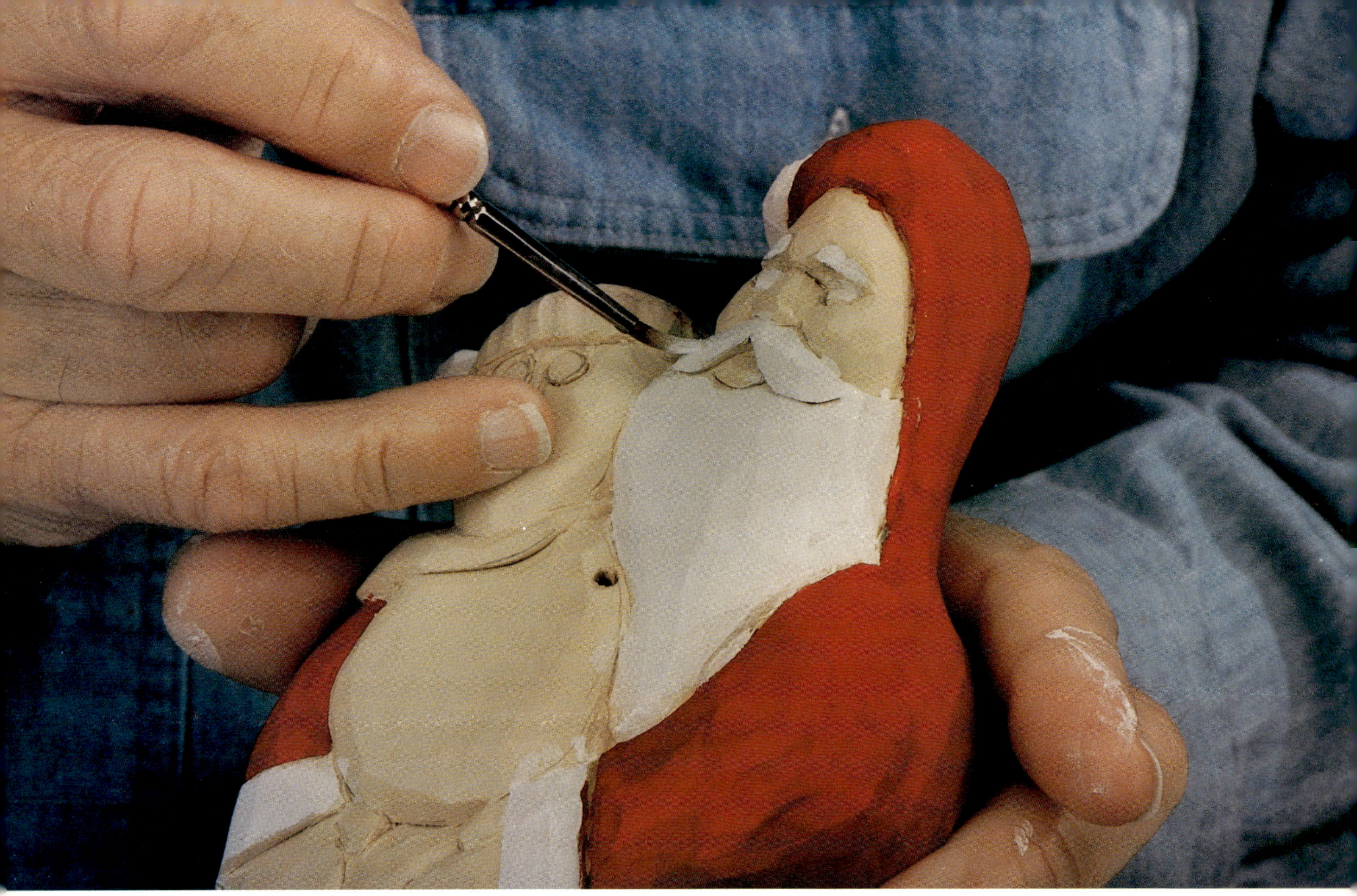

Use the #3 brush to get into the smaller areas around the beard, eyebrows and eyes.

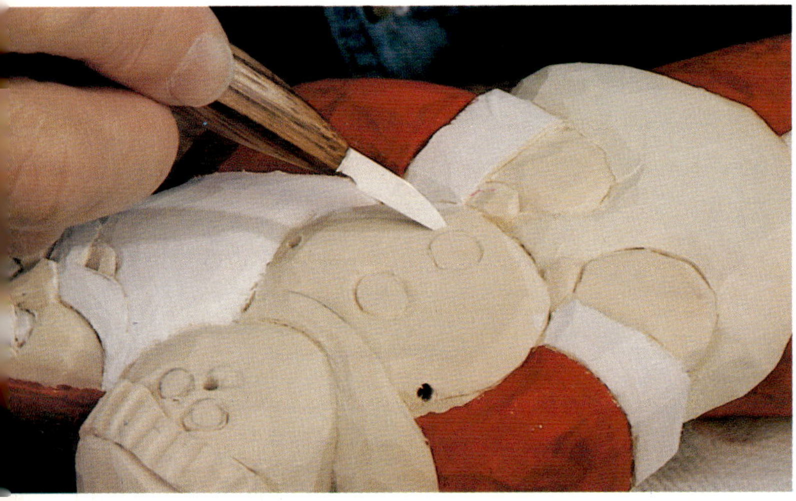

Use antique white on the snowman to show some contrast between the two whites used so close together. It would be boring to use the same white on the snowman and Santa's beard and fur cuffs. Anyway, this snowman has been out in the weather and has some soot on him. As I was getting ready to paint the snowman, I realized I had forgotten to carve in coal buttons. To carve them, first incise them and then carve at a shallow angle around them. The buttons may also be painted on of course.

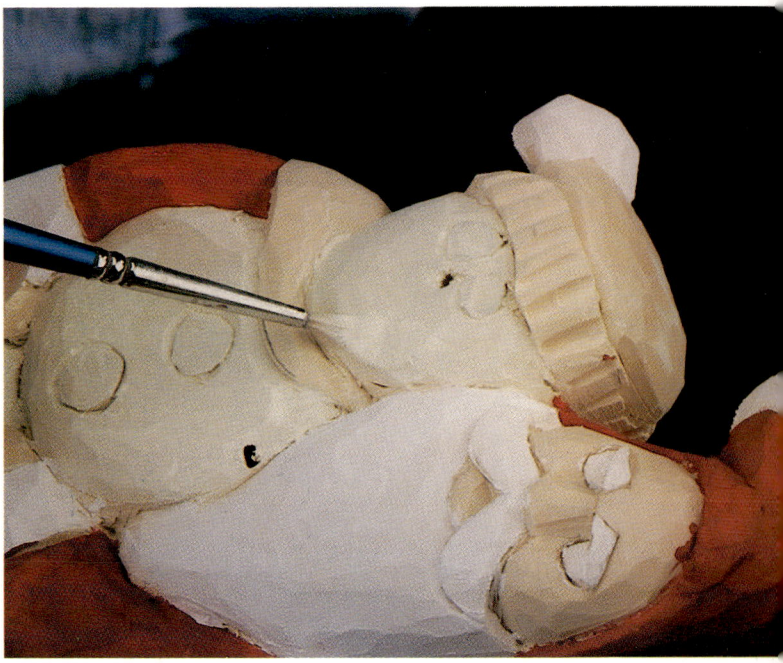

Note that when applying the antique white I have covered the areas of the coal buttons and eyes. These will be painted in with black later.

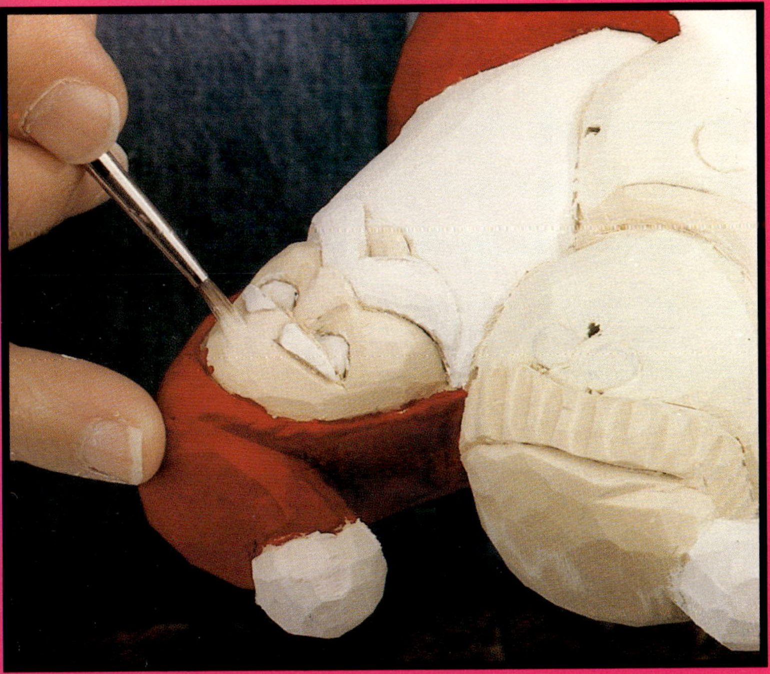

Apply Santa's Flesh now to the face. Be very careful when applying the flesh. This color is very close to that of the bass-wood. However, any area left uncovered will appear as a dark spot when the figure is antiqued.

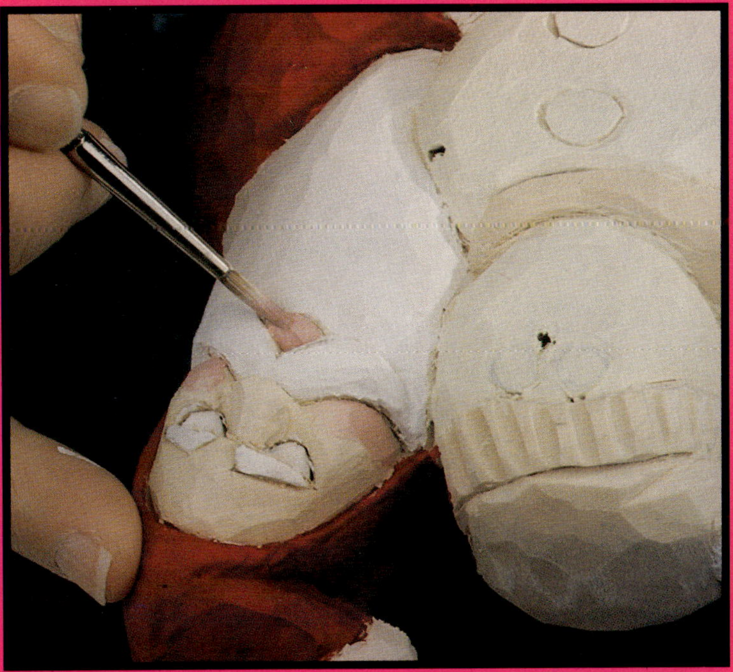

The same mix with just a bit more red is used on the lip.

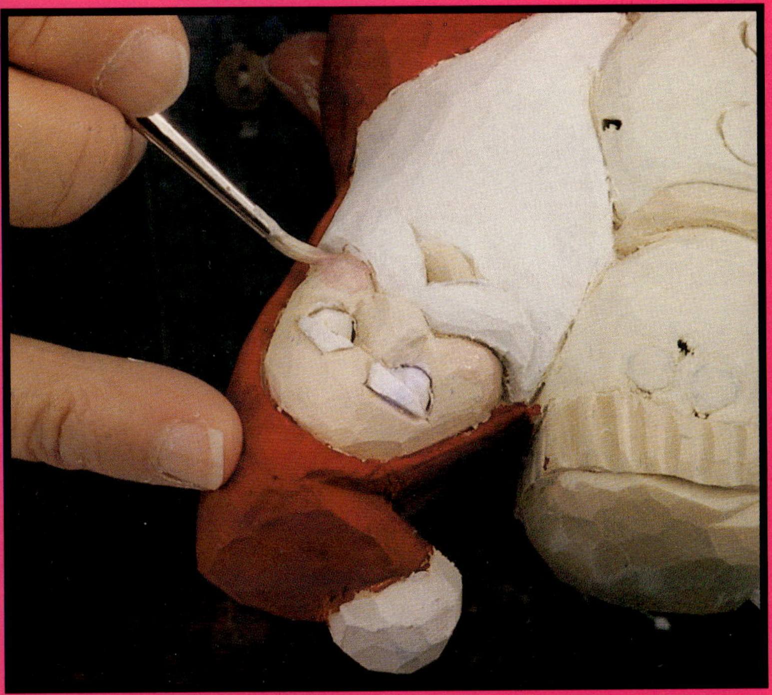

Mix in a little red with the flesh and apply to the cheeks. Don't apply this blush in circles or Santa will look like a clown.

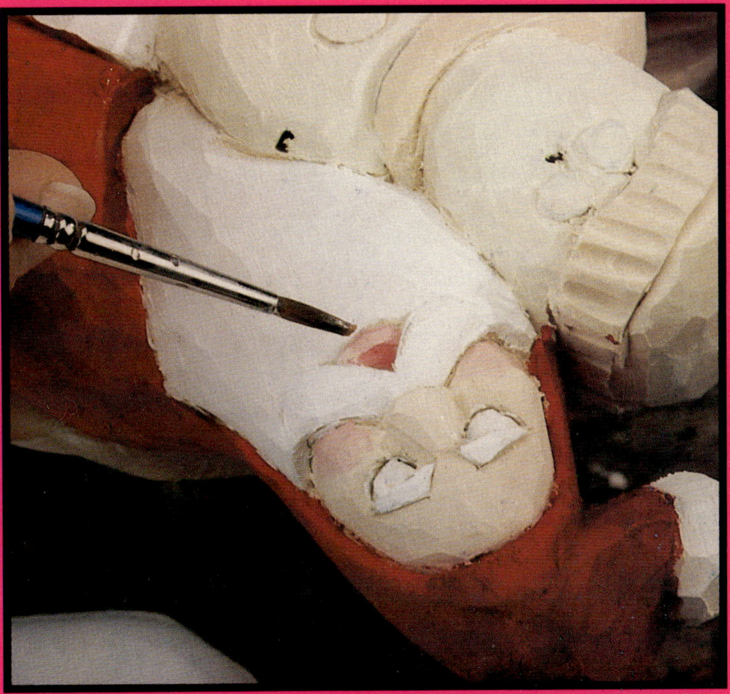

Paint the inner lip a little darker as it recedes back into the mouth.

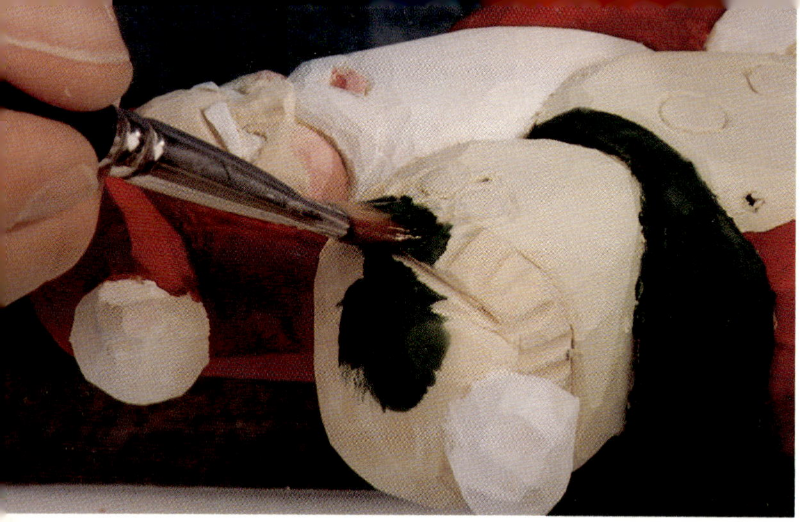

Christmas Green is used on the scarf and the toboggan. We will come back with white when the green has dried to make stripes on the toboggan's roll.

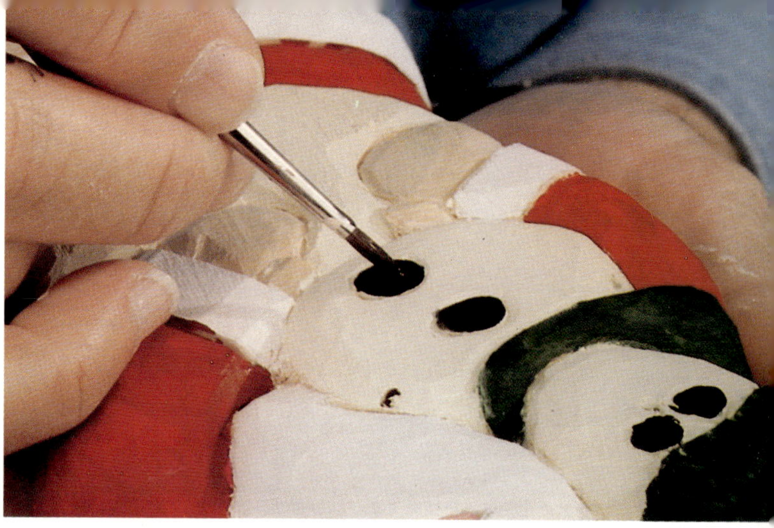

While I have the black out I'll paint the coal eyes and buttons on the snowman (if you don't know what coal is, check your dictionary).

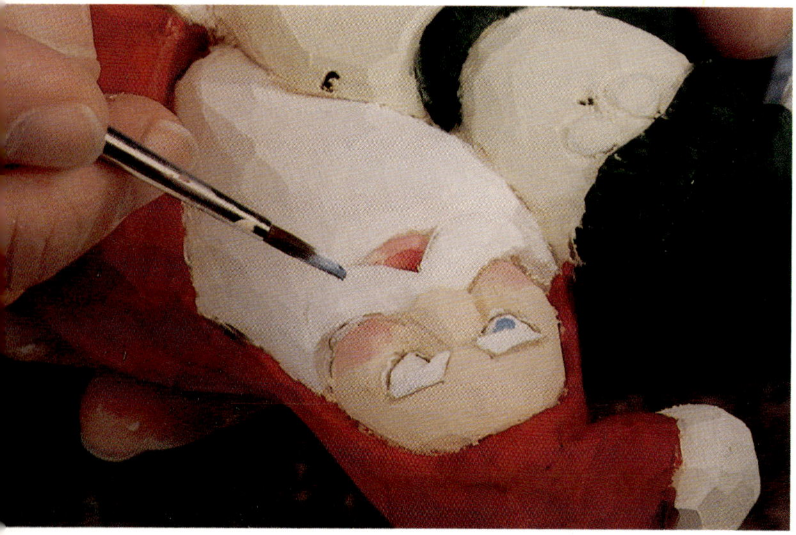

To paint Santa's eyeballs we are using Navy Blue with a little white in it. Use the #3 or smaller brush to apply. Paint the pupil up into the upper lid of the eye unless you want Santa to look like he has been goosed.

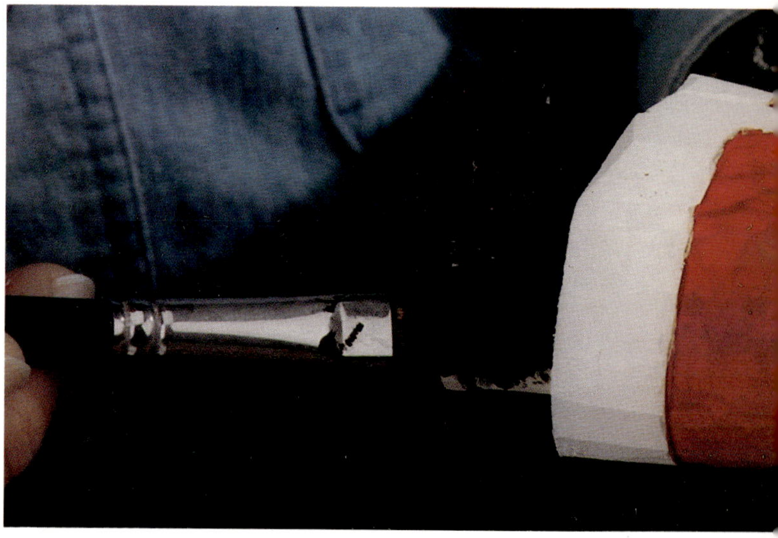

Paint the boots black as well.

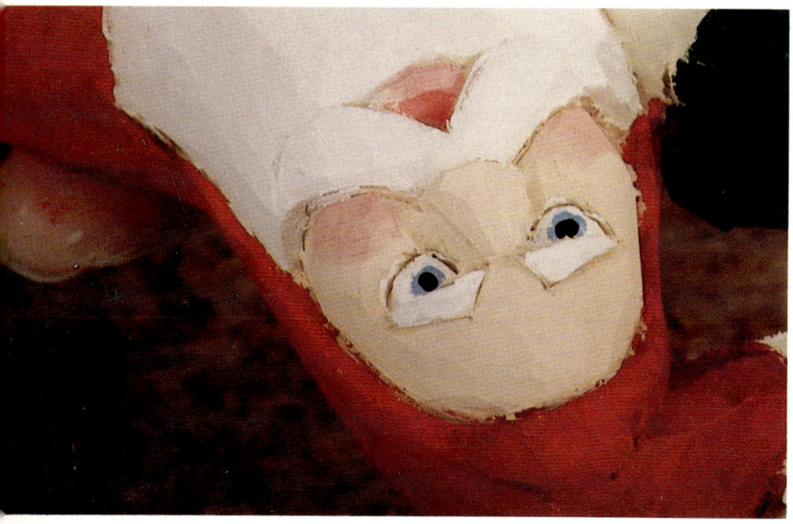

Use undiluted black for the pupils. Apply with a very small brush.

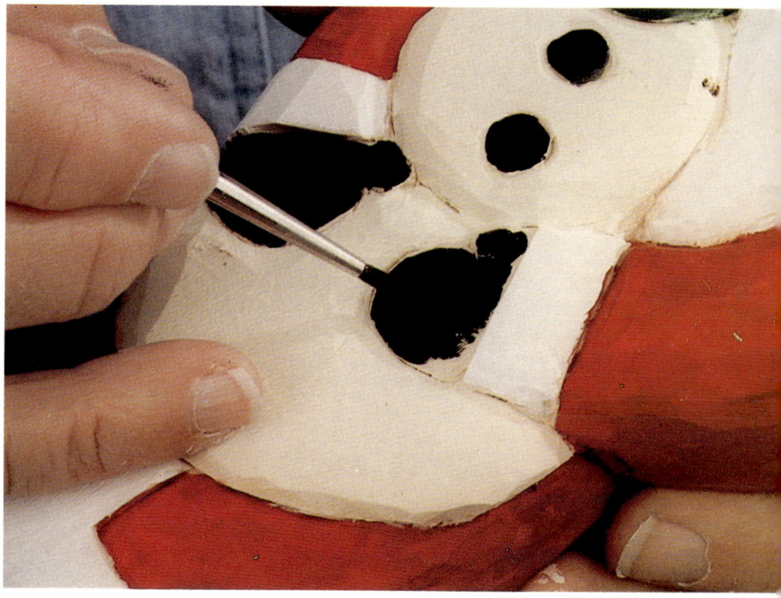

Use black on the mittens. This is how your hands look when you handle coal (see dictionary).

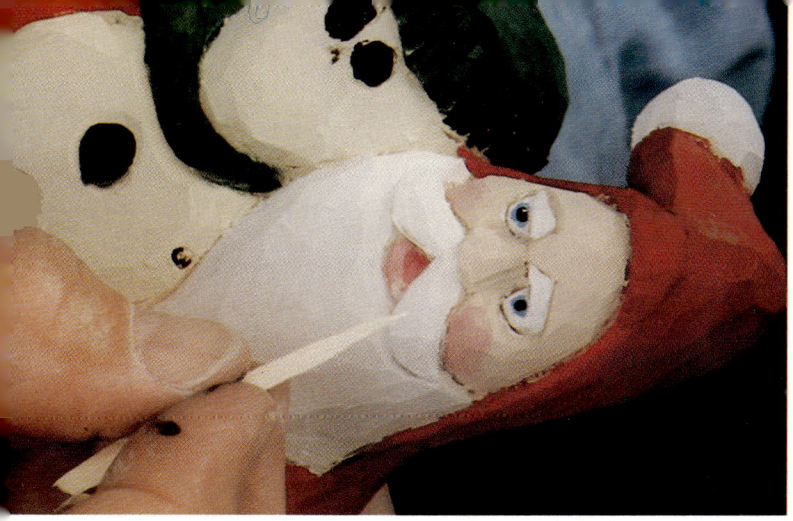

I've sharpened a little scrap of wood to apply a small white highlight in each eye. Apply the highlights in the same place on each eye. If one is at 11 o'clock the other needs to be there too.

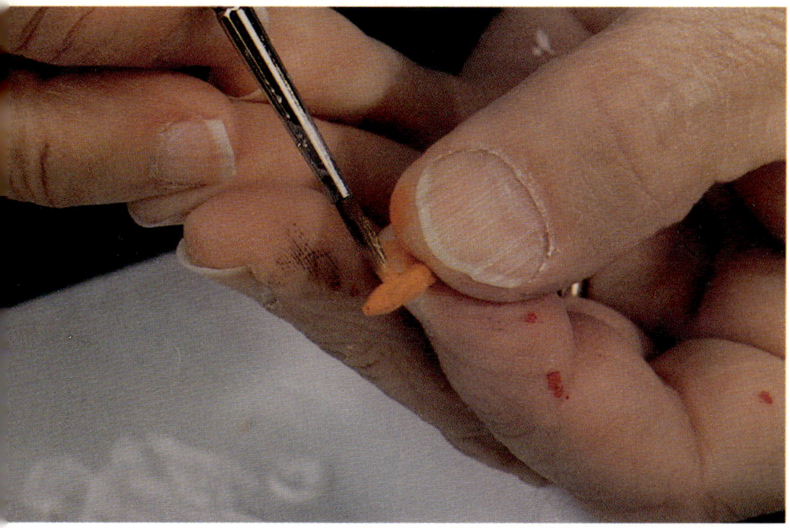

Use Pumpkin to paint the carrot nose for the snowman. When it dries, insert the nose into the hole drilled earlier. I do not glue the nose in place. This way, if it breaks, it is easier to remove and replace.

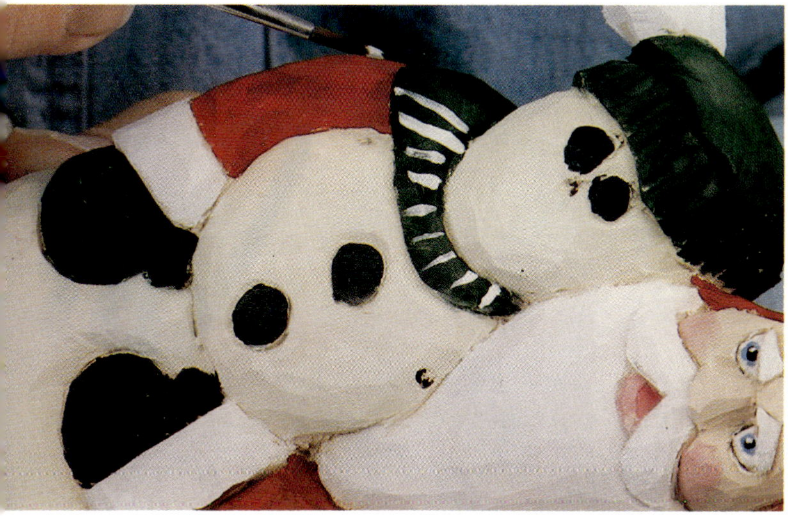

We're going to put a white criss-cross pattern on the scarf. Begin with the vertical lines on the scarf.

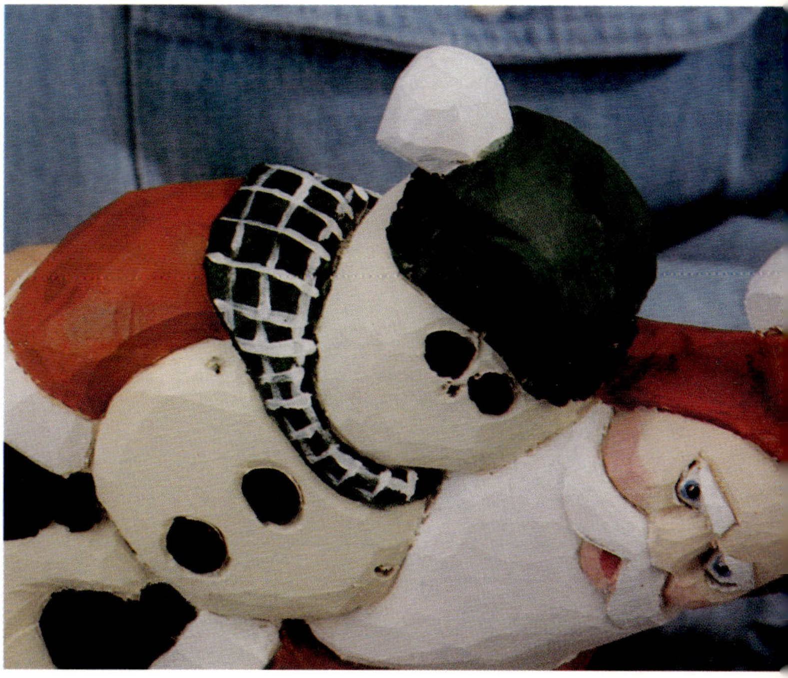

The finished pattern on the scarf.

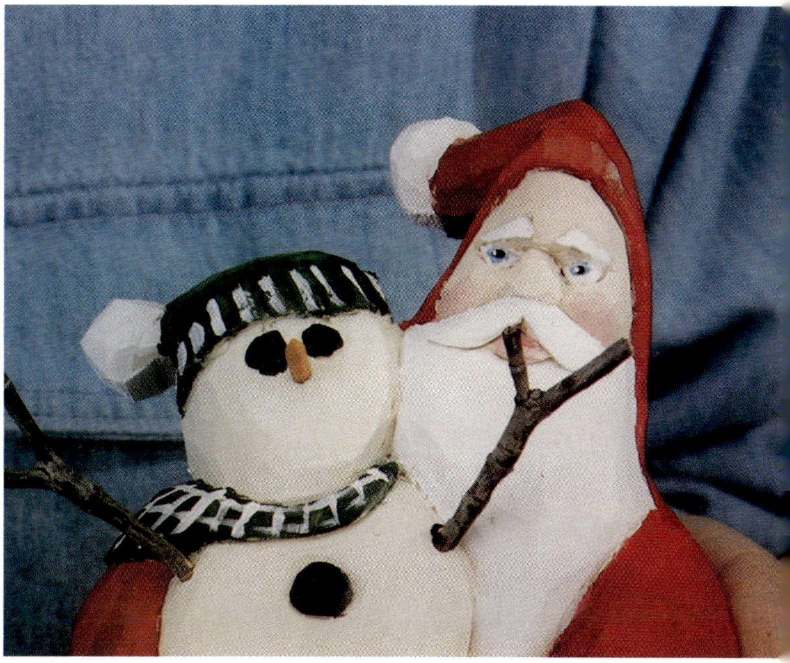

Paint the raised portions of the roll on the toboggan white. The carrot nose and the dogwood limbs are in place on the snowman as well.

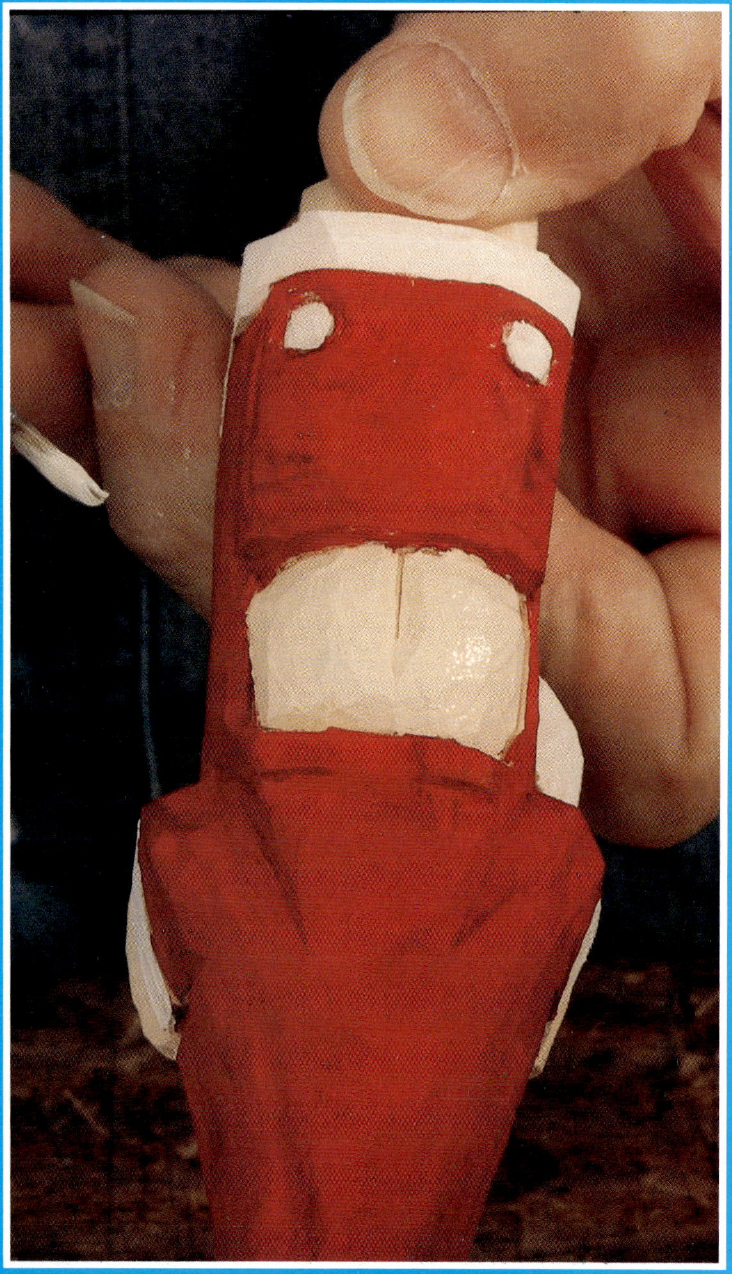

On the "night after" Santa, follow the previous instructions for the robe, boots, fur trim, face, beard and hands. I am going to show you how to paint the "other" cheeks. Someday you may carve nudes and need to know this after all. First apply a coat of Santa's Flesh.

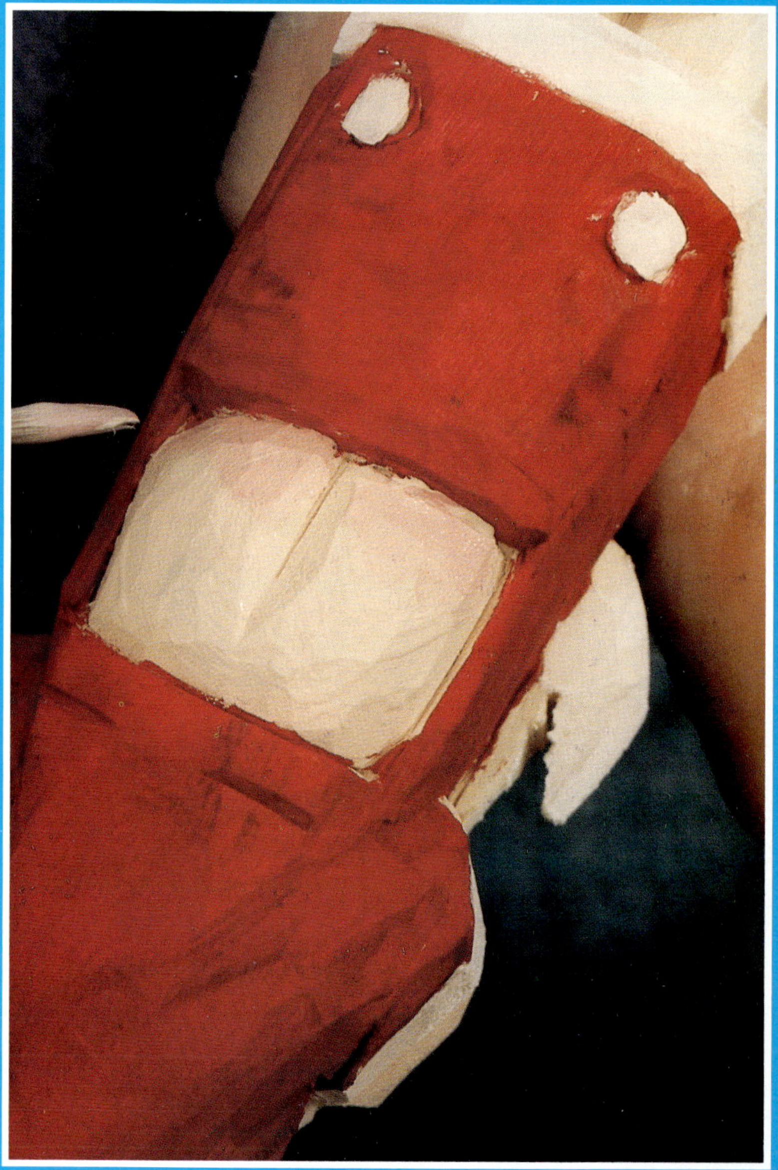

Mix a little red with the flesh to create a little blush. You will also notice I have painted the buttons white.

Coating and Antiquing the Carving

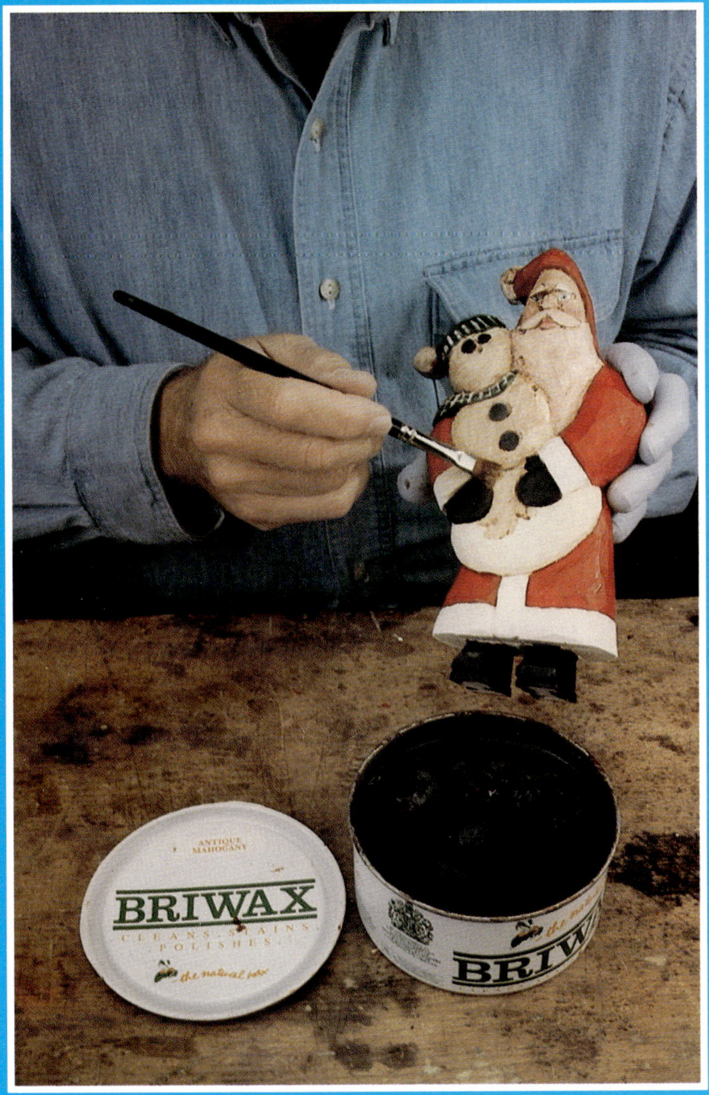

It's extremely important after your acrylic has dried to spray it with Krylon Clear Coat #1301 aerosol before you coat the entire figure with Briwax. Now that Griffin has gone out of business their polish is really hard to find. So I am now using Briwax. They have been in business since 1860 so I feel sure they will be in business for a long time. I'm using the Antique Mahogany.

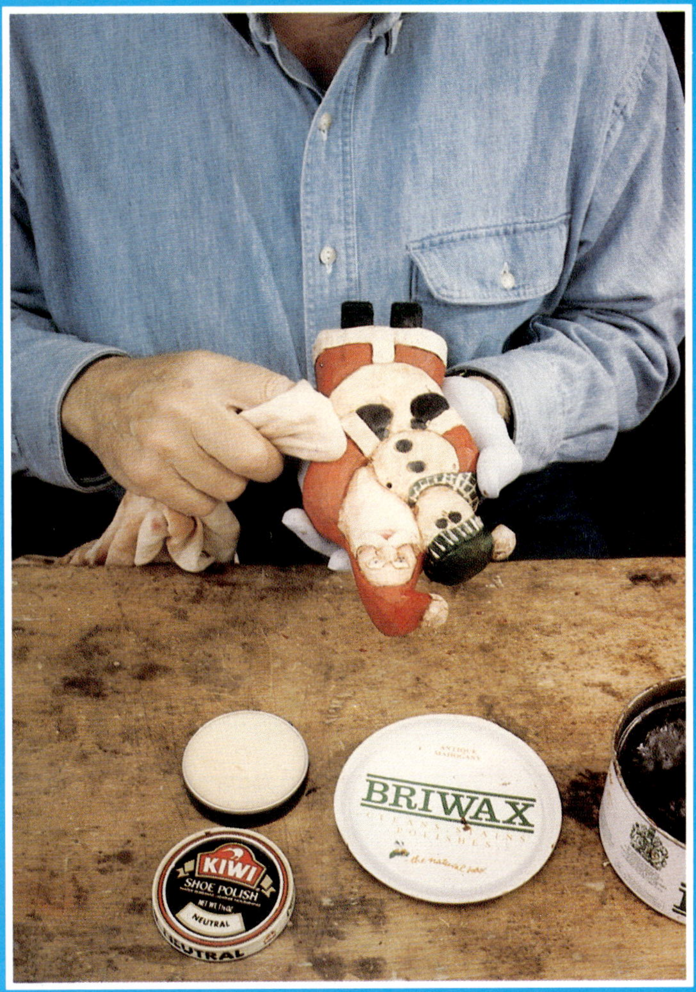

The next step is to take an old tee shirt or diaper and rub with a neutral shoe polish. Kiwi works fine. This takes off enough of the Briwax to give it that antique look. I like my pieces dark, not garish. If you like, after the shoe polish has dried, you may buff it with a shoe brush.

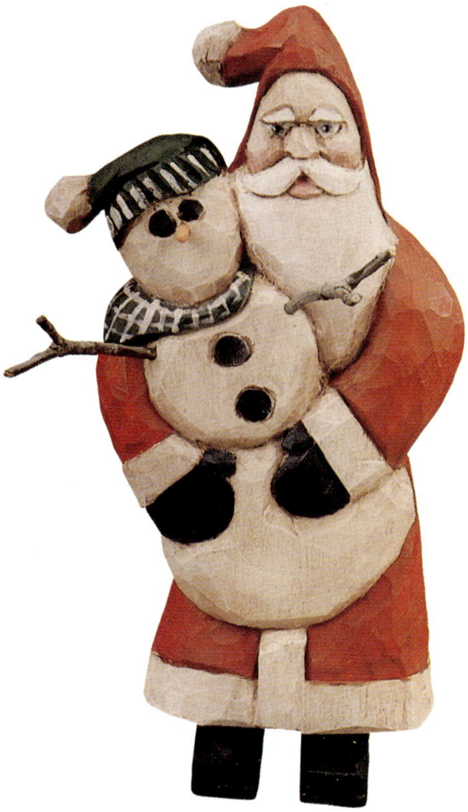

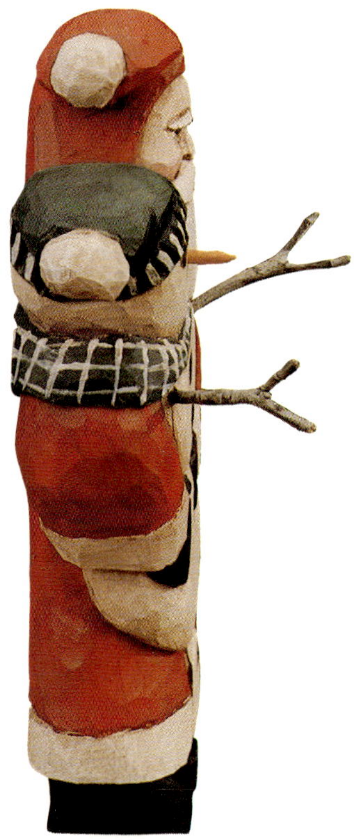

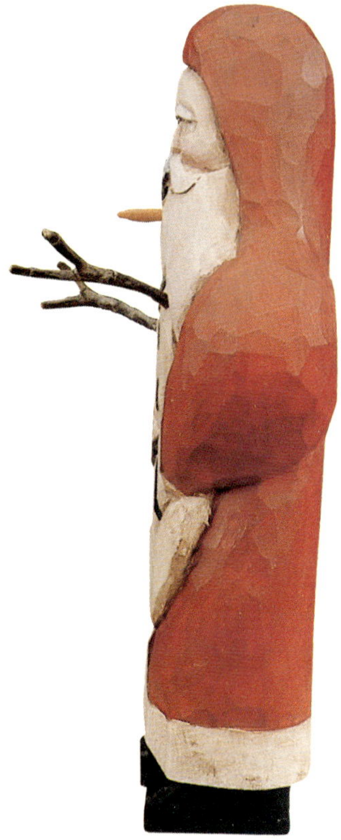

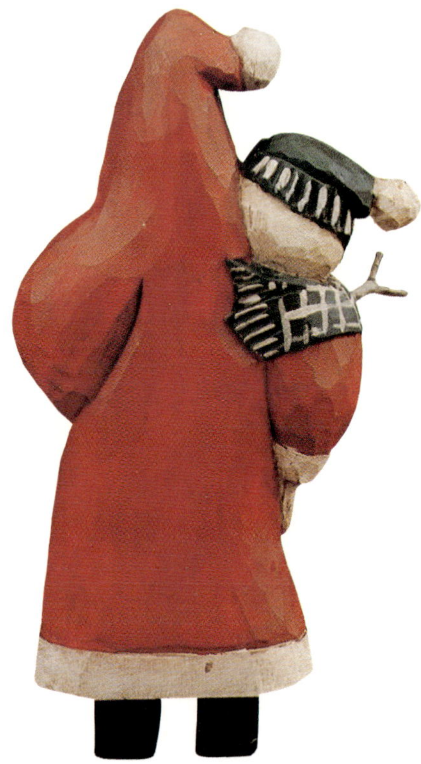

The finished Santa and Snowman.

The Gallery

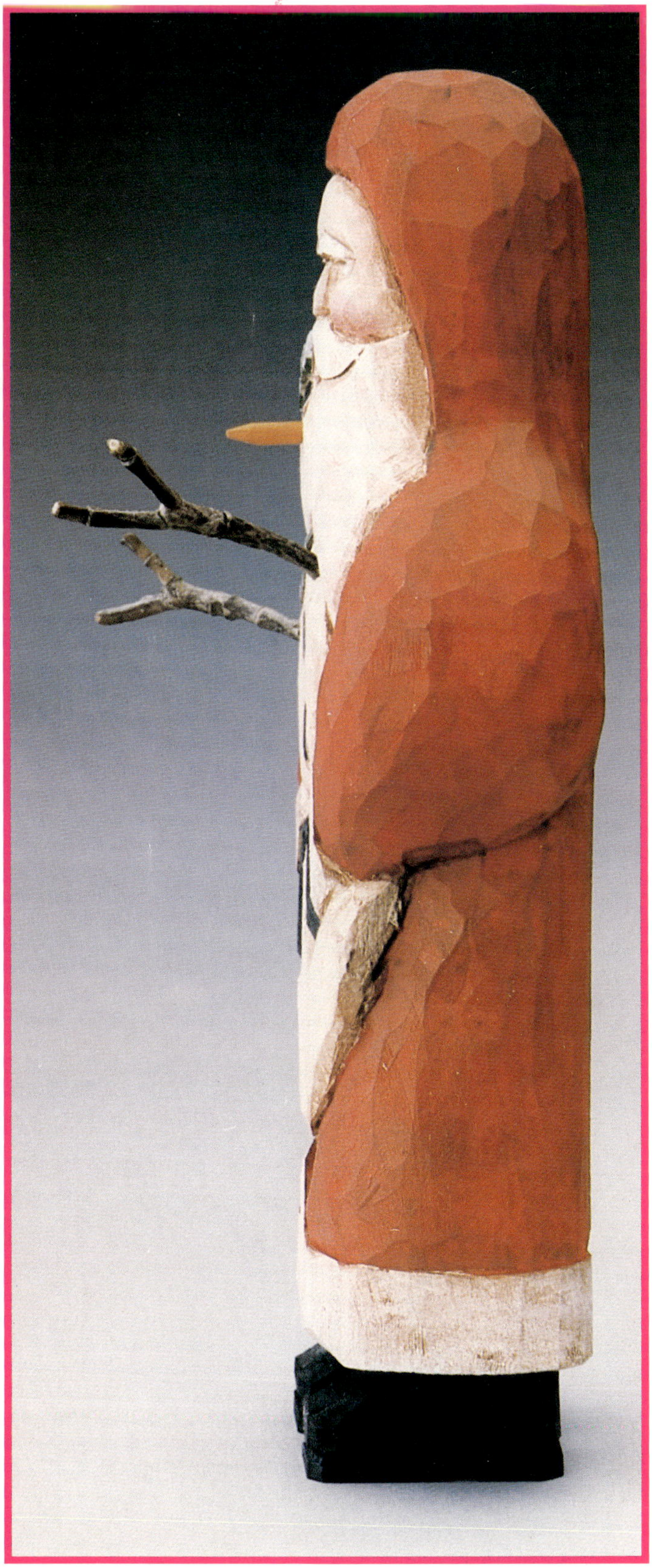

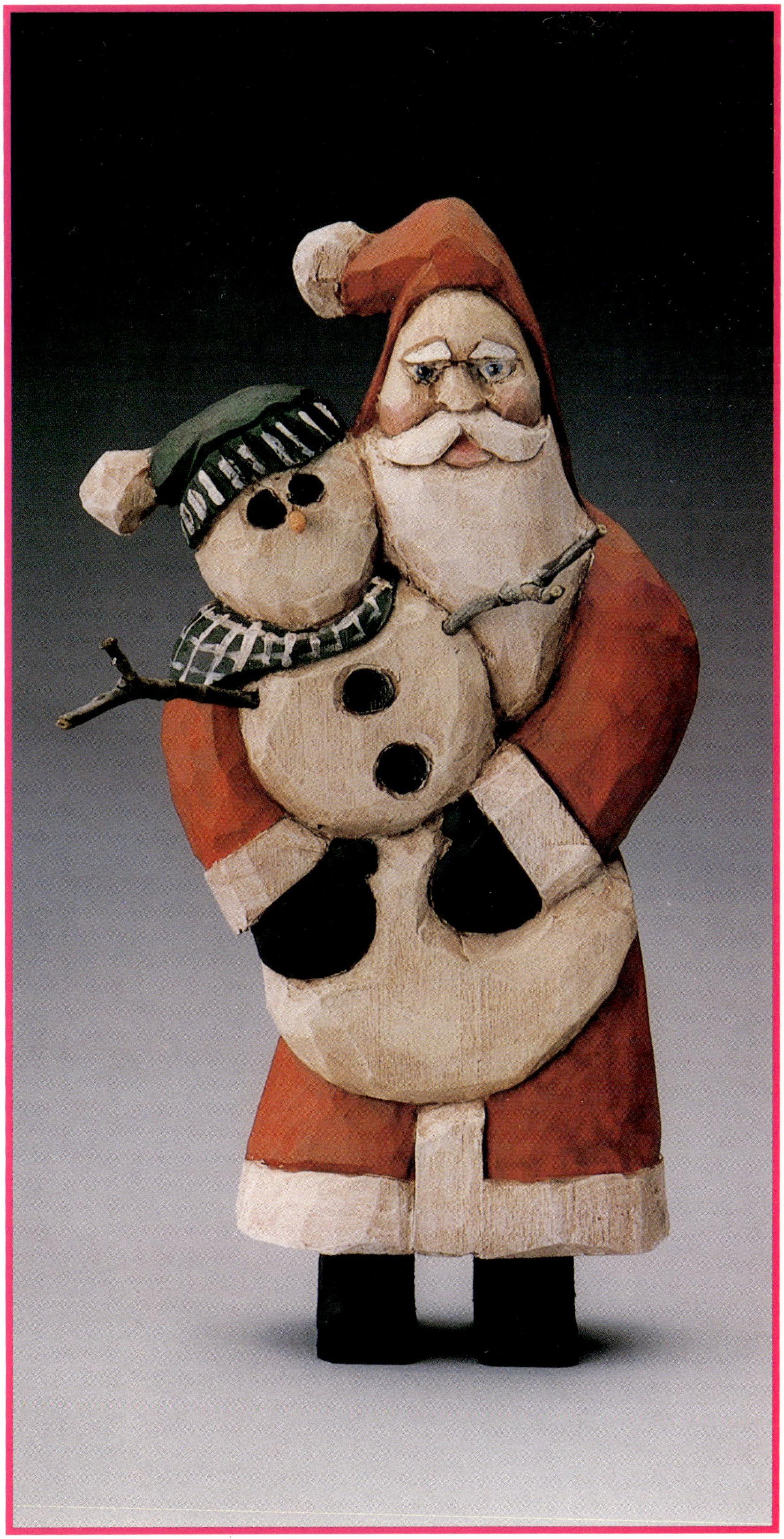

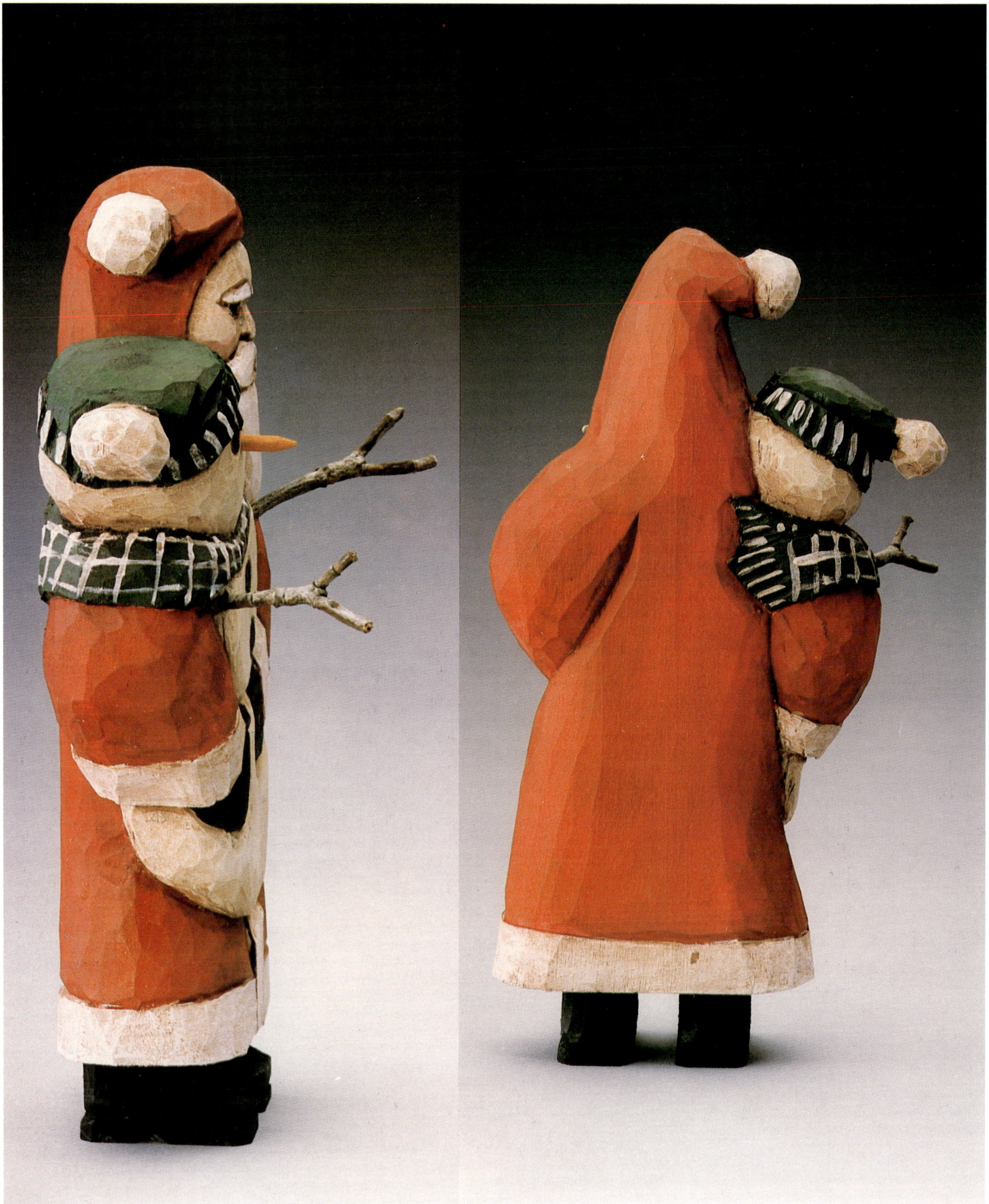

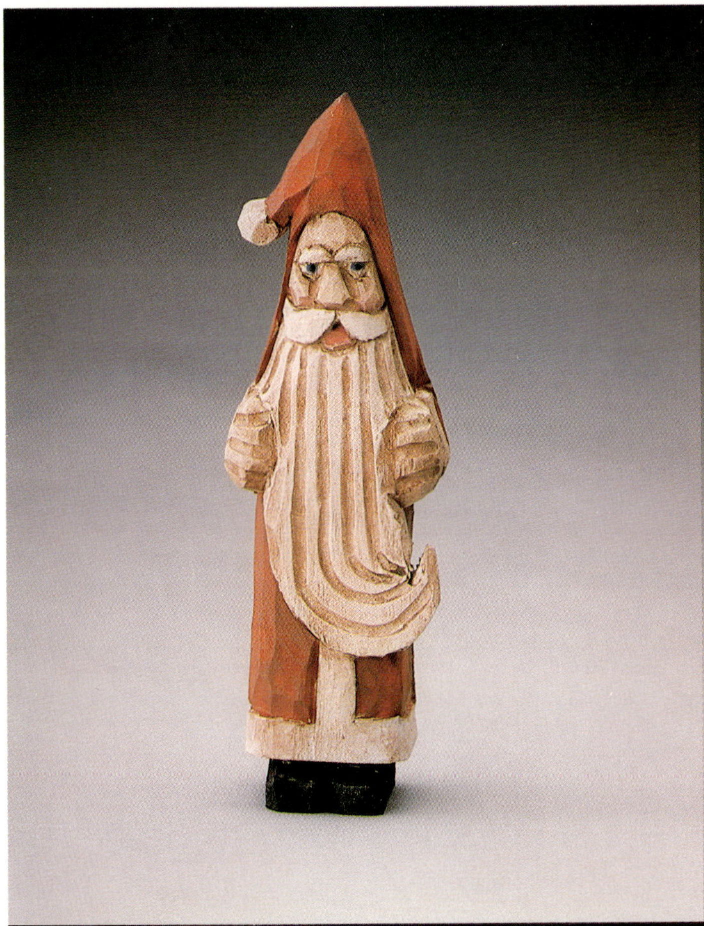
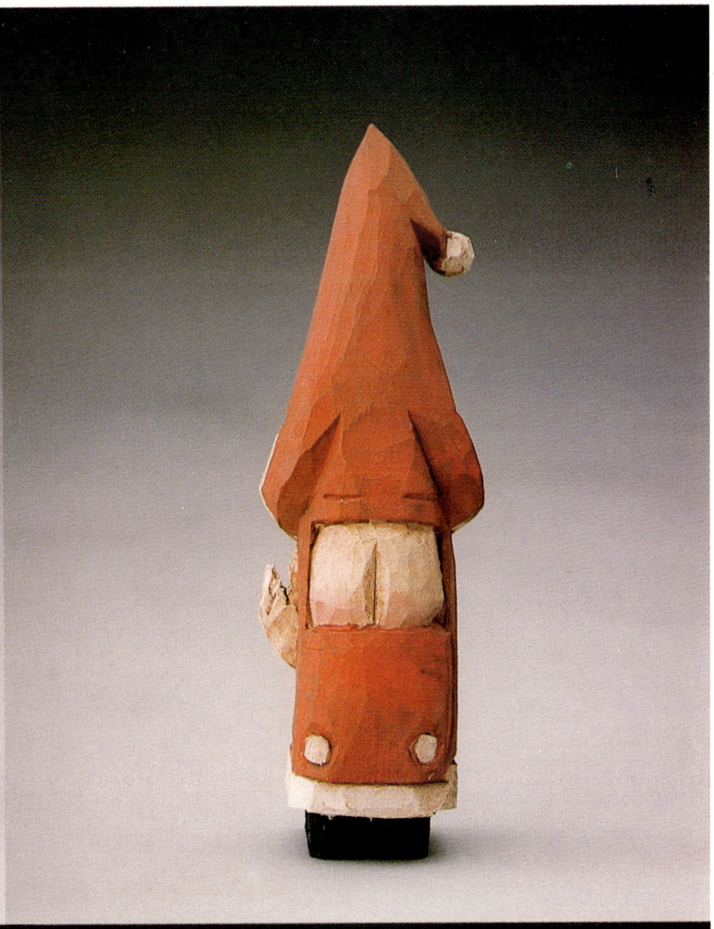
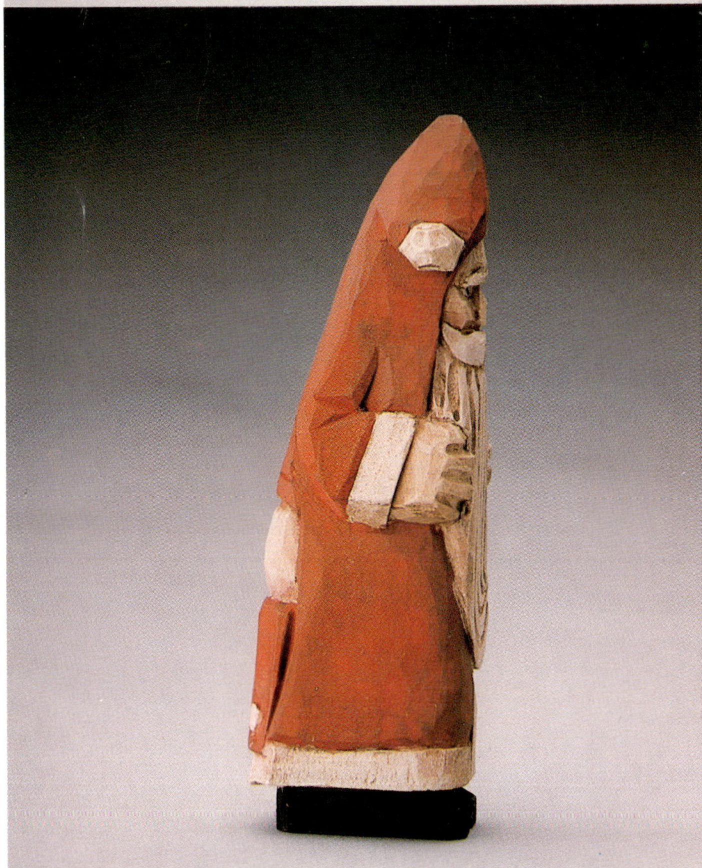
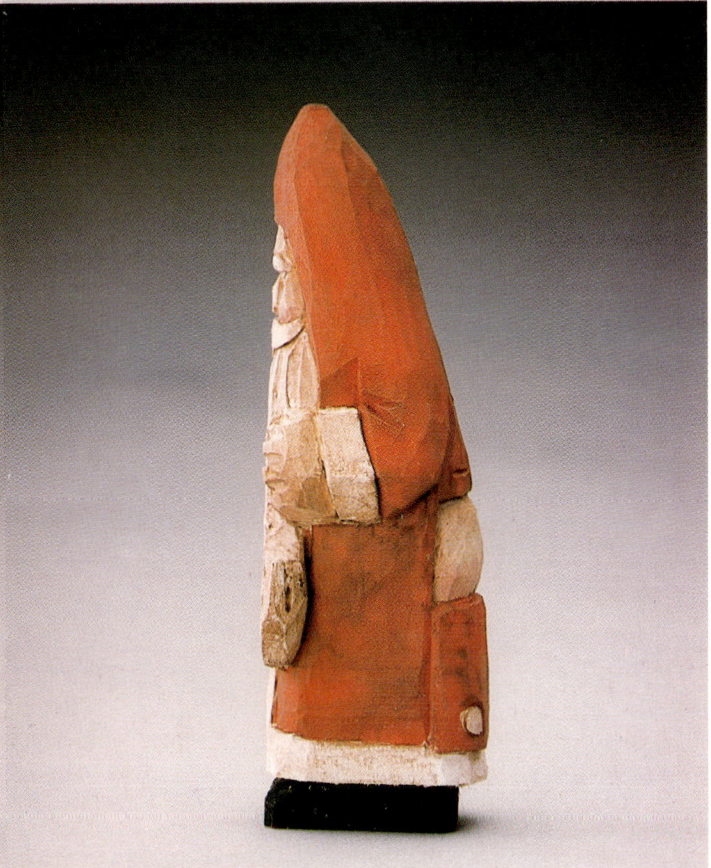

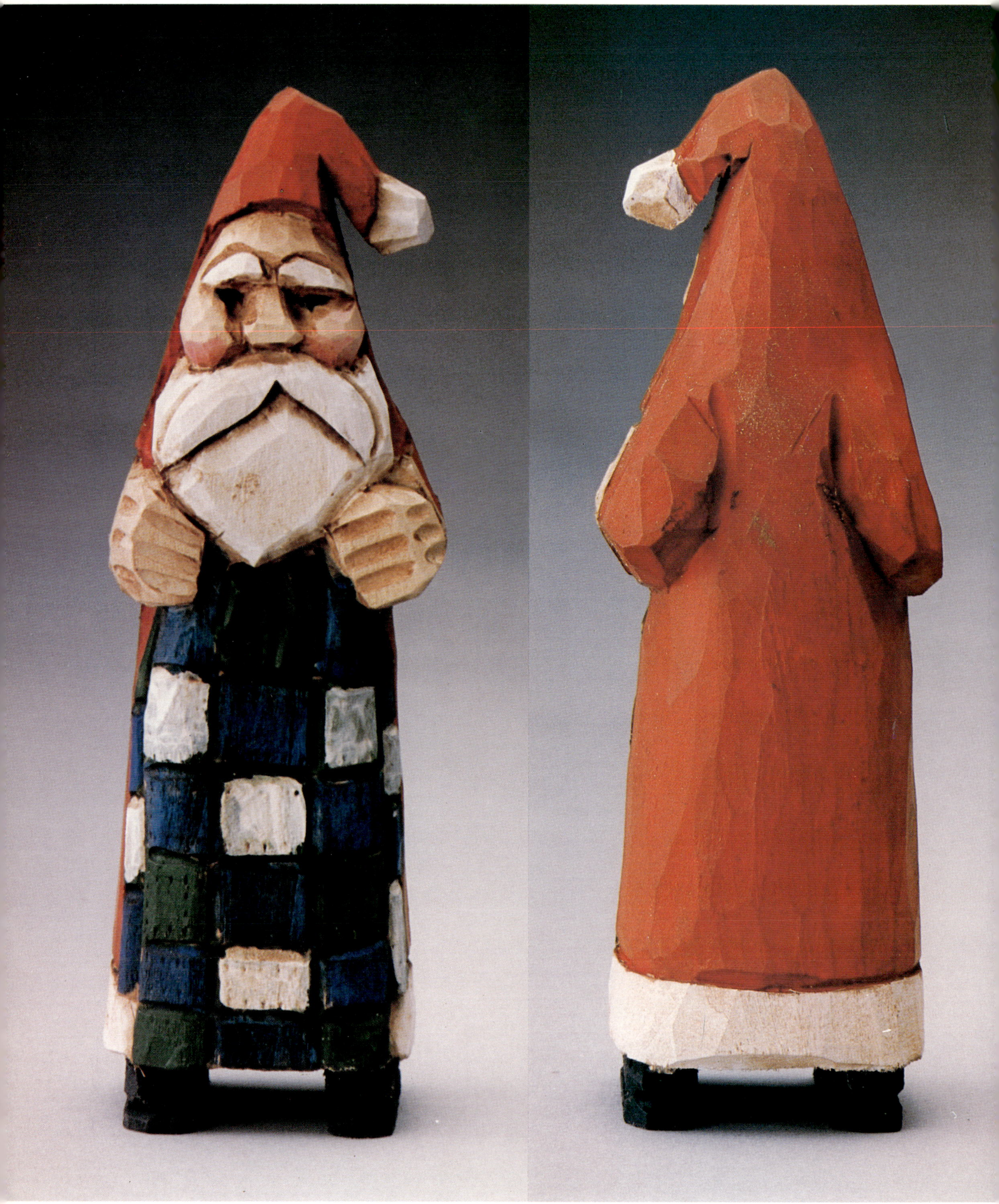

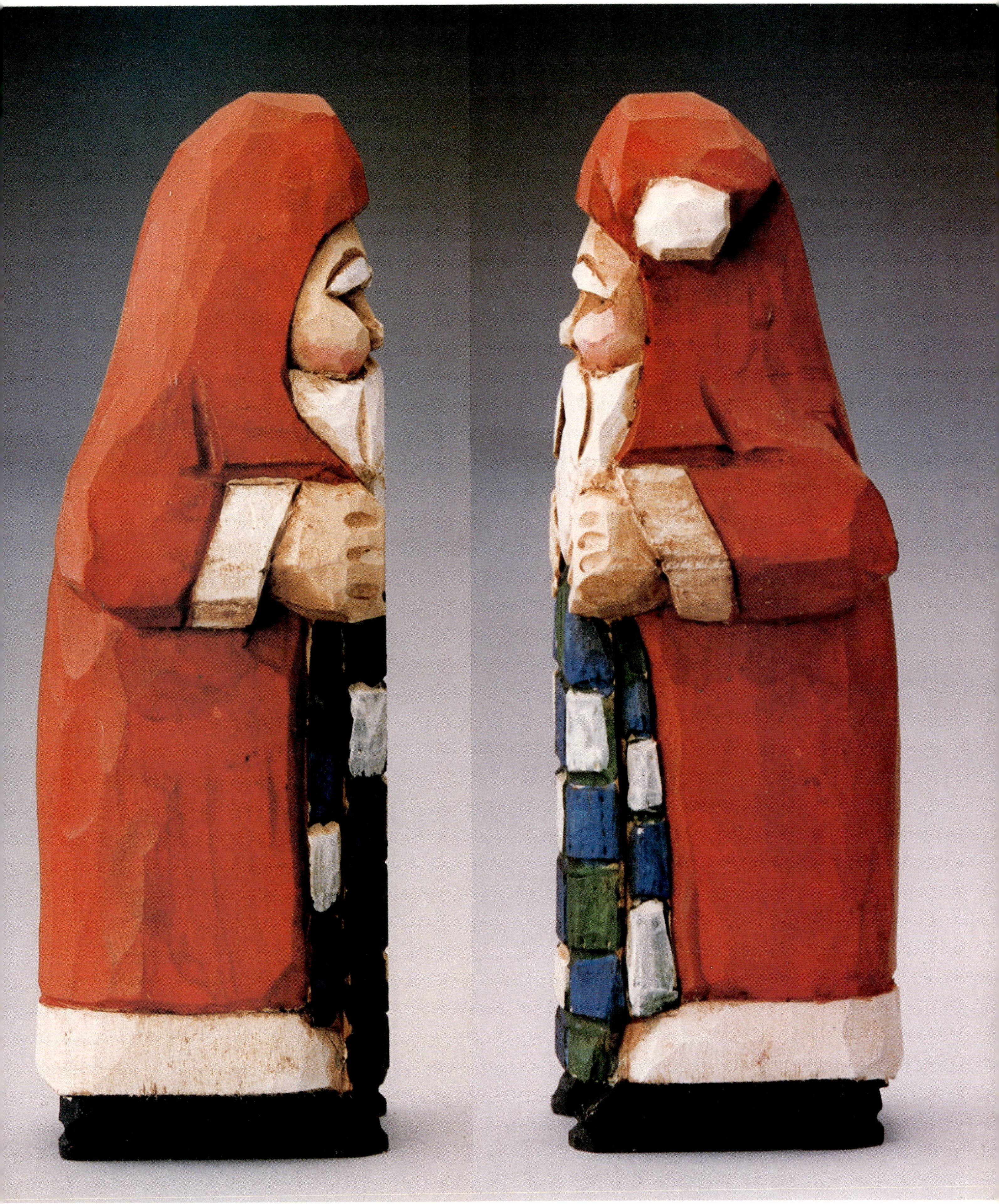

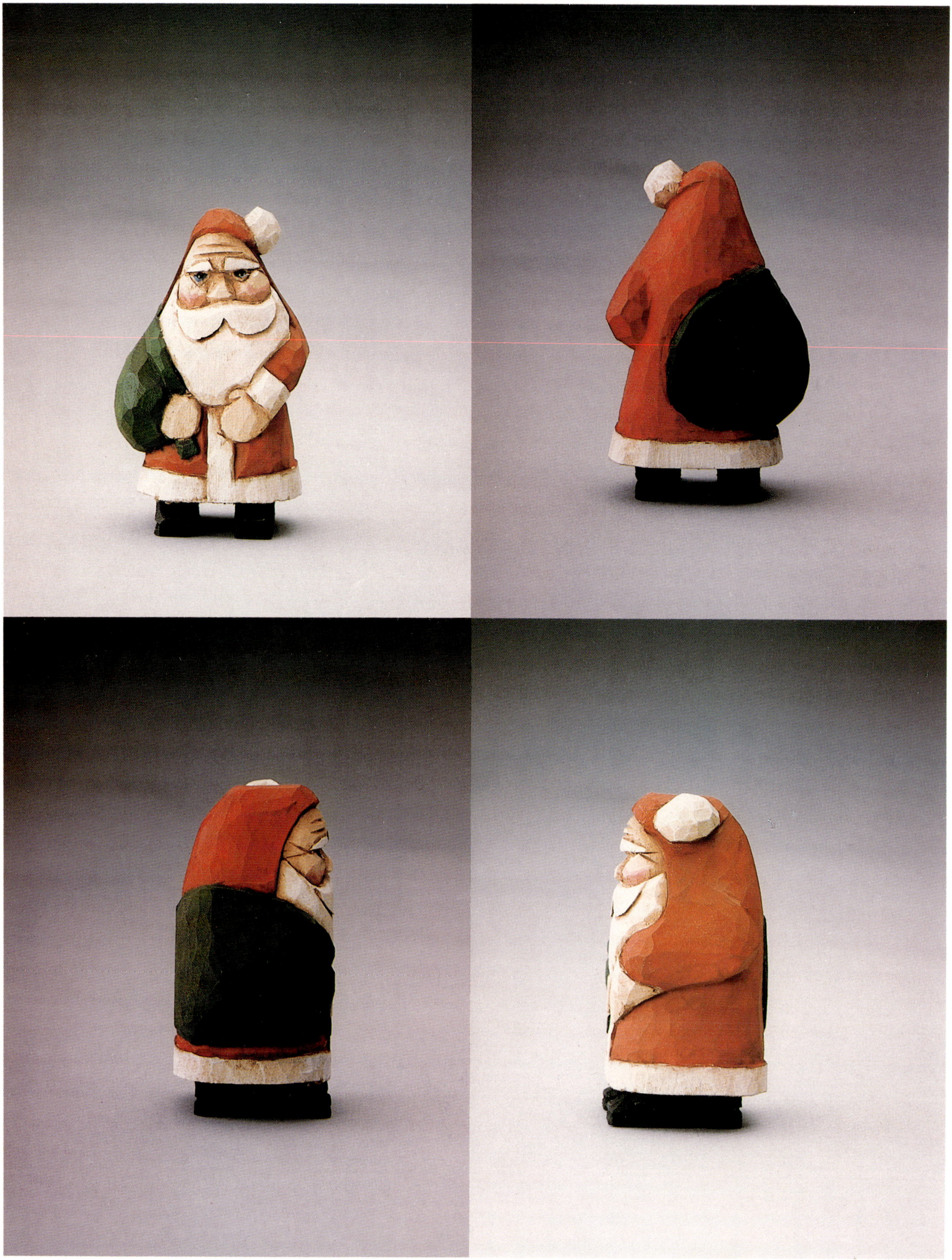